A Student Grammar of Modern Standard Arabic

This accessible grammar provides a concise and user-friendly guide to the structure of Modern Standard Arabic. Using familiar terminology and keeping theory to a minimum, it is suitable for beginning students as well as those at a more advanced level. Detailed descriptions of all types of sentence are given, and numerous tables provide a clear presentation of verbs and nouns. The most familiar grammatical terms are given in Arabic as well as in English in order to help the student identify them, and the index is also presented in both languages for fast and straightforward cross-referencing. Each pattern or rule described is illustrated with authentic examples from a range of real-life contexts such as newspapers, magazines, business communications and the internet, as well as from Arabic literary texts. Clearly organized and practical, this book will be an invaluable reference resource for all learners and teachers of Modern Standard Arabic.

- Concise, accessible and practical
- Clearly organized, with detailed descriptions of all types of sentence, and tabular presentation of verbs and nouns
- Uses familiar terminology and keeps complex theory to a minimum
- Suitable for beginners as well as more advanced students
- Examples are illustrated with authentic examples from real-life contexts

Eckehard Schulz is Professor of Arabic Language and Linguistics at the University of Leipzig, and an experienced teacher and translator of the language. His previous books include *Lehrbuch des modernen Arabisch* (1995), *Modernes Arabisch für Fortgeschrittene* (1995), and *Standard Arabic: An elementary-intermediate course* (Cambridge University Press, 2000).

A STUDENT GRAMMAR OF MODERN STANDARD ARABIC

ECKEHARD SCHULZ

CAMBRIDGE
UNIVERSITY PRESS

PUBLISHED BY THE PRESS SYNDICATE OF THE UNIVERSITY OF CAMBRIDGE
The Pitt Building, Trumpington Street, Cambridge, United Kingdom

CAMBRIDGE UNIVERSITY PRESS
The Edinburgh Building, Cambridge CB2 2RU, UK
40 West 20th Street, New York, NY 10011–4211, USA
477 Williamstown Road, Port Melbourne, VIC 3207, Australia
Ruiz de Alarcón 13, 28014 Madrid, Spain
Dock House, The Waterfront, Cape Town 8001, South Africa

http://www.cambridge.org

First published 2004

Printed in the United Kingdom at the University Press, Cambridge

Typeface Times New Roman 11pt and Traditional Arabic 16pt   *System* LaTeX 2_ε [TB]

A catalogue record for this book is available from the British Library

Library of Congress Cataloguing in Publication data

ISBN 0 521 83377 9 hardback
ISBN 0 521 54159 X paperback

FOR VERONIKA

CONTENTS

PREFACE

This book is intended for beginners, intermediate and advanced students, for scholars in linguistics and related fields and also for Arabs grown up in an English-speaking environment who often try to learn Arabic and find difficulties when consulting traditional Arabic grammars.

The Arabic portrayed in this book is not only literary Arabic, rather it is based on contemporary professional practice, i.e. the type of modern Arabic used in newspapers, magazines, official and business communications and the internet, too. On the other hand, it is clear for those who know the history of Arabic that the classical tradition is still alive in quotations from the Koran or from ancient literature and poetry.

This book is slightly different from other grammars because it follows a different approach. Its focus is on Modern Standard Arabic and it pays special attention to what is in use today but does not leave out what else can occur. The terminology is both in English and Arabic and the approach is influenced by the traditional Arabic system of writing grammar, i.e. not to try to press Arabic as a Semitic language into the terminology of English grammar.

In general, I have tried to use the most intelligible and familiar terminology and not to overload the book with too much theory. Arabic terms, although not in full, are given to open the way for the user to find the according passages in traditional Arabic grammars to gain more information about a certain topic and to help the learner to identify these terms when attending Arabic courses in the Arab world.

Not all the rules are explained in detail since the book assumes that the user already knows Arabic and should be able to deduce the rule in question from the examples quoted. In some cases examples are given in which the usage nowadays is different from what Arab grammarians considered acceptable a thousand years ago. To accept this usage does not mean to accept whatever is written, but certain changes, not only in the field of the vocabulary, are in my opinion a quite natural development.

The Arabic dialects are not included in this book because its focus is on (official) written usage, and this usage does not differ dramatically between Morocco in the West and Iraq in the East in the field of grammar.

Finally, I take this opportunity to express my great thanks to all those who helped me with hints and examples and their valuable assistance in checking the text.

I wish to express my deep gratitude to my friend Monem Jumaili who generously provided valuable observations and excellent advice. I am indebted to Yvonne Stägemann who took responsibility for the index. Any remaining errors are my responsibility.

Leipzig 2004   ECKEHARD SCHULZ

NOTES FOR THE USER

Abbreviations

a., acc.	accusative case	part.	participle
cf.	compare	prep.	preposition
collect.	collective noun	q.	quadriliteral
colloq.	colloquial	R1	1st radical
def.	definite	R2	2nd radical
e.g.	for example	R3	3rd radical
Eg.	Egyptian	Russ.	Russian
Engl.	English	s.o.	someone
f., fem.	feminine	s.o.'s.	someone's
fig.	figurative sense	sg., sing.	singular
foll.	following	s.th.	something
Fr.	French	Syr.	Syrian
g.	genitive case	th.s.	the same
gram.	grammar	to sb.	to somebody
indef.	indefinite	trans.	transitive
intrans.	intransitive	Yem.	Yemeni
lit.	literal	ث	*muṯannan* = dual
m., masc.	masculine	ج	*ǧam'* = plural
n.	nominative case	م	*mu'annaṯ* = feminine
off.	official	☞	see
p.	person		
pl., plur.	plural		

Transliteration. The transliteration of the Arabic script follows the pronunciation and not the spelling, e.g.: أَلشَّنْطَة *aš-šanṭa* and not *al-šanṭa*. The transliteration in this book ignores *Hamza* in initial position, e.g.: إنّ is given as *inna*, and not as *'inna*.

Vocalizing (Pointing) and *Hamza*. The Arabic terms and texts in this book are nearly fully vocalized, except *Hamzat al-waṣl* in the definite article. *Hamzat al-qaṭ'* is always indicated. *Hamzat al-waṣl* ٱ is written as *Alif* without any auxiliary sign.

Patterns and Forms: The numerous patterns of Arabic are represented by means of *fa'ala* as model root and its various patterns. The derived forms (stems) of the verbs are indicated by Roman letters (II … X).

Index. The index, which is subdivided into an English and an Arabic index, comprises all essential English and Arabic grammatical and linguistic terms which are used in this book. Its purpose is to facilitate finding the relevant passages.

LETTERS, PRONUNCIATION, AUXILIARY SIGNS, WRITING

Arabic has 29 characters (حَرْفٌ ج حُرُوفٌ): 26 consonants (حُرُوفٌ سَاكِنَةٌ) and 3 vowels (حُرُوفٌ مُتَحَرِّكَةٌ). Two (و، ي) of the three, however, occur both as vowels and consonants.

THE CHARACTERS AND THEIR PRONUNCIATION

The following consonants have more or less similar equivalents in English.

'	ء	Hamza	like 'a in 'arm, like 'i in 'inn, like 'oo in 'ooze (initial occlusive element, glottal stop)
b	ب	Bāʾ	like b in big
t	ت	Tāʾ	like t in tea
ṯ	ث	Ṯāʾ	like th in three
ğ	ج	Ğīm	like g in gentle
ḥ	خ	Ḥāʾ	like ch in Scottish English, loch
d	د	Dāl	like d in door
ḏ	ذ	Ḏāl	like th in the
r	ر	Rāʾ	like r in Scottish English, room
z	ز	Zāy	like z in zero
s	س	Sīn	like s in sun
š	ش	Šīn	like s in sure
f	ف	Fāʾ	like f in fog
k	ك	Kāf	like k in key
l	ل	Lām	like l in long, live or luck
m	م	Mīm	like m in monkey
n	ن	Nūn	like n in noon
h	ه	Hāʾ	like h in hot
w	و	Wāw	like w in wall
y	ي	Yāʾ	like y in year

Arabic has the following long vowels:

ā	ا	Alif	like a in far
ī	ي	Yāʾ	like ee in deer
ū	و	Wāw	like oo in school

The short vowels a (hut, pat), i (lift) and u (look) as well as the diphthongs ay (write) and aw (like in how, but short) are also the same as in English.

The following letters are typical Arabic consonants which do not have equivalents in English and can only be learned through regular practice with native speakers:

ḥ	ح	Ḥā'	like *h* articulated with friction
'	ع	'Ayn	like *a* articulated in the pharynx with friction
ġ	غ	Ġayn	like the Parisian *r* in *renaissance*
ṣ	ص	Ṣād	like *s* articulated with emphasis
ḍ	ض	Ḍād	like *d* articulated with emphasis
ṭ	ط	Ṭā'	like *t* articulated with emphasis
ẓ	ظ	Ẓā'	like *dh* articulated with emphasis
q	ق	Qāf	like *k* articulated with emphasis

The last five of these consonants are the so-called emphatic consonants. They normally affect the pronunciation of adjacent consonants, vowels and diphthongs. Their correct pronunciation and the modifications in the adjacent sounds need special practising.

The Persian characters چ for *ch* (*chapter*), پ for *p* (*politics*), ژ for (French) *j* (*Jacques*), ڤ for *v* (*vehicle*) *and* گ for *g* (*go*) are sometimes used to write words or names of Persian or foreign origin.

The order of the Arabic consonants according to the place where they are articulated:

bilabial:	*b, m, w*
labiodental:	*f*
interdental:	*ḏ, ṯ, ẓ*
dental:	*d, t, ḍ, ṭ*
prepalatal:	*n, l, r, z, s, ṣ, š, ǧ, y*
postpalatal:	*k*
velar:	*ġ, q, ḫ*
pharyngeal:	*', ḥ*
laryngeal:	*', h*

AUXILIARY SIGNS (أَلْحَرَكَاتُ)

Since Arabic expresses only long vowels by special characters, a system of auxiliary signs was developed to distinguish whether or not a consonant is followed by a short vowel. But normally these signs do not appear in printed or written texts, since the reader who is familiar with the morphology of Arabic will be able to read the words correctly without such signs.

The auxiliary signs are mainly used in the Koran, poetry and children's books. Texts which contain such signs are called vocalized or pointed texts, whereas those without them are referred to as unvocalized.

The signs may be divided into two main groups:

a) Short vowels (for which Arabic has no characters)

Fatḥa   =   a short oblique stroke (´) written on top of the letter

بَ ba, فَ fa, وَ wa

denoting that the consonant is followed by a short *a*.

(*Fatḥa* followed by *Alif* = long *ā*: مَا *mā*)

Kasra   =   a short oblique stroke ( ) written below the consonant

بِ bi, لِ li, مِ mi

denoting that the consonant is followed by a short *i*.

(*Kasra* followed by *Yā'* = long *ī*: كَبِير *kabīr*)

Ḍamma =   a sign similar in shape to a small *Wāw* ( ) written on top of the letter

مُدُن *mudun*, كُم *kum*, هُم *hum*

denoting that the consonant is followed by a short *u*.

(*Ḍamma* followed by *Wāw* = long *ū*: نُون *Nūn*)

b) OTHER SIGNS

Sukūn   =   a small circle (°) on top of the letter

تَحْتَ *taḥta*, نَحْنُ *naḥnu*, مِنْ *min*

denoting that the consonant is not followed by any vowel.

Šadda =   a small *Sīn* ( ) written on top of the letter denoting that the consonant is doubled, which is pronounced in a somewhat prolonged way then. *Fatḥa* and *Ḍamma* are written on top of *Šadda*, whereas *Kasra* may be placed either below *Šadda* or below the doubled letter:

شُبَّاك *šubbāk*, مُعَلِّم/ مُعَلِّم *mu'allim*, تَقَدُّم *taqaddum*

Madda   =   a sign on top of *Alif* (آ) denoting a long *ā*.

الآنَ *al-āna*, القُرْآن *al-qur'ān*

DIPHTHONGS:

Fatḥa followed by a و with *Sukūn* denotes the diphthong *aw*, whereas *Fatḥa* followed by a ي with *Sukūn* denotes the diphthong *ay*: لَوْح *lawḥ*, بَيْت *bayt*

HAMZA (ء) AND TĀ' MARBŪṬA (ة)

Hamza, which has the shape of a small *'Ayn*, normally needs a character to "carry" it. The characters which carry *Hamza* are أ (*Alif*), ؤ (*Wāw*) and ئ (*Yā'*), and they are referred to as chairs of *Hamza*. (☞ Spelling of *Hamza*)

At the beginning of a word, the chair of *Hamza* is always *Alif*:

أَنْتَ *'anta*, أُمٌّ *'umm*, إِن *'in*

The *Tā' marbūṭa* ة is a special form of the *Tā'*. It only occurs in final position. It is pronounced as a short *a* when the word occurs isolated. However, if the word is the 1ˢᵗ term of a genitive construction, it turns into *t*. (☞ Genitive)

NUNATION / TANWĪN (التَّنْوِين)

The *Tanwīn* is used to mark that a noun is indefinite in the nominative, genitive or accusative case. The *Tā' marbūṭa* with *Tanwīn* turns into *t* and is pronounced – *atun, -atin, -atan*. The *Tanwīn* is also combined with *Šadda*:

n. (un)		g. (in)		a. (an)	
ṭālibatun	*kitābun*	*ṭālibatin*	*kitābin*	*ṭālibatan*	*kitāban*
طَالِبَةٌ	كِتَابٌ	طَالِبَة	كِتَاب	طَالِبَةً	كِتَابًا
ṭibbun		*ṭibbin*		*ṭibban*	
طِبٌّ		طِبٍّ		طِبًّا	

WRITING

Arabic is written from right to left. The letters differ in size, but there are no capitals. Each of them has a basic form, but modifications in their shapes occur according to their positions in words. Thus, each letter has a different shape in initial, medial, final and isolated position:

isolated position	final position	medial position	initial position
ب	ـب	ـبـ	بـ

- The shapes of Arabic letters are generally similar both in script and printed form. However, a few differences occur.
- A number of letters share the same shape and are only distinguished by diacritic dots: ـن *Nūn*, ـت *Tā'*, ـث *Thā'*, ـب *Bā'*, ـي *Yā'*. The letters و ز ر ذ د ا are only connected with the preceding letter, whereas all the others are connected with both sides.
- *Yā'* (ى) without diacritical dots in final position is always preceded by *Fatḥa* and is pronounced as the long vowel *ā*: إِلَى *ilā*, عَلَى *'alā*, مَتَى *matā*
- Final *Yā'* (ي) with diacritical dots is usually preceded by *Kasra*: فِي *fī*, كِتَابِي *kitābī*. However, many texts do not seem to be consistent in regard to the use of diacritical dots with ي when it occurs in the final position.
- *Allāh* (God) is mostly written in the form of الله. The *Šadda* above the *Lām* shows that the *Lām* is doubled here; the small *Alif* above the *Šadda* means that a long *ā* has to be pronounced after it. This small *Alif* is also used in the word *raḥmān* (*the Merciful*) and others.

***Table 1*: THE ALPHABET** (أَلْحُرُوفُ الأَبْجَدِيَّةُ)

The first letter of the alphabet is actually *Hamza*, but since *Alif* is the chair of *Hamza* in most cases, it appears in its place as the first letter.

The alphabet in its traditional order:

name of the letter	translitera-tion	isolated position	final position	medial position	initial position
Alif	ā	ا	ـا	ـا	ا
Bā'	b	ب	ـب	ـبـ	بـ
Tā'	t	ت	ـت	ـتـ	تـ
Ṯā'	ṯ	ث	ـث	ـثـ	ثـ
Ǧīm	ǧ	ج	ـج	ـجـ	جـ
Ḥā'	ḥ	ح	ـح	ـحـ	حـ
Ḫā'	ḫ	خ	ـخ	ـخـ	خـ
Dāl	d	د	ـد	ـد	د
Ḏāl	ḏ	ذ	ـذ	ـذ	ذ
Rā'	r	ر	ـر	ـر	ر
Zāy	z	ز	ـز	ـز	ز
Sīn	s	س	ـس	ـسـ	سـ
Šīn	š	ش	ـش	ـشـ	شـ
Ṣād	ṣ	ص	ـص	ـصـ	صـ
Ḍād	ḍ	ض	ـض	ـضـ	ضـ
Ṭā'	ṭ	ط	ـط	ـطـ	طـ
Ẓā'	ẓ	ظ	ـظ	ـظـ	ظـ
'Ayn	'	ع	ـع	ـعـ	عـ
Ġayn	ġ	غ	ـغ	ـغـ	غـ
Fā'	f	ف	ـف	ـفـ	فـ
Qāf	q	ق	ـق	ـقـ	قـ
Kāf	k	ك	ـك	ـكـ	كـ
Lām	l	ل	ـل	ـلـ	لـ
Mīm	m	م	ـم	ـمـ	مـ
Nūn	n	ن	ـن	ـنـ	نـ
Ha'	h	ه	ـه	ـهـ	هـ
Wāw	w, ū	و	ـو	ـو	و
Yā'	y, ī	ي	ـي	ـيـ	يـ

SPELLING OF *HAMZA*

The key to the spelling of *Hamza* is to determine whether ا ، و or ى is the chair of *Hamza* or whether *Hamza* occurs without a chair. To determine which spelling must be chosen depends on which vowel precedes or follows *Hamza*. The formal order principle for the following rules distinguishes between initial, medial and final *Hamza* in the word.

Initial *Hamza*

Alif invariably is the chair of *Hamza*:

to take	أَخَذَ
mother	أُمّ
production	إِنْتَاجٌ
delegation	إِيفَادٌ

This also applies if the word is preceded by a preposition which is written together with it:

for my mother	لِأُمِّي
by the production of the cars	بِإِنْتَاجِ السَّيَّارَاتِ

Medial *Hamza*

a) If *Hamza* is not followed by a vowel, the chair of *Hamza* is determined by the vowel immediately preceding *Hamza*, i.e. *Alif* is used with *a/ā*, *Wāw* with *u/ū* and *Yā'* (without diacritical dots) with *i/ī*:

opinion	رَأْيٌ
well/spring	بِئْرٌ
(infinitive of رَأَى)	رُؤْيَة

b) If *Hamza* is followed by a vowel, but if the consonant immediately preceding *Hamza* is vowelless, the chair of *Hamza* is determined by the vowel which follows *Hamza*:

he asks	يَسْأَلُ
questions	أَسْئِلَة
responsible	مَسْؤُولٌ

Exception: If the vowelless consonant preceding *Hamza* is a *Yā'*, the chair of *Hamza* is *Yā'* as well: هَيْئَة *"form/shape/appearance; group/body/committee"*.

c) If *Hamza* is preceded by a vowel as well as followed by a vowel,
Alif is the chair of *Hamza* if both vowels are *a*,
Wāw is the chair of *Hamza* if one of the two vowels is *u* and
Yā' is the chair of *Hamza* if one of the two vowels is *i*.
If *u* and *i* meet, *Yā'* is the chair of *Hamza*:

he has asked	سَأَلَ
presidents	رُؤَسَاء
question	سُؤَال
hundred	مِئَة
president	رَئِيس
he was asked	سُئِلَ

If the sequence of vowels is *-ā a, -ā ā* or *-ū a, Hamza* is written in its isolated form on the line:

reading (infinitive of قَرَأَ)	قِرَاءَة
experts, chief performers	كَفَاءَاتٌ
manliness	مُرُوءَة

Final *Hamza*
a) If *Hamza* is preceded by a short vowel, this vowel determines the chair of *Hamza*:

he has read	قَرَأَ
he reads	يَقْرَأُ
it was read	قُرِئَ
to be manly	مَرُؤَ

b) If *Hamza* is preceded by a long vowel or a vowelless consonant, *Hamza* occurs without a chair:

| friends | أَصْدِقَاء |

read (pass. part.)	مَقْرُوءٌ
coming (infinitive of جاء)	مَجِيءٌ
one (impers. pron.), man	أَلْمَرْءُ
building	بِنَاءٌ

c) The following applies to the spelling of the indefinite accusative of nouns with final *Hamza*:

The *Alif* of the indefinite accusative is omitted if the chair of *Hamza* is an *Alif* or if *Hamza* follows *Alif* (= long vowel *ā* without chair اِبْتِدَاءً، مُبْتَدَأً).

The *Alif* of the indefinite accusative is used if *Hamza* occurs without chair (except after the long vowel *ā*) (جُزْءًا).

It has *Yā'* as its chair if it is preceded by ي (شَيْئًا).

d) Final *Hamza* may become medial *Hamza* by means of a suffix. In this case the rules for *Hamza* in medial position apply:

friends	أَصْدِقَاءُ
your friends	أَصْدِقَاؤُكَ
with your friends	مَعَ أَصْدِقَائِكَ
he reads	يَقْرَأُ
they read	يَقْرَؤُونَ
you (f.) read	تَقْرَئِينَ

e) *Hamza* together with the long vowel *ā* following is written as *Madda* (آ):

August	آبُ
minarets	مَآذِن

This rule does not apply if *Hamza* is also preceded by the long vowel *ā*:

experts, chief performers	كَفَاءَاتٌ
measures	إِجْرَاءَاتٌ
exemptions, excuses	إِعْفَاءَاتٌ

STRESS

Stress, i.e. to pronounce a syllable with more emphasis, is regular in Arabic. In general, it is not difficult to stress the Arabic words in the correct way. The stressed syllable is shown in italics in the following rules and examples:

1. Only the last three syllables of a word can be stressed. If *Nunation* is pronounced, it is included.

2. The last syllable that contains a long vowel is stressed:
ki-*tāb*   ki-*tā*-bun
ǧa-*dīd*   ǧa-*dī*-dun
ma-*ḫā*-zin   ma- *ḫā*-zi-nu
however, the vocalic final sound of the word is never stressed:
hu-nā
kur-sī *(but:* kur-*sī*-yun*)*

3. If the last three syllables do not contain a long vowel, the second to last syllable is stressed if it is a closed syllable (sequence of sounds: consonant - short vowel - consonant):
mu-ʿ*al*-lim
mu-*tar*-ǧim,
and the same applies if the word consists of only two syllables:
an-ta
ra-ǧul
Otherwise the third to last syllable is stressed, regardless of its structure:
mu-ʿ*al*-li-ma
muǧ-*ta*-hi-dun

4. It is accepted in modern Arabic language that the stress may not advance beyond the last syllable but two. This requires the stress to be shifted if the number of syllables changes, when the *Nunation* is pronounced or suffixes are added.

ṭā-li-ba	ṭā-*li*-ba-tun
mu-ʿ*al*-li-ma	mu-ʿal-*li*-ma-tun
ku-tu-bun	ku-*tu*-bu-nā *(our books)*
mu-ʿ*al*-li-mun	mu-ʿal-*li*-mu-nā *(our teacher)*
ṭā-li-ba	ṭa-*li*-ba-tun
	ṭā-li-*ba*-tu-nā *(our student (f.))*
mu-ʿ*al*-li-ma	mu-ʿal-*li*-ma-tun
	mu-ʿal-li-*ma*-tu-nā *(our teacher (f.))*

5. The definite article, and the first syllable of verbal Forms VII, VIII, IX and X are never stressed.

RADICAL, ROOT, PATTERN

The majority of Arabic words can be reduced to a triliteral root consisting of three consonants (ثُلاثِيّ). They are called *radicals* (R1, R2 and R3). There is also quite a number of quadriliteral roots (رُبَاعِيّ).

The root expresses a certain conceptual content, e.g. the meaning *"to write"* is inherent in the root K-T-B (ك - ت - ب), *"to go"* in D - H - B (ذ - ه - ب), and *"to drink"* in Š - R - B (ش - ر - ب).

This conceptual content is specified by short and long vowels between the consonants and by prefixes, infixes and suffixes regarding the part of speech (verb, noun, adjective) as well as regarding the grammatical category (tense, mood, number, case etc.). Simplified, one can say that the root consonants (*Radicals*) fulfil a semantic and the vowels a grammatical function in the Arabic word:

KaTaBa	(كَتَبَ)	= *he wrote / has written*
KāTiB	(كاتب)	= *writing; writer, author*
KiTāB	(كتَاب)	= *book*
KuTuB	(كُتُب)	= *books*
maKTūB	(مَكْتُوب)	= *written; letter*
maKTaBa	(مَكْتَبَة)	= *library, bookshop*

The Arab grammarians use ف for R1 (1st Radical), ع for R2 (2nd Radical) and ل for R3 (3rd Radical) in order to describe the numerous word forms systematically. *Fā'*, *'Ayn* and *Lām* fulfil the function of variables in the patterns, for which theoretically any consonant can be substituted.

فَعَلَ	*fa'ala*	is the pattern used for the perfect tense (3rd p.sg.m.):	كَتَبَ، ذَهَبَ
فَاعِل	*fā'il*	is the pattern used for the active participle:	كاتِبٌ، طَالِبٌ
فَعِيل	*fa'īl*	is a typical pattern of the adjective:	كبِيرٌ، صَغِيرٌ
فِعَال	*fi'āl*	is a typical pattern of the broken plural:	كبَارٌ، طِوَالٌ
أَفْعَال	*af'āl*	is another typical pattern of the broken plural:	أَقْلامٌ، أَعْوَامٌ

A reliable knowledge of the patterns and their general meaning is very useful for obtaining a good command of the language, and enables the learner to deduce the meanings of derived nouns and verbal forms by knowing the meaning of the root.

VERBS (الأَفْعَالُ)

GENERAL

Most Arabic verbs are triliteral (ثُلَاثِيّ) and some are quadriliteral (رُبَاعِيّ). The Arabic verb has basically **two tenses**:

    1. Perfect tense (الْمَاضِي)

    2. Imperfect tense (الْمُضَارِعُ)

conjugational patterns for the perfect and imperfect tense for:

    1. Singular (الْمُفْرَدُ)

    2. Dual (الْمُثَنَّى)

    3. Plural (الْجَمْعُ)

four groups of verbs:

    1. Sound verbs (الْفِعْلُ الصَّحِيحُ/السَّالِمُ)

    2. Hamzated verbs (الْفِعْلُ الْمَهْمُوزُ)

    3. Doubled Verbs R2=R3 (الْفِعْلُ الْمُضَاعَفُ)

    4. Weak verbs (الأَفْعَالُ الْمُعْتَلَّةُ)

four moods

    1. Indicative perfect (الْمَاضِي) **and indicative imperfect** (الْمُضَارِعُ الْمَرْفُوعُ)

    2. Subjunctive (الْمُضَارِعُ الْمَنْصُوبُ)

    3. Jussive (الْمُضَارِعُ الْمَجْزُومُ)

    4. Imperative (الأَمْرُ)

two voices

    1. Active voice (الْمَاضِي/الْمُضَارِعُ الْمَبْنِيُّ لِلْمَعْلُومِ) = Indicative perfect and indicative imperfect

    2. Passive voice (الْمَاضِي/الْمُضَارِعُ الْمَبْنِيُّ لِلْمَجْهُولِ) occurring as indicative perfect and indicative imperfect as well as as subjunctive and jussive

and in addition to basic **Form I** the **derived or increased forms** (الْفِعْلُ الْمَزِيدُ) (**Forms II …X**) occurring also in all the tenses, groups, moods and voices.

Any full verb (أَلْفِعْلُ التَّامُّ) needs a subject (أَلْفَاعِلُ). The only exceptions are some auxiliary verbs which do not always have a subject (كَانَ وَأَخَوَاتُهَا وَكَادَ وَأَخَوَاتُهَا ☞).
All these verbs may be **transitive** (أَلْفِعْلُ الْمُتَعَدِّيُ), i.e. they are followed by one or more objects (أَلْمَفْعُولُ), or **intransitive** (أَلْفِعْلُ اللازِمُ/أَلْفِعْلُ غَيْرُ الْمُتَعَدِّيُ), i.e. the verb has only a subject and not necessarily an object.

SOUND VERBS (أَلْفِعْلُ السَّالِمُ)

PERFECT TENSE (أَلْمَاضِي)

The perfect tense is one of the two simple forms of the verb and basically narrative in function. In most cases it denotes a completed event or action. The perfect form can also be used to express actions that (will) take place in the present and future, like e.g. in maledictions, in conditional sentences and optative clauses, because the Arabic perfect tense does not actually express a certain tense; it merely states the verbal action. The Arabic perfect tense corresponds – depending on the context - to both the English past tense and present perfect.

He wrote. / He has written.	كَتَبَ

The Arabic dictionary entry form is the 3rd p. sg. m. of the perfect tense. The vocabulary in this grammar is given according to the common practice in both languages: كَتَبَ "*to write*" (instead of the exact equivalent "*he wrote/ has written*").

The vowel *a* (*Fatha*) invariably follows R1 and R3 in the perfect tense. R2 is mostly followed by *a* (*Fatha*): كَتَبَ "*to write*" ذَهَبَ "*to go*" فَعَلَ "*to do*", often by *i* (*Kasra*): شَرِبَ "*to drink*" سَمِعَ "*to hear*"
Verbs in which *u* (*Damma*) follows R2 are relatively rare. They are always intransitives, occur only in literary language and are equivalent to groups of verbs consisting of an adjective + auxiliary verb (e. g. حَسُنَ "*sth. was [or became] good, nice*", كَبُرَ "*sth. became big*" a. o.).

CONJUGATION OF THE SOUND VERB (تَصْرِيفُ الفِعْلِ السَّالِمِ)

The order of persons in the Arabic conjugational paradigm is 3rd person - 2nd person - 1st person. This complies with Arab tradition and the practice pursued in nearly all Arabic textbooks. The persons are expressed by means of suffixes. In the following paradigm, the independent pronoun has been added in parentheses to be able to do without additional information about person, gender and number. The verbal dual forms are used to denote that the verbal action is done by two persons or things by adding the suffix *–ā* / *-āni* to the 3rd p.sg. m. and f. and to the 2nd p.pl.m. of the perfect / imperfect tense. However, there is no verbal dual form attested in any modern Arabic dialect.

***Table 2*: PERFECT TENSE** (أَلْمَاضِي)

plural				singular			
sample verbs							
سَمِعَ	كَبُرَ	ذَهَبَ		سَمِعَ	كَبُرَ	ذَهَبَ	
فَعَلُوا	فَعَلُوا	فَعَلُوا	(هُمْ)	فَعَلَ	فَعَلَ	فَعَلَ	(هُوَ)
فَعَلْنَ	فَعَلْنَ	فَعَلْنَ	(هُنَّ)	فَعَلَتْ	فَعَلَتْ	فَعَلَتْ	(هِيَ)
فَعَلْتُمْ	فَعَلْتُمْ	فَعَلْتُمْ	(أَنْتُمْ)	فَعَلْتَ	فَعَلْتَ	فَعَلْتَ	(أَنْتَ)
فَعَلْتُنَّ	فَعَلْتُنَّ	فَعَلْتُنَّ	(أَنْتُنَّ)	فَعَلْتِ	فَعَلْتِ	فَعَلْتِ	(أَنْتِ)
فَعَلْنَا	فَعَلْنَا	فَعَلْنَا	(نَحْنُ)	فَعَلْتُ	فَعَلْتُ	فَعَلْتُ	(أَنَا)
			dual 3rd p.m.	فَعَلَا	فَعَلَا	فَعَلَا	(هُمَا)
			dual 3rd p.f.	فَعَلَتَا	فَعَلَتَا	فَعَلَتَا	(هُمَا)
			dual 2nd p.pl.	فَعَلْتُمَا	فَعَلْتُمَا	فَعَلْتُمَا	(أَنْتُمَا)

The 3rd p. pl. m., i.e. the form فَعَلُوا, is also used to express the impersonal "one". The *Alif* in فَعَلُوا is not pronounced and omitted in writing if suffixes are added. The auxiliary vowel of فَعَلْتُمْ is *u*, of فَعَلَتْ it is *i*, when followed by the definite article.

IMPERFECT TENSE/INDICATIVE (أَلْمُضَارِعُ الْمَرْفُوعُ)

The imperfect tense/indicative is the second of the two simple verb forms in Arabic. It almost always indicates an action or state taking place in the present (أَلْحَاضِرُ) or future tense (أَلْمُسْتَقْبَلُ) and may express a habitual, progressive, future or stative meaning.

The imperfect tense can sometimes be employed to express actions having taken place in the past, as is the case in some subordinate clauses, because the imperfect tense is actually neutral regarding tense and merely describes the verbal action in its course.

It is characteristic for the imperfect tense/indicative that R1 is vowelless and that R2 is followed by a so-called **imperfect stem vowel**, which can be *a (Fatha)* as well as *i (Kasra)* or *u (Damma)*. The imperfect stem vowel is invariably *a (Fatha)* when the second vowel of the perfect tense is *i* (شَرِبَ / يَشْرَبُ).

The vowel *u* or a suffix follows R3. The persons are expressed by prefixes.

***Table 3*: IMPERFECT/INDICATIVE (أَلْمُضَارِعُ الْمَرْفُوعُ)**

pl.				sg.			
sample verbs							
عَرَفَ	كَبُرَ	ذَهَبَ		عَرَفَ	كَبُرَ	ذَهَبَ	
يَفْعَلُونَ	يَفْعُلُونَ	يَفْعِلُونَ	هُمْ	يَفْعَلُ	يَفْعُلُ	يَفْعِلُ	هُوَ
يَفْعَلْنَ	يَفْعُلْنَ	يَفْعِلْنَ	هُنَّ	تَفْعَلُ	تَفْعُلُ	تَفْعِلُ	هِيَ
تَفْعَلُونَ	تَفْعُلُونَ	تَفْعِلُونَ	أَنْتُمْ	تَفْعَلُ	تَفْعُلُ	تَفْعِلُ	أَنْتَ
تَفْعَلْنَ	تَفْعُلْنَ	تَفْعِلْنَ	أَنْتُنَّ	تَفْعَلِينَ	تَفْعُلِينَ	تَفْعِلِينَ	أَنْتِ
نَفْعَلُ	نَفْعُلُ	نَفْعِلُ	نَحْنُ	أَفْعَلُ	أَفْعُلُ	أَفْعِلُ	أَنَا
			dual 3rd p.m.	يَفْعَلَانِ	يَفْعُلَانِ	يَفْعِلَانِ	هُمَا
			dual 3rd p.f.	تَفْعَلَانِ	تَفْعُلَانِ	تَفْعِلَانِ	هُمَا
			dual 2nd p.pl.	تَفْعَلَانِ	تَفْعُلَانِ	تَفْعِلَانِ	أَنْتُمَا

The particle سَوْفَ or its abridged form ـــسَ (as a prefix) can be placed in front of the imperfect tense to emphasize its future aspect:

He will definitely write to you. / He is sure to write to you.	سَوْفَ يَكْتُبُ لَكَ ، سَيَكْتُبُ لَكَ.

The particle قَدْ + **imperfect tense** meaning "*perhaps, may, might, probably*" also denotes a future action or event as a possibility:

Perhaps he will write.	قَدْ يَكْتُبُ.

MOODS OF THE IMPERFECT TENSE

The imperfect tense consists of several moods. The indicative generally serves to express an action (an event, also a state). The same applies to the **subjunctive** (أَلْمُضَارِعُ الْمَنْصُوب) and the **jussive** (أَلْمُضَارِعُ الْمَجْزُوم), which, however, never occur alone, but are only used after certain conjunctions and particles (☞ أَنْ "*that*", أَلَّا "*that ... not*", (لِأَنْ = لِ + أَنْ) لِ ، (كَيْ لا) كَيْ and لِكَيْ (لِكَيْ لا) "*in order that*", حَتَّى "*so that, until*"and the negations لَنْ, لَمْ and لا).

The subjunctive and the jussive differ from the indicative by an *a* (subjunctive) replacing the short vowel *u* after R3 or by R3 being vowelless (jussive) and by the suffixes *-īna* and *-ūna* being abridged. In the latter case an *Alif*, which is not pronounced, is added in spelling to the long vowel *-ū*, which has become final now - like in the 3rd p.pl.m. of the perfect tense.

Only the imperfect tense has the subjunctive and the jussive. The perfect tense has only one mood, the indicative. The ending ن is omitted in the dual of the subjunctive and in the jussive.

Table 4: SUBJUNCTIVE AND JUSSIVE (وَأَلْمُضَارِعُ الْمَجْزُوم أَلْمُضَارِعُ الْمَنْصُوب)

Jussive	Subjunctive	Indicative	
يَفْعَلْ	يَفْعَلَ	يَفْعَلُ	هُوَ
تَفْعَلْ	تَفْعَلَ	تَفْعَلُ	هِيَ
تَفْعَلْ	تَفْعَلَ	تَفْعَلُ	أَنْتَ
تَفْعَلِي	تَفْعَلِي	تَفْعَلِينَ	أَنْتِ
أَفْعَلْ	أَفْعَلَ	أَفْعَلُ	أَنا
يَفْعَلُوا	يَفْعَلُوا	يَفْعَلُونَ	هُمْ
يَفْعَلْنَ	يَفْعَلْنَ	يَفْعَلْنَ	هُنَّ
تَفْعَلُوا	تَفْعَلُوا	تَفْعَلُونَ	أَنْتُمْ
تَفْعَلْنَ	تَفْعَلْنَ	تَفْعَلْنَ	أَنْتُنَّ
نَفْعَلْ	نَفْعَلَ	نَفْعَلُ	نَحْنُ
يَفْعَلَا	يَفْعَلَا	يَفْعَلَانِ	هُمَا
تَفْعَلَا	تَفْعَلَا	تَفْعَلَانِ	هُمَا (f.)
تَفْعَلَا	تَفْعَلَا	تَفْعَلَانِ	أَنْتُمَا

IMPERATIVE (صِيغَةُ الْأَمْر)

Forming: The 2ⁿᵈ p. sg. and pl. of the jussive is the form to start from. The prefix *ta-* is omitted, and the double consonant, which has now been formed, is resolved by a prosthetic vowel. The prosthetic vowel is represented in writing by an *Alif* with *Hamza* (**in the interior of the sentence *Hamzat waṣl*!**). The vowel is *i-* in verbs with the imperfect stem vowel *a* or *i*, and it is *u-* in verbs with the imperfect stem vowel *u*. There is also one dual form for the imperative.

أُدْخُلْ	اعْرِفْ	افْعَلْ	أَنْتَ
أُدْخُلِي	اعْرِفِي	افْعَلِي	أَنْتِ

أُدْخُلُوا	اعْرِفُوا	افْعَلُوا	أَنْتُمْ
أُدْخُلْنَ	اعْرِفْنَ	افْعَلْنَ	أَنْتُنَّ
أُدْخُلَا	dual	افْعَلَا	أَنْتُمَا

The indirect command (hortative) is expressed by the preposition لِ + jussive.

Let's go!	لِنَذْهَبْ!
He shall do that!	لِيَفْعَلْ ذلك!

The imperative of the verbs R1 = و and of some verbs R1 = أ is formed without a prosthetic vowel: خُذْ "*Take!*", كُلُوا "*Eat!*" (☞ the respective tables).

Another mood of the imperfect tense is the so-called energetic mood to express emphasis. It is formed by adding the suffix ـَنَّ or ـَنْ to the imperative or jussive. However, it is extremely rare in modern Arabic.

PASSIVE VOICE (صِيغَةُ الْمَجْهُول)

The passive voice (أَلْمَبْنِيُّ لِلْمَجْهُول) can be formed from the perfect tense and imperfect tense (الْمُضَارِعُ الْمَبْنِيُّ لِلْمَجْهُول) and (الْمَاضِي الْمَبْنِيُّ لِلْمَجْهُول) differs from the active voice (مَبْنِيٌّ لِلْمَعْلُوم) with respect to function in the possibility of the actor (الفَاعِل) being left unmentioned. The object of a transitive verb turns into the subject of the predicate (نَائِبُ الفَاعِل) in the passive voice. However, preference is given in Arabic to the use of the active voice.

The passive voice formally only differs from the active voice in the sequence of vowels. The characteristic sequence of vowels in the passive voice of the perfect tense is *u - i – a* and of the imperfect tense *u - a - a*.

The verbal government by means of prepositions is preserved in the passive voice. In such constructions the masculine singular form of the verb is always used, even if the subject is feminine (☞ Passive Participle):

The guests are welcomed.	يُرَحَّبُ بِالضُّيُوف.
Many opinions were expressed.	عُبِّرَ عن آراءٍ كثيرة.

In modern Arabic, however, the rule of the actor (الفَاعِل) being left unmentioned is frequently broken, and the actor is added after مِنْ قَبَل "*by*":

The book was written by the president.	كُتِبَ الْكِتَابُ مِنْ قِبَل الرَّئِيس.

The periphrasis of the passive voice is also possible through the use of the infinitive preceded by the perfect or imperfect tense of تَمَّ / يَتِمُّ (*to come about, to be performed, to be accomplished, to take place, to happen*) or جَرَى / يَجْري (*to occur, to come to pass, to take place, to happen*).

The papers were delivered. ~ (*lit.: The delivery... took place.*)	سُلِّمَتِ الأَوْرَاقُ . تَمَّ / جَرَى تَسْلِيمُ الأَوْرَاقِ.

However, it is to be observed in colloquial and written usage that تَمَّ is often used in its masculine form although it is followed by a feminine noun:

The project was / is studied.	تَمَّ / يَتِمُّ دِرَاسَةُ الْمَشْرُوعِ.

The passive imperfect tense, when occurring in conjunction with the negation لا, is often used in the form of an attributive relative clause, which can be replaced by an attributive adjective in English:

an event which is not forgotten = an unforgettable event	حَفْلَةٌ لا تُنْسَى

Table 5: PASSIVE VOICE (أَلْمَاضِي الْمَبْنِيُّ لِلْمَجْهُولِ وَالْمُضَارِعُ الْمَبْنِيُّ لِلْمَجْهُولِ)

Imperfect		Perfect		
Passive	Active	Passive	Active	
يُفْعَلُ	يَفْعَلُ	فُعِلَ	فَعَلَ	هُوَ
تُفْعَلُ	تَفْعَلُ	فُعِلَتْ	فَعَلَتْ	هِيَ
تُفْعَلُ	تَفْعَلُ	فُعِلْتَ	فَعَلْتَ	أَنْتَ
تُفْعَلِينَ	تَفْعَلِينَ	فُعِلْتِ	فَعَلْتِ	أَنْتِ
أُفْعَلُ	أَفْعَلُ	فُعِلْتُ	فَعَلْتُ	أَنَا
يُفْعَلُونَ	يَفْعَلُونَ	فُعِلُوا	فَعَلُوا	هُمْ
يُفْعَلْنَ	يَفْعَلْنَ	فُعِلْنَ	فَعَلْنَ	هُنَّ
تُفْعَلُونَ	تَفْعَلُونَ	فُعِلْتُمْ	فَعَلْتُمْ	أَنْتُمْ
تُفْعَلْنَ	تَفْعَلْنَ	فُعِلْتُنَّ	فَعَلْتُنَّ	أَنْتُنَّ
نُفْعَلُ	نَفْعَلُ	فُعِلْنَا	فَعَلْنَا	نَحْنُ
يُفْعَلَانِ	يَفْعَلَانِ	فُعِلَا	فَعَلَا	هُمَا
تُفْعَلَانِ	تَفْعَلَانِ	فُعِلَتَا	فَعَلَتَا	هُمَا
تُفْعَلَانِ	تَفْعَلَانِ	فُعِلْتُمَا	فَعَلْتُمَا	أَنْتُمَا

Table 6: SOUND VERBS (فَعَلَ) : FORM I (أَلْفِعْلُ السَّالِمُ)

Passive		Active						
Imperfect	Perfect	Imperative	Imperfect			Perfect		
Indicative			Jussive	Subjunctive	Indicative			
يُفْعَلُ	فُعِلَ		يَفْعَلْ	يَفْعَلَ	يَفْعَلُ	فَعَلَ	(هُوَ)	
تُفْعَلُ	فُعِلَتْ		تَفْعَلْ	تَفْعَلَ	تَفْعَلُ	فَعَلَتْ	(هِيَ)	
تُفْعَلُ	فُعِلْتَ	اِفْعَلْ/اُفْعُلْ*	تَفْعَلْ	تَفْعَلَ	تَفْعَلُ	فَعَلْتَ	(أَنْتَ)	
تُفْعَلِينَ	فُعِلْتِ	اِفْعَلِي/اُفْعُلِي*	تَفْعَلِي	تَفْعَلِي	تَفْعَلِينَ	فَعَلْتِ	(أَنْتِ)	
أُفْعَلُ	فُعِلْتُ		أَفْعَلْ	أَفْعَلَ	أَفْعَلُ	فَعَلْتُ	(أَنَا)	
يُفْعَلُونَ	فُعِلُوا		يَفْعَلُوا	يَفْعَلُوا	يَفْعَلُونَ	فَعَلُوا	(هُمْ)	
يُفْعَلْنَ	فُعِلْنَ		يَفْعَلْنَ	يَفْعَلْنَ	يَفْعَلْنَ	فَعَلْنَ	(هُنَّ)	
تُفْعَلُونَ	فُعِلْتُمْ	اِفْعَلُوا/اُفْعُلُوا*	تَفْعَلُوا	تَفْعَلُوا	تَفْعَلُونَ	فَعَلْتُمْ	(أَنْتُمْ)	
تُفْعَلْنَ	فُعِلْتُنَّ	اِفْعَلْنَ/اُفْعُلْنَ*	تَفْعَلْنَ	تَفْعَلْنَ	تَفْعَلْنَ	فَعَلْتُنَّ	(أَنْتُنَّ)	
نُفْعَلُ	فُعِلْنَا		نَفْعَلْ	نَفْعَلَ	نَفْعَلُ	فَعَلْنَا	(نَحْنُ)	
يُفْعَلَانِ	فُعِلَا		يَفْعَلَا	يَفْعَلَا	يَفْعَلَانِ	فَعَلَا	(هُمَا)	
تُفْعَلَانِ	فُعِلَتَا		تَفْعَلَا	تَفْعَلَا	تَفْعَلَانِ	فَعَلَتَا	(هُمَا)	
تُفْعَلَانِ	فُعِلْتُمَا	اِفْعَلَا/اُفْعُلَا*	تَفْعَلَا	تَفْعَلَا	تَفْعَلَانِ	فَعَلْتُمَا	(أَنْتُمَا)	

* This is the form of the imperative when the imperfect stem vowel is *u*.

DERIVED FORMS OF THE VERBS (أَلْفِعْلُ الْمَزِيدُ)

The base form (Form I) of the Arabic verb (فَعَلَ / يَفْعُلُ) can be extended by gemination of consonants, prolongation of vowels, prefixation or infixation, or a combination of the two possibilities. The extensions of the base form, like the base form itself, are called Forms.

There are 15 Forms, of which only 10, however, are in common use. They are referred to by Roman numerals in European grammar books and dictionaries: base Form = Form I, derived Forms = Form II, III, ... X. Theoretically, all forms can be derived from any verb. However, a verb rarely occurs in more than 4 or 5 forms, and in fact it often occurs only in its basic form or a derived form.

Table 7: SOUND VERBS (فَعَّلَ) : FORM II

Characteristic: doubling of R2.

The sequence of vowels in the imperfect form is **u - a - i**.

Perfect tense:							فَعَّلَ
Imperfect tense:							يُفَعِّلُ

Passive		Active					
Imperfect	Perfect	Imperative	Imperfect			Perfect	
Indicative			Jussive	Subjunctive	Indicative		
يُفَعَّلُ	فُعِّلَ		يُفَعِّلْ	يُفَعِّلَ	يُفَعِّلُ	فَعَّلَ	(هُوَ)
تُفَعَّلُ	فُعِّلَتْ		تُفَعِّلْ	تُفَعِّلَ	تُفَعِّلُ	فَعَّلَتْ	(هِيَ)
تُفَعَّلُ	فُعِّلْتَ	فَعِّلْ	تُفَعِّلْ	تُفَعِّلَ	تُفَعِّلُ	فَعَّلْتَ	(أَنْتَ)
تُفَعَّلِينَ	فُعِّلْتِ	فَعِّلِي	تُفَعِّلِي	تُفَعِّلِي	تُفَعِّلِينَ	فَعَّلْتِ	(أَنْتِ)
أُفَعَّلُ	فُعِّلْتُ		أُفَعِّلْ	أُفَعِّلَ	أُفَعِّلُ	فَعَّلْتُ	(أَنَا)
يُفَعَّلُونَ	فُعِّلُوا		يُفَعِّلُوا	يُفَعِّلُوا	يُفَعِّلُونَ	فَعَّلُوا	(هُمْ)
يُفَعَّلْنَ	فُعِّلْنَ		يُفَعِّلْنَ	يُفَعِّلْنَ	يُفَعِّلْنَ	فَعَّلْنَ	(هُنَّ)
تُفَعَّلُونَ	فُعِّلْتُمْ	فَعِّلُوا	تُفَعِّلُوا	تُفَعِّلُوا	تُفَعِّلُونَ	فَعَّلْتُمْ	(أَنْتُمْ)
تُفَعَّلْنَ	فُعِّلْتُنَّ	فَعِّلْنَ	تُفَعِّلْنَ	تُفَعِّلْنَ	تُفَعِّلْنَ	فَعَّلْتُنَّ	(أَنْتُنَّ)
نُفَعَّلُ	فُعِّلْنَا		نُفَعِّلْ	نُفَعِّلَ	نُفَعِّلُ	فَعَّلْنَا	(نَحْنُ)
يُفَعَّلَانِ	فُعِّلَا		يُفَعِّلَا	يُفَعِّلَا	يُفَعِّلَانِ	فَعَّلَا	(هُمَا)
تُفَعَّلَانِ	فُعِّلَتَا		تُفَعِّلَا	تُفَعِّلَا	تُفَعِّلَانِ	فَعَّلَتَا	(هُمَا)
تُفَعَّلَانِ	فُعِّلْتُمَا	فَعِّلَا	تُفَعِّلَا	تُفَعِّلَا	تُفَعِّلَانِ	فَعَّلْتُمَا	(أَنْتُمَا)

The quadriliteral verb has the same vocalization of the imperfect form.

to translate		تَرْجَمَ ، يَتَرْجِمُ		فَعْلَلَ ، يُفَعْلِلُ

Table 40 supplies a full survey about all forms of the quadriliteral verb.

Table 8: SOUND VERBS (فَاعَلَ) : FORM III

Characteristic: prolongation of the vowel that follows R₁.

The sequence of vowels in the imperfect form is ***u - ā - i***.

Passive		Active					
Imperfect	Perfect	Imperative	Imperfect			Perfect	فَاعَلَ (Perfect) / يُفَاعِلُ (Imperfect)
Indicative			Jussive	Subjunctive	Indicative		
يُفَاعَلُ	فُوعِلَ		يُفَاعِلْ	يُفَاعَلَ	يُفَاعِلُ	فَاعَلَ	(هُوَ)
تُفَاعَلُ	فُوعِلَتْ		تُفَاعِلْ	تُفَاعِلَ	تُفَاعِلُ	فَاعَلَتْ	(هِيَ)
تُفَاعَلُ	فُوعِلْتَ	فَاعِلْ	تُفَاعِلْ	تُفَاعِلَ	تُفَاعِلُ	فَاعَلْتَ	(أَنْتَ)
تُفَاعَلِينَ	فُوعِلْتِ	فَاعِلِي	تُفَاعِلِي	تُفَاعِلِي	تُفَاعَلِينَ	فَاعَلْتِ	(أَنْتِ)
أُفَاعَلُ	فُوعِلْتُ		أُفَاعِلْ	أُفَاعِلَ	أُفَاعِلُ	فَاعَلْتُ	(أَنَا)
يُفَاعَلُونَ	فُوعِلُوا		يُفَاعِلُوا	يُفَاعِلُوا	يُفَاعِلُونَ	فَاعَلُوا	(هُمْ)
يُفَاعَلْنَ	فُوعِلْنَ		يُفَاعِلْنَ	يُفَاعِلْنَ	يُفَاعِلْنَ	فَاعَلْنَ	(هُنَّ)
تُفَاعَلُونَ	فُوعِلْتُمْ	فَاعِلُوا	تُفَاعِلُوا	تُفَاعِلُوا	تُفَاعِلُونَ	فَاعَلْتُمْ	(أَنْتُمْ)
تُفَاعَلْنَ	فُوعِلْتُنَّ	فَاعِلْنَ	تُفَاعِلْنَ	تُفَاعِلْنَ	تُفَاعِلْنَ	فَاعَلْتُنَّ	(أَنْتُنَّ)
نُفَاعَلُ	فُوعِلْنَا		نُفَاعِلْ	نُفَاعِلَ	نُفَاعِلُ	فَاعَلْنَا	(نَحْنُ)
يُفَاعَلَانِ	فُوعِلَا		يُفَاعِلَا	يُفَاعِلَا	يُفَاعَلَانِ	فَاعَلَا	(هُمَا)
تُفَاعَلَانِ	فُوعِلَتَا		تُفَاعِلَا	تُفَاعِلَا	تُفَاعَلَانِ	فَاعَلَتَا	(هُمَا)
تُفَاعَلَانِ	فُوعِلْتُمَا	فَاعِلَا	تُفَاعِلَا	تُفَاعِلَا	تُفَاعَلَانِ	فَاعَلْتُمَا	(أَنْتُمَا)

Table 9: SOUND VERBS (أَفْعَلَ) : FORM IV

Characteristic: prefix *a-* أ, vowellessness of R1

The prefixed *Hamza* of Form IV is a *Hamzat al-qaṭ'*. The sequence of vowels in the imperfect form is **u - i**.

Perfect tense:							أَفْعَلَ
Imperfect tense:							يُفْعِلُ
Passive		Active					
Imperfect	Perfect	Imperative	Imperfect			Perfect	
Indicative			Jussive	Subjunctive	Indicative		
يُفْعَلُ	أُفْعَلَ		يُفْعِلْ	يُفْعِلَ	يُفْعِلُ	أَفْعَلَ	(هُوَ)
تُفْعَلُ	أُفْعِلَتْ		تُفْعِلْ	تُفْعِلَ	تُفْعِلُ	أَفْعَلَتْ	(هِيَ)
تُفْعَلُ	أُفْعِلْتَ	اَفْعِلْ	تُفْعِلْ	تُفْعِلَ	تُفْعِلُ	أَفْعَلْتَ	(أَنْتَ)
تُفْعَلِينَ	أُفْعِلْتِ	اَفْعِلِي	تُفْعِلِي	تُفْعِلِي	تُفْعِلِينَ	أَفْعَلْتِ	(أَنْتِ)
أُفْعَلُ	أُفْعِلْتُ		أُفْعِلْ	أُفْعِلَ	أُفْعِلُ	أَفْعَلْتُ	(أَنَا)
يُفْعَلُونَ	أُفْعِلُوا		يُفْعِلُوا	يُفْعِلُوا	يُفْعِلُونَ	أَفْعَلُوا	(هُم)
يُفْعَلْنَ	أُفْعِلْنَ		يُفْعِلْنَ	يُفْعِلْنَ	يُفْعِلْنَ	أَفْعَلْنَ	(هُنَّ)
تُفْعَلُونَ	أُفْعِلْتُم	اَفْعِلُوا	تُفْعِلُوا	تُفْعِلُوا	تُفْعِلُونَ	أَفْعَلْتُمْ	(أَنْتُم)
تُفْعَلْنَ	أُفْعِلْتُنَّ	اَفْعِلْنَ	تُفْعِلْنَ	تُفْعِلْنَ	تُفْعِلْنَ	أَفْعَلْتُنَّ	(أَنْتُنَّ)
نُفْعَلُ	أُفْعِلْنَا		نُفْعِلْ	نُفْعِلَ	نُفْعِلُ	أَفْعَلْنَا	(نَحْنُ)
يُفْعَلَانِ	أُفْعِلَا		يُفْعِلَا	يُفْعِلَا	يُفْعِلَانِ	أَفْعَلَا	(هُمَا)
تُفْعَلَانِ	أُفْعِلَتَا		تُفْعِلَا	تُفْعِلَا	تُفْعِلَانِ	أَفْعَلَتَا	(هُمَا)
تُفْعَلَانِ	أُفْعِلْتُمَا	اَفْعِلَا	تُفْعِلَا	تُفْعِلَا	تُفْعِلَانِ	أَفْعَلْتُمَا	(أَنْتُمَا)

The imperfect tense of Forms II and IV are neither distinguishable from each other nor from the basic Form without auxiliary signs.

Table 10 : SOUND VERBS (تَفَعَّلَ) : FORM V

Form V has the same basic structure as Form II. The prefix *ta-* ـتَ is added as a distinguishing characteristic. The sequence of vowels in the perfect and imperfect tense is - *a* - throughout.

| Perfect tense | | | | | | | تَفَعَّلَ |
| Imperfect tense | | | | | | | يَتَفَعَّلُ |

Passive		Active					
Imperfect	Perfect	Imperative	Imperfect			Perfect	
Indicative			Jussive	Subjunctive	Indicative		
يُتَفَعَّلُ	تُفُعِّلَ		يَتَفَعَّلْ	يَتَفَعَّلَ	يَتَفَعَّلُ	تَفَعَّلَ	(هُوَ)
تُتَفَعَّلُ	تُفُعِّلَتْ		تَتَفَعَّلْ	تَتَفَعَّلَ	تَتَفَعَّلُ	تَفَعَّلَتْ	(هِيَ)
تُتَفَعَّلُ	تُفُعِّلْتَ	تَفَعَّلْ	تَتَفَعَّلْ	تَتَفَعَّلَ	تَتَفَعَّلُ	تَفَعَّلْتَ	(أَنْتَ)
تُتَفَعَّلِينَ	تُفُعِّلْتِ	تَفَعَّلِي	تَتَفَعَّلِي	تَتَفَعَّلِي	تَتَفَعَّلِينَ	تَفَعَّلْتِ	(أَنْتِ)
أُتَفَعَّلُ	تُفُعِّلْتُ		أَتَفَعَّلْ	أَتَفَعَّلَ	أَتَفَعَّلُ	تَفَعَّلْتُ	(أَنَا)
يُتَفَعَّلُونَ	تُفُعِّلُوا		يَتَفَعَّلُوا	يَتَفَعَّلُوا	يَتَفَعَّلُونَ	تَفَعَّلُوا	(هُمْ)
يُتَفَعَّلْنَ	تُفُعِّلْنَ		يَتَفَعَّلْنَ	يَتَفَعَّلْنَ	يَتَفَعَّلْنَ	تَفَعَّلْنَ	(هُنَّ)
تُتَفَعَّلُونَ	تُفُعِّلْتُمْ	تَفَعَّلُوا	تَتَفَعَّلُوا	تَتَفَعَّلُوا	تَتَفَعَّلُونَ	تَفَعَّلْتُمْ	(أَنْتُم)
تُتَفَعَّلْنَ	تُفُعِّلْتُنَّ	تَفَعَّلْنَ	تَتَفَعَّلْنَ	تَتَفَعَّلْنَ	تَتَفَعَّلْنَ	تَفَعَّلْتُنَّ	(أَنْتُنَّ)
نُتَفَعَّلُ	تُفُعِّلْنَا		نَتَفَعَّلْ	نَتَفَعَّلَ	نَتَفَعَّلُ	تَفَعَّلْنَا	(نَحْنُ)
يُتَفَعَّلَانِ	تُفُعِّلَا		يَتَفَعَّلَا	يَتَفَعَّلَا	يَتَفَعَّلَانِ	تَفَعَّلَا	(هُمَا)
تُتَفَعَّلَانِ	تُفُعِّلَتَا		تَتَفَعَّلَا	تَتَفَعَّلَا	تَتَفَعَّلَانِ	تَفَعَّلَتَا	(هُمَا)
تُتَفَعَّلَانِ	تُفُعِّلْتُمَا	تَفَعَّلَا	تَتَفَعَّلَا	تَتَفَعَّلَا	تَتَفَعَّلَانِ	تَفَعَّلْتُمَا	(أَنْتُمَا)

The imperative of Form V is used with only a few verbs.

Table 11 : SOUND VERBS (تَفَاعَلَ) : FORM VI

Form VI has the same basic structure as Form III. The prefix *ta-* ـَت is added as a distinguishing characteristic. The sequence of vowels in the perfect and imperfect tense is - *a* - throughout.

Perfect tense							تَفَاعَلَ
Imperfect tense							يَتَفَاعَلُ
Passive		Active					
Imperfect	Perfect	Imperative	Imperfect			Perfect	
Indicative			Jussive	Subjunctive	Indicative		
يُتَفَاعَلُ	تُفُوعِلَ		يَتَفَاعَلْ	يَتَفَاعَلَ	يَتَفَاعَلُ	تَفَاعَلَ	(هُوَ)
تُتَفَاعَلُ	تُفُوعِلَتْ		تَتَفَاعَلْ	تَتَفَاعَلَ	تَتَفَاعَلُ	تَفَاعَلَتْ	(هِيَ)
تُتَفَاعَلُ	تُفُوعِلْتَ	تَفَاعَلْ	تَتَفَاعَلْ	تَتَفَاعَلَ	تَتَفَاعَلُ	تَفَاعَلْتَ	(أَنْتَ)
تُتَفَاعَلِينَ	تُفُوعِلْتِ	تَفَاعَلِي	تَتَفَاعَلِي	تَتَفَاعَلِي	تَتَفَاعَلِينَ	تَفَاعَلْتِ	(أَنْتِ)
أُتَفَاعَلُ	تُفُوعِلْتُ		أَفَاعَلْ	أَفَاعَلَ	أَفَاعَلُ	تَفَاعَلْتُ	(أَنَا)
يُتَفَاعَلُونَ	تُفُوعِلُوا		يَتَفَاعَلُوا	يَتَفَاعَلُوا	يَتَفَاعَلُونَ	تَفَاعَلُوا	(هُمْ)
يُتَفَاعَلْنَ	تُفُوعِلْنَ		يَتَفَاعَلْنَ	يَتَفَاعَلْنَ	يَتَفَاعَلْنَ	تَفَاعَلْنَ	(هُنَّ)
تُتَفَاعَلُونَ	تُفُوعِلْتُمْ	تَفَاعَلُوا	تَتَفَاعَلُوا	تَتَفَاعَلُوا	تَتَفَاعَلُونَ	تَفَاعَلْتُمْ	(أَنْتُم)
تُتَفَاعَلْنَ	تُفُوعِلْتُنَّ	تَفَاعَلْنَ	تَتَفَاعَلْنَ	تَتَفَاعَلْنَ	تَتَفَاعَلْنَ	تَفَاعَلْتُنَّ	(أَنْتُنَّ)
نُتَفَاعَلُ	تُفُوعِلْنَا		نَتَفَاعَلْ	نَتَفَاعَلَ	نَتَفَاعَلُ	تَفَاعَلْنَا	(نَحْنُ)
يُتَفَاعَلَانِ	تُفُوعِلَا		يَتَفَاعَلَا	يَتَفَاعَلَا	يَتَفَاعَلَانِ	تَفَاعَلَا	(هُمَا)
تُتَفَاعَلَانِ	تُفُوعِلَتَا		تَتَفَاعَلَا	تَتَفَاعَلَا	تَتَفَاعَلَانِ	تَفَاعَلَتَا	(هُمَا)
تُتَفَاعَلَانِ	تُفُوعِلْتُمَا	تَفَاعَلَا	تَتَفَاعَلَا	تَتَفَاعَلَا	تَتَفَاعَلَانِ	تَفَاعَلْتُمَا	(أَنْتُمَا)

The imperative of Form VI is used with only a few verbs.

Table 12 : SOUND VERBS (انْفَعَلَ): FORM VII

Characteristic of Form VII: prefix *n-* ‍ان

The consonant cluster at the beginning of the verb due to the prefix is dissolved by the prosthetic vowel *i-: (i)n-* ‍ان . The *Hamza*, as the chair of the vowel *i*, is a *Hamzat al-waṣl*. The sequence of vowels in the perfect tense is *a* throughout - with the exception of the prosthetic vowel. The prosthetic vowel is omitted in the imperfect tense; the sequence of vowels is: *a - a - i*.

Perfect tense						انْفَعَلَ
Imperfect tense						يَنْفَعِلُ

Passive		Active				
Imperfect	Perfect	Imperative	Imperfect			Perfect
Indicative			Jussive	Subjunctive	Indicative	
يُنْفَعَلُ	انْفُعِلَ		يَنْفَعِلْ	يَنْفَعِلَ	يَنْفَعِلُ	انْفَعَلَ	(هُوَ)
تُنْفَعَلُ	انْفُعِلَتْ		تَنْفَعِلْ	تَنْفَعِلَ	تَنْفَعِلُ	انْفَعَلَتْ	(هِيَ)
تُنْفَعَلُ	انْفُعِلْتَ	انْفَعِلْ	تَنْفَعِلْ	تَنْفَعِلَ	تَنْفَعِلُ	انْفَعَلْتَ	(أَنْتَ)
تُنْفَعَلِينَ	انْفُعِلْتِ	انْفَعِلِي	تَنْفَعِلِي	تَنْفَعِلِي	تَنْفَعِلِينَ	انْفَعَلْتِ	(أَنْتِ)
أُنْفَعَلُ	انْفُعِلْتُ		أَنْفَعِلْ	أَنْفَعِلَ	أَنْفَعِلُ	انْفَعَلْتُ	(أَنَا)
يُنْفَعَلُونَ	انْفُعِلُوا		يَنْفَعِلُوا	يَنْفَعِلُوا	يَنْفَعِلُونَ	انْفَعَلُوا	(هُمْ)
يُنْفَعَلْنَ	انْفُعِلْنَ		يَنْفَعِلْنَ	يَنْفَعِلْنَ	يَنْفَعِلْنَ	انْفَعَلْنَ	(هُنَّ)
تُنْفَعَلُونَ	انْفُعِلْتُمْ	انْفَعِلُوا	تَنْفَعِلُوا	تَنْفَعِلُوا	تَنْفَعِلُونَ	انْفَعَلْتُمْ	(أَنْتُمْ)
تُنْفَعَلْنَ	انْفُعِلْتُنَّ	انْفَعِلْنَ	تَنْفَعِلْنَ	تَنْفَعِلْنَ	تَنْفَعِلْنَ	انْفَعَلْتُنَّ	(أَنْتُنَّ)
نُنْفَعَلُ	انْفُعِلْنَا		نَنْفَعِلْ	نَنْفَعِلَ	نَنْفَعِلُ	انْفَعَلْنَا	(نَحْنُ)
يُنْفَعَلَانِ	انْفُعِلَا		يَنْفَعِلَا	يَنْفَعِلَا	يَنْفَعِلَانِ	انْفَعَلَا	(هُمَا)
تُنْفَعَلَانِ	انْفُعِلَتَا		تَنْفَعِلَا	تَنْفَعِلَا	تَنْفَعِلَانِ	انْفَعَلَتَا	(هُمَا)
تُنْفَعَلَانِ	انْفُعِلْتُمَا	انْفَعِلَا	تَنْفَعِلَا	تَنْفَعِلَا	تَنْفَعِلَانِ	انْفَعَلْتُمَا	(أَنْتُمَا)

Table 13 : SOUND VERBS (اِفْتَعَلَ): FORM VIII

Characteristic of Form VIII: infix *t(a)*- ـتـ between R1 and R2; R1 *is not followed by a vowel*. The *Hamza*, as the chair of the vowel *i*, is a *Hamzat al-waṣl*. The sequence of vowels in the perfect tense is *a* throughout - with the exception of the prosthetic vowel. The prosthetic vowel is omitted in the imperfect tense; the succession of vowels is: *a - a - i*.

Perfect tense						افْتَعَلَ
Imperfect tense						يَفْتَعِلُ
Passive		Active				
Imperfect	Perfect	Imperative	Imperfect			Perfect
Indicative			Jussive	Subjunctive	Indicative	
يُفْتَعَلُ	افْتُعِلَ		يَفْتَعِلْ	يَفْتَعِلَ	يَفْتَعِلُ	افْتَعَلَ	(هُوَ)
تُفْتَعَلُ	افْتُعِلَتْ		تَفْتَعِلْ	تَفْتَعِلَ	تَفْتَعِلُ	افْتَعَلَتْ	(هِيَ)
تُفْتَعَلُ	افْتُعِلْتَ	افْتَعِلْ	تَفْتَعِلْ	تَفْتَعِلَ	تَفْتَعِلُ	افْتَعَلْتَ	(أَنْتَ)
تُفْتَعَلِينَ	افْتُعِلْتِ	افْتَعِلِي	تَفْتَعِلِي	تَفْتَعِلِي	تَفْتَعِلِينَ	افْتَعَلْتِ	(أَنْتِ)
أُفْتَعَلُ	افْتُعِلْتُ		أَفْتَعِلْ	أَفْتَعِلَ	أَفْتَعِلُ	افْتَعَلْتُ	(أَنَا)
يُفْتَعَلُونَ	افْتُعِلُوا		يَفْتَعِلُوا	يَفْتَعِلُوا	يَفْتَعِلُونَ	افْتَعَلُوا	(هُمْ)
يُفْتَعَلْنَ	افْتُعِلْنَ		يَفْتَعِلْنَ	يَفْتَعِلْنَ	يَفْتَعِلْنَ	افْتَعَلْنَ	(هُنَّ)
تُفْتَعَلُونَ	افْتُعِلْتُمْ	افْتَعِلُوا	تَفْتَعِلُوا	تَفْتَعِلُوا	تَفْتَعِلُونَ	افْتَعَلْتُمْ	(أَنْتُم)
تُفْتَعَلْنَ	افْتُعِلْتُنَّ	افْتَعِلْنَ	تَفْتَعِلْنَ	تَفْتَعِلْنَ	تَفْتَعِلْنَ	افْتَعَلْتُنَّ	(أَنْتُنَّ)
نُفْتَعَلُ	افْتُعِلْنَا		نَفْتَعِلْ	نَفْتَعِلَ	نَفْتَعِلُ	افْتَعَلْنَا	(نَحْنُ)
يُفْتَعَلَانِ	افْتُعِلَا		يَفْتَعِلَا	يَفْتَعِلَا	يَفْتَعِلَانِ	افْتَعَلَا	(هُمَا)
تُفْتَعَلَانِ	افْتُعِلَتَا		تَفْتَعِلَا	تَفْتَعِلَا	تَفْتَعِلَانِ	افْتَعَلَتَا	(هُمَا)
تُفْتَعَلَانِ	افْتُعِلْتُمَا	افْتَعِلَا	تَفْتَعِلَا	تَفْتَعِلَا	تَفْتَعِلَانِ	افْتَعَلْتُمَا	(أَنْتُمَا)

There are various rules for the assimilation of the infix *t-* to R1 = ط، ض، ص، ز، ظ ذ، د، ث، ت،

The most important rules are as follows:

R1 = ت + infix ت > تّ ـــ	اتَّبَعَ	to follow, to succeed (sb./sth.), to pursue, to observe
R1 = د + infix ت > دّ ـــ	ادَّفَأ	to warm o.s.
R1 = ذ + infix ت > دّ ـــ	ادَّخَرَ	to keep, to save
R1 = ز + infix ت > زد	ازْدَهَرَ	to blossom, to flourish, to prosper
R1 = ص + infix ت > ـصط ـــ	اصْطَدَمَ بِ	to collide with
R1 = ض + infix ت > ـضط ـــ	اضْطَهَدَ	to suppress, to oppress
R1= ط + infix ت > طّ ـــ	اطَّلَعَ عَلَى	to look at, to inspect, to examine
R1= ظ + infix ت > ظّ ـــ	اظَّلَمَ	to suffer injustice

Table 14 : SOUND VERBS (اِفْعَلَّ): FORM IX

Form IX is rare because it is primarily used in conjunction with colours and defects.

	verbal noun	verb
to be or to turn/become white	اِبْيِضَاضٌ	أَبْيَضُ < اِبْيَضَّ
to be or to turn/become red	اِحْمِرَارٌ	أَحْمَرُ < اِحْمَرَّ
to be or to turn/become blue	اِزْرِقَاقٌ	أَزْرَقُ < اِزْرَقَّ
to be or to turn/become brown	اِسْمِرَارٌ	أَسْمَرُ < اِسْمَرَّ
to be or to turn/become black	اِسْوِدَادٌ	أَسْوَدُ < اِسْوَدَّ
to be or to turn/become yellow	اِصْفِرَارٌ	أَصْفَرُ < اِصْفَرَّ

The initial *Hamza* is *Hamzat al-waṣl*, as in Forms VII, VIII and X. The verbs of Form IX are virtually only used in the 3ʳᵈ p.sg.m. or f.

Another pattern with the same function is:

	verbal noun	verb	verbal noun	verb
to be or to turn/ become red/to redden	اِحْمَارٌّ	اِحْمَارَّ	اِفْعَالٌّ	اِفْعَالَّ

Table 15 : SOUND VERBS (اِسْتَفْعَلَ): FORM X

Characteristic of Form X: prefix *st(a)*- اِسْت; R1 is not followed by a vowel. The *Hamza*, as the chair of the vowel *i*, is a *Hamzat al-waṣl*. The succession of vowels in the perfect tense is *a* throughout - with the exception of the prosthetic vowel. The prosthetic vowel is omitted in the imperfect tense; the sequence of vowels is: *a - a - i*.

perfect tense							اِسْتَفْعَلَ
imperfect tense							يَسْتَفْعِلُ
Passive		Active					
Imperfect	Perfect	Imperative	Imperfect			Perfect	
Indicative			Jussive	Subjunctive	Indicative		
يُسْتَفْعَلُ	أُسْتُفْعِلَ		يَسْتَفْعِلْ	يَسْتَفْعِلَ	يَسْتَفْعِلُ	اِسْتَفْعَلَ	(هُوَ)
تُسْتَفْعَلُ	أُسْتُفْعِلَتْ		تَسْتَفْعِلْ	تَسْتَفْعِلَ	تَسْتَفْعِلُ	اِسْتَفْعَلَتْ	(هِيَ)
تُسْتَفْعَلُ	أُسْتُفْعِلْتَ	اِسْتَفْعِلْ	تَسْتَفْعِلْ	تَسْتَفْعِلَ	تَسْتَفْعِلُ	اِسْتَفْعَلْتَ	(أَنْتَ)
تُسْتَفْعَلِينَ	أُسْتُفْعِلْتِ	اِسْتَفْعِلِي	تَسْتَفْعِلِي	تَسْتَفْعِلِي	تَسْتَفْعِلِينَ	اِسْتَفْعَلْتِ	(أَنْتِ)
أُسْتَفْعَلُ	أُسْتُفْعِلْتُ		أَسْتَفْعِلْ	أَسْتَفْعِلَ	أَسْتَفْعِلُ	اِسْتَفْعَلْتُ	(أَنَا)
يُسْتَفْعَلُونَ	أُسْتُفْعِلُوا		يَسْتَفْعِلُوا	يَسْتَفْعِلُوا	يَسْتَفْعِلُونَ	اِسْتَفْعَلُوا	(هُمْ)
يُسْتَفْعَلْنَ	أُسْتُفْعِلْنَ		يَسْتَفْعِلْنَ	يَسْتَفْعِلْنَ	يَسْتَفْعِلْنَ	اِسْتَفْعَلْنَ	(هُنَّ)
تُسْتَفْعَلُونَ	أُسْتُفْعِلْتُمْ	اِسْتَفْعِلُوا	تَسْتَفْعِلُوا	تَسْتَفْعِلُوا	تَسْتَفْعِلُونَ	اِسْتَفْعَلْتُمْ	(أَنْتُمْ)
تُسْتَفْعَلْنَ	أُسْتُفْعِلْتُنَّ	اِسْتَفْعِلْنَ	تَسْتَفْعِلْنَ	تَسْتَفْعِلْنَ	تَسْتَفْعِلْنَ	اِسْتَفْعَلْتُنَّ	(أَنْتُنَّ)
نُسْتَفْعَلُ	أُسْتُفْعِلْنَا		نَسْتَفْعِلْ	نَسْتَفْعِلَ	نَسْتَفْعِلُ	اِسْتَفْعَلْنَا	(نَحْنُ)
يُسْتَفْعَلَانِ	أُسْتُفْعِلَا		يَسْتَفْعِلَا	يَسْتَفْعِلَا	يَسْتَفْعِلَانِ	اِسْتَفْعَلَا	(هُمَا)
تُسْتَفْعَلَانِ	أُسْتُفْعِلَتَا		تَسْتَفْعِلَا	تَسْتَفْعِلَا	تَسْتَفْعِلَانِ	اِسْتَفْعَلَتَا	(هُمَا)
تُسْتَفْعَلَانِ	أُسْتُفْعِلْتُمَا	اِسْتَفْعِلَا	تَسْتَفْعِلَا	تَسْتَفْعِلَا	تَسْتَفْعِلَانِ	اِسْتَفْعَلْتُمَا	(أَنْتُمَا)

Table 16 : SOUND VERBS (أَلْفِعْلُ السَّالِمُ) : FORMS II – X (SUMMARY)

Passive		Active					
Imperfect	Perfect	Imperative	Imperfect			Perfect	
Indicative			Jussive	Subjunctive	Indicative		
يُفَعَّلُ	فُعِّلَ	فَعِّلْ	يُفَعِّلْ	يُفَعِّلَ	يُفَعِّلُ	فَعَّلَ	II
يُفَاعَلُ	فُوعِلَ	فَاعِلْ	يُفَاعِلْ	يُفَاعِلَ	يُفَاعِلُ	فَاعَلَ	III
يُفْعَلُ	أُفْعِلَ	أَفْعِلْ	يُفْعِلْ	يُفْعِلَ	يُفْعِلُ	أَفْعَلَ	IV
يُتَفَعَّلُ	تُفُعِّلَ	تَفَعَّلْ	يَتَفَعَّلْ	يَتَفَعَّلَ	يَتَفَعَّلُ	تَفَعَّلَ	V
يُتَفَاعَلُ	تُفُوعِلَ	تَفَاعَلْ	يَتَفَاعَلْ	يَتَفَاعَلَ	يَتَفَاعَلُ	تَفَاعَلَ	VI
يُنْفَعَلُ	أُنْفُعِلَ	اِنْفَعِلْ	يَنْفَعِلْ	يَنْفَعِلَ	يَنْفَعِلُ	اِنْفَعَلَ	VII
يُفْتَعَلُ	اُفْتُعِلَ	اِفْتَعِلْ	يَفْتَعِلْ	يَفْتَعِلَ	يَفْتَعِلُ	اِفْتَعَلَ	VIII
يُسْتَفْعَلُ	اُسْتُفْعِلَ	اِسْتَفْعِلْ	يَسْتَفْعِلْ	يَسْتَفْعِلَ	يَسْتَفْعِلُ	اِسْتَفْعَلَ	X

CHARACTERISTIC FEATURES OF THE DERIVED FORMS

Originally, the derived Forms are variants of Form I which serve to express aspects as well as the character of the respective verb. A functional-semantic description of the Forms is possible, however, it provides little benefit for language practice. The learner does not need to create certain Forms anew himself. Knowing the basic meaning of a certain Form can, however, enable him to understand an unfamiliar verb without referring to a dictionary.

Changes with regard to meaning correspond to the formal extensions of the base form as well. Thus e.g. an intensifying, causative and denominative meaning is stated for Form II, a reflexive meaning for Form VII. However, as every individual verb is lexically fixed, the original "value of the form" is often not identifiable any more. Basically, it must be stated here that many verbs do not fit into a general semantic system of the individual Forms. Therefore, it is simply not enough to memorize only the root or Form I of a verb. Every verb must be learned according to its respective Form. Knowing the Forms is necessary to ensure their correct technical use.

In the following we provide some characteristic features of the derived Forms.

Form II	فَعَّلَ – يُفَعِّلُ
Intensifying, causative, denominative (it is productive in modern Arabic in this function)	nearly all its verbs are transitive, most frequent after Form I
Form III	فَاعَلَ – يُفَاعِلُ
denoting an aim (attempted) effect on a person or thing	many verbs do not show this meaning of the Form, nearly all verbs are transitive.
Form IV	أَفْعَلَ – يُفْعِلُ
causative, denominative, and occurs in various other meanings which are hard to summarize	most verbs of this Form are transitive
Form V	تَفَعَّلَ – يَتَفَعَّلُ
intransitives in relation to Form II as well as some denominatives	mostly intransitive
Form VI	تَفَاعَلَ – يَتَفَاعَلُ
Mostly a reciprocal meaning in relation to Form III	transitive and intransitive, rare
Form VII	انْفَعَلَ – يَنْفَعِلُ
intransitives and reflexives	in colloquial language used as passive voice of verbs of Form I, all intransitive
Form VIII	افْتَعَلَ – يَفْتَعِلُ
various meanings, which are partially very different from each other, some verbs are reciprocal variants of Form I.	partly transitive, partly intransitive
Form IX	افْعَلَّ – يَفْعَلُّ
almost always used in conjunction with colours and defects, denotes both the arising of the respective state and its existence, which is often characterized by intensity	always intransitive, very rare
Form X	اسْتَفْعَلَ – يَسْتَفْعِلُ
often occurs in the meaning *"to request sth., to ask s.o. for s.th."* which is included in the meaning of the root	primarily transitive

HAMZATED VERBS (اَلأَفْعَالُ الْمَهْمُوزَةُ)

GENERAL

In principle, Verbs with *Hamza* as R1, R2 or R3 follow the same conjugational patterns of the sound verb (اَلْفِعْلُ السَّالِمُ). Their peculiarities are nearly exclusively a question of correct spelling (☞ Spelling of *Hamza*). The phonetical peculiarities as compared with the sound verb are limited to a few patterns of the verbs in which *Hamza* is the 1st radical. This is due to the following phonetic rule: *'a'* becomes *'ā, 'i'* ⇨ *'ī* and *'u'* ⇨ *'ū*. However, this rule does not apply throughout.

Form I

أَخَذَ	=	فَعَلَ
يَأْخُذُ	=	يَفْعَلُ
آخُذُ (أَأْخُذُ >)	=	أَفْعَلُ
آخِذٌ (أَاخِذٌ >)	=	فَاعِلٌ
خُذْ	=	إِفْعَلْ

The two imperatives كُلْ "*Eat!*" and مُرْ "*Order!*", which are derived from the verbs أَكَلَ "*to eat*" and أَمَرَ "*to order*", have the same form as خُذْ "*take*"; otherwise the imperative is formed by R1 being included, accordingly: اُومُلْ ⇨ أُؤْمُلْ "*Hope!*" derived from the verb أَمَلَ "*to hope*".

Form III

آخَذَ (أَاخَذَ >)	=	فَاعَلَ

Form IV

آخَذَ (أَأْخَذَ >)	=	أَفْعَلَ
أُوخِذَ (أُؤْخِذَ >)	=	أُفْعِلَ
أُوخِذُ (أُؤْخِذُ >)	=	أُفْعِلُ
إِيخَاذٌ (إِئْخَاذٌ >)	=	إِفْعَالٌ

Form VIII

اتَّخَذَ	=	اِفْتَعَلَ

R1 is not assimilated to the infix *t* in the other verbs R1 = *Hamza*, but the vowel is not prolonged either:

إِئْتَلَفَ	(instead of)	إِيتَلَفَ
إِئْتِلاف	(instead of)	إِيتِلاف

Table 17 : HAMZATED VERBS R1 = ء (أَخَذَ) : FORM I (أَلْفِعْلُ الْمَهْمُوزُ الْأَوَّلُ)

Passive			Active				
Imperfect	Perfect			Imperfect			Perfect
Indicative		Imperative	Jussive	Subjunctive	Indicative		
يُؤْخَذُ	أُخِذَ		يَأْخُذْ	يَأْخُذَ	يَأْخُذُ	أَخَذَ	(هُوَ)
تُؤْخَذُ	أُخِذَتْ		تَأْخُذْ	تَأْخُذَ	تَأْخُذُ	أَخَذَتْ	(هِيَ)
تُؤْخَذُ	أُخِذْتَ	خُذْ	تَأْخُذْ	تَأْخُذَ	تَأْخُذُ	أَخَذْتَ	(أَنْتَ)
تُؤْخَذِينَ	أُخِذْت	خُذِي	تَأْخُذِي	تَأْخُذِي	تَأْخُذِينَ	أَخَذْت	(أَنْتِ)
أُوخَذُ	أُخِذْتُ		آخُذْ	آخُذَ	آخُذُ	أَخَذْتُ	(أَنَا)
يُؤْخَذُونَ	أُخِذُوا		يَأْخُذُوا	يَأْخُذُوا	يَأْخُذُونَ	أَخَذُوا	(هُمْ)
يُؤْخَذْنَ	أُخِذْنَ		يَأْخُذْنَ	يَأْخُذْنَ	يَأْخُذْنَ	أَخَذْنَ	(هُنَّ)
تُؤْخَذُونَ	أُخِذْتُمْ	خُذُوا	تَأْخُذُوا	تَأْخُذُوا	تَأْخُذُونَ	أَخَذْتُمْ	(أَنْتُمْ)
تُؤْخَذْنَ	أُخِذْتُنَّ	خُذْنَ	تَأْخُذْنَ	تَأْخُذْنَ	تَأْخُذْنَ	أَخَذْتُنَّ	(أَنْتُنَّ)
نُؤْخَذُ	أُخِذْنَا		نَأْخُذْ	نَأْخُذَ	نَأْخُذُ	أَخَذْنَا	(نَحْنُ)
يُؤْخَذَانِ	أُخِذَا		يَأْخُذَا	يَأْخُذَا	يَأْخُذَانِ	أَخَذَا	(هُمَا)
تُؤْخَذَانِ	أُخِذَتَا		تَأْخُذَا	تَأْخُذَا	تَأْخُذَانِ	أَخَذَتَا	(هُمَا)
تُؤْخَذَانِ	أُخِذْتُمَا	خُذَا	تَأْخُذَا	تَأْخُذَا	تَأْخُذَانِ	أَخَذْتُمَا	(أَنْتُمَا)

Table 18 : HAMZATED VERBS R1 = ء (أَخَذَ) : FORMS II - X

Passive			Active				
Imperfect	Perfect			Imperfect			Perfect
Indicative		Imperative	Jussive	Subjunctive	Indicative		
يُؤَخَّذُ	أُخِّذَ	أَخِّذْ	يُؤَخِّذْ	يُؤَخِّذَ	يُؤَخِّذُ	أَخَّذَ	II
يُؤَاخَذُ	أُوخِذَ	آخِذْ	يُؤَاخِذْ	يُؤَاخِذَ	يُؤَاخِذُ	آخَذَ	III
يُؤْخَذُ	أُوخِذَ	آخِذْ	يُؤْخِذْ	يُؤْخِذَ	يُؤْخِذُ	آخَذَ	IV
يُتَأَخَّذُ	تُؤُخِّذَ	تَأَخَّذْ	يَتَأَخَّذْ	يَتَأَخَّذَ	يَتَأَخَّذُ	تَأَخَّذَ	V
يُتَآخَذُ	تُؤُوخِذَ	تَآخَذْ	يَتَآخَذْ	يَتَآخَذَ	يَتَآخَذُ	تَآخَذَ	VI
no forms							VII
يُتَّخَذُ	اُتُّخِذَ	اِتَّخِذْ	يَتَّخِذْ	يَتَّخِذَ	يَتَّخِذُ	اِتَّخَذَ	VIII
يُسْتَأْخَذُ	اُسْتُوخِذَ	اِسْتَأْخِذْ	يَسْتَأْخِذْ	يَسْتَأْخِذَ	يَسْتَأْخِذُ	اِسْتَأْخَذَ	X

Table 19 : HAMZATED VERBS R2 = ء (سَأَلَ) : FORM I (اَلْفِعْلُ الْمَهْمُوزُ الثَّانِي)

Passive		Active					
Imperfect	Perfect			Imperfect		Perfect	
Indicative		Imperative	Jussive	Subjunctive	Indicative		
يُسْأَلُ	سُئِلَ		يَسْأَلْ	يَسْأَلَ	يَسْأَلُ	سَأَلَ	(هُوَ)
تُسْأَلُ	سُئِلَتْ		تَسْأَلْ	تَسْأَلَ	تَسْأَلُ	سَأَلَتْ	(هِيَ)
تُسْأَلُ	سُئِلْتَ	اِسْأَلْ	تَسْأَلْ	تَسْأَلَ	تَسْأَلُ	سَأَلْتَ	(أَنْتَ)
تُسْأَلِينَ	سُئِلْتِ	اِسْأَلِي	تَسْأَلِي	تَسْأَلِي	تَسْأَلِينَ	سَأَلْتِ	(أَنْتِ)
أُسْأَلُ	سُئِلْتُ		أَسْأَلْ	أَسْأَلَ	أَسْأَلُ	سَأَلْتُ	(أَنَا)
يُسْأَلُونَ	سُئِلُوا		يَسْأَلُوا	يَسْأَلُوا	يَسْأَلُونَ	سَأَلُوا	(هُمْ)
يُسْأَلْنَ	سُئِلْنَ		يَسْأَلْنَ	يَسْأَلْنَ	يَسْأَلْنَ	سَأَلْنَ	(هُنَّ)
تُسْأَلُونَ	سُئِلْتُمْ	اِسْأَلُوا	تَسْأَلُوا	تَسْأَلُوا	تَسْأَلُونَ	سَأَلْتُمْ	(أَنْتُمْ)
تُسْأَلْنَ	سُئِلْتُنَّ	اِسْأَلْنَ	تَسْأَلْنَ	تَسْأَلْنَ	تَسْأَلْنَ	سَأَلْتُنَّ	(أَنْتُنَّ)
نُسْأَلُ	سُئِلْنَا		نَسْأَلْ	نَسْأَلَ	نَسْأَلُ	سَأَلْنَا	(نَحْنُ)
يُسْأَلَانِ	سُئِلَا		يَسْأَلَا	يَسْأَلَا	يَسْأَلَانِ	سَأَلَا	(هُمَا)
تُسْأَلَانِ	سُئِلَتَا		تَسْأَلَا	تَسْأَلَا	تَسْأَلَانِ	سَأَلَتَا	(هُمَا)
تُسْأَلَانِ	سُئِلْتُمَا	اِسْأَلَا	تَسْأَلَا	تَسْأَلَا	تَسْأَلَانِ	سَأَلْتُمَا	(أَنْتُمَا)

Table 20 : HAMZATED VERBS R2 = ء (سَأَلَ) : FORMS II - X

Passive		Active					
Imperfect	Perfect			Imperfect		Perfect	
Indicative		Imperative	Jussive	Subjunctive	Indicative		
يُسَأَّلُ	سُئِّلَ	سَئِّلْ	يُسَئِّلْ	يُسَئِّلَ	يُسَئِّلُ	سَأَّلَ	II
يُسَاءَلُ	سُوئِلَ	سَائِلْ	يُسَائِلْ	يُسَائِلَ	يُسَائِلُ	سَاءَلَ	III
يُسْأَلُ	أُسْئِلَ	أَسْئِلْ	يُسْئِلْ	يُسْئِلَ	يُسْئِلُ	أَسْأَلَ	IV
يُتَسَأَّلُ	تُسُئِّلَ	تَسَأَّلْ	يَتَسَأَّلْ	يَتَسَأَّلَ	يَتَسَأَّلُ	تَسَأَّلَ	V
يُتَسَاءَلُ	تُسُوئِلَ	تَسَاءَلْ	يَتَسَاءَلْ	يَتَسَاءَلَ	يَتَسَاءَلُ	تَسَاءَلَ	VI
يُنْسَأَلُ	أُنْسِئِلَ	اِنْسَئِلْ	يَنْسَئِلْ	يَنْسَئِلَ	يَنْسَئِلُ	اِنْسَأَلَ	VII
يُسْتَأَلُ	أُسْتُئِلَ	اِسْتَئِلْ	يَسْتَئِلْ	يَسْتَئِلَ	يَسْتَئِلُ	اِسْتَأَلَ	VIII
يُسْتَسْأَلُ	أُسْتُسْئِلَ	اِسْتَسْئِلْ	يَسْتَسْئِلْ	يَسْتَسْئِلَ	يَسْتَسْئِلُ	اِسْتَسْأَلَ	X

Table 21 : HAMZATED VERBS R3 = ء ‏(قَرَأَ)‏ : FORM I ‏(أَلْفِعْلُ الْمَهْمُوزُ الآخِرِ)‏

Passive Imperfect Indicative	Passive Perfect	Active Imperative	Active Jussive	Active Subjunctive	Active Imperfect Indicative	Active Perfect	
يُقْرَأُ	قُرِئَ		يَقْرَأْ	يَقْرَأَ	يَقْرَأُ	قَرَأَ	‏(هُوَ)‏
تُقْرَأُ	قُرِئَتْ		تَقْرَأْ	تَقْرَأَ	تَقْرَأُ	قَرَأَتْ	‏(هِيَ)‏
تُقْرَأُ	قُرِئْتَ	اِقْرَأْ	تَقْرَأْ	تَقْرَأَ	تَقْرَأُ	قَرَأْتَ	‏(أَنْتَ)‏
تُقْرَئِينَ	قُرِئْتِ	اِقْرَئِي	تَقْرَئِي	تَقْرَئِي	تَقْرَئِينَ	قَرَأْتِ	‏(أَنْتِ)‏
أُقْرَأُ	قُرِئْتُ		أَقْرَأْ	أَقْرَأَ	أَقْرَأُ	قَرَأْتُ	‏(أَنَا)‏
يُقْرَؤُونَ	قُرِئُوا		يَقْرَؤُوا	يَقْرَؤُوا	يَقْرَؤُونَ	قَرَؤُوا	‏(هُمْ)‏
يُقْرَأْنَ	قُرِئْنَ		يَقْرَأْنَ	يَقْرَأْنَ	يَقْرَأْنَ	قَرَأْنَ	‏(هُنَّ)‏
تُقْرَؤُونَ	قُرِئْتُمْ	اِقْرَؤُوا	تَقْرَؤُوا	تَقْرَؤُوا	تَقْرَؤُونَ	قَرَأْتُمْ	‏(أَنْتُمْ)‏
تُقْرَأْنَ	قُرِئْتُنَّ	اِقْرَأْنَ	تَقْرَأْنَ	تَقْرَأْنَ	تَقْرَأْنَ	قَرَأْتُنَّ	‏(أَنْتُنَّ)‏
نُقْرَأُ	قُرِئْنَا		نَقْرَأْ	نَقْرَأَ	نَقْرَأُ	قَرَأْنَا	‏(نَحْنُ)‏
يُقْرَآنِ	قُرِآ		يَقْرَآ	يَقْرَآ	يَقْرَآنِ	قَرَآ	‏(هُمَا)‏
تُقْرَآنِ	قُرِئَتَا		تَقْرَآ	تَقْرَآ	تَقْرَآنِ	قَرَأَتَا	‏(هُمَا)‏
تُقْرَآنِ	قُرِئْتُمَا	اِقْرَآ	تَقْرَآ	تَقْرَآ	تَقْرَآنِ	قَرَأْتُمَا	‏(أَنْتُمَا)‏

Table 22 : HAMZATED VERBS R3 = ء ‏(قَرَأَ)‏ : FORMS II - X

Passive Imperfect Indicative	Passive Perfect	Active Imperative	Active Jussive	Active Subjunctive	Active Imperfect Indicative	Active Perfect	
يُقَرَّأُ	قُرِّئَ	قَرِّئْ	يُقَرِّئْ	يُقَرِّئَ	يُقَرِّئُ	قَرَّأَ	II
يُقَارَأُ	قُورِئَ	قَارِئْ	يُقَارِئْ	يُقَارِئَ	يُقَارِئُ	قَارَأَ	III
يُقْرَأُ	أُقْرِئَ	أَقْرِئْ	يُقْرِئْ	يُقْرِئَ	يُقْرِئُ	أَقْرَأَ	IV
يُتَقَرَّأُ	تُقُرِّئَ	تَقَرَّأْ	يَتَقَرَّأْ	يَتَقَرَّأَ	يَتَقَرَّأُ	تَقَرَّأَ	V
يُتَقَارَأُ	تُقُورِئَ	تَقَارَأْ	يَتَقَارَأْ	يَتَقَارَأَ	يَتَقَارَأُ	تَقَارَأَ	VI
يُنْقَرَأُ	اُنْقُرِئَ	اِنْقَرِئْ	يَنْقَرِئْ	يَنْقَرِئَ	يَنْقَرِئُ	اِنْقَرَأَ	VII
يُقْتَرَأُ	اُقْتُرِئَ	اِقْتَرِئْ	يَقْتَرِئْ	يَقْتَرِئَ	يَقْتَرِئُ	اِقْتَرَأَ	VIII
يُسْتَقْرَأُ	اُسْتُقْرِئَ	اِسْتَقْرِئْ	يَسْتَقْرِئْ	يَسْتَقْرِئَ	يَسْتَقْرِئُ	اِسْتَقْرَأَ	X

DOUBLED VERBS R2 = R3 (أَلْفِعْلُ الْمُضَاعَفُ)

The 2nd and the 3rd radical of the verbs R2 = R3 are identical.

Example: R1 = م , R2 = ر , R3 = ر ⇨ مَرَّ "he (has) passed (by)"

The special feature of these verbs, compared with the sound triliteral verb, is that R2 and R3 are contracted in some of their forms, but not in others. As a rule, R2 and R3 are contracted if a vowel follows R3:

imperfect		perfect		
يَفْعَلُ	يَمُرُّ	فَعَلَ	مَرَّ	هُوَ
تَفْعَلُ	تَمُرُّ	فَعَلَتْ	مَرَّتْ	هِيَ
يَفْعَلُونَ	يَمُرُّونَ	فَعَلُوا	مَرُّوا	هُمْ

R2 and R3 are not contracted if R3 is vowelless in the new form which was formed according to the pattern of the sound verbs:

يَفْعَلْنَ = يَمْرُرْنَ | فَعَلْنَا = مَرَرْنَا | فَعَلْتُ = مَرَرْتُ

or if there is a long vowel between R2 and R3:

فَعُولٌ = مُرُورٌ   مَفْعُولٌ = مَمْرُورٌ

The imperfect stem vowel may be *a*, *i* or *u* as is the case with the sound verbs; the vowel that follows R2 in the non-contracted patterns of the perfect tense is almost always *a*.

active participle	مَارٌّ
passive participle	مَمْرُورٌ

(☞ respective tables)

Derived Forms: All patterns of Forms II and V are formed according to the pattern of the sound verbs:

	V		II	
perfect	تَفَعَّلَ = تَمَرَّرَ		فَعَّلَ = مَرَّرَ	
imperfect	يَتَفَعَّلُ = يَتَمَرَّرُ		يُفَعِّلُ = يُمَرِّرُ	

In the other Forms R2 and R3 are contracted in the 3rd p.sg.m. The individual conjugational forms follow the rules given above. (☞ the following tables)

In most dialects, these verbs are conjugated in the perfect tense like مَشَى , analog to the verbs R3 = ى , accordingly:

Table 23 : DOUBLED VERBS R2 = R3 (مَرَّ) : FORM I (اَلْفِعْلُ الْمُضَاعَفُ)

Passive		Active					
Imperfect	Perfect				Imperfect		Perfect
Indicative		Imperative	Jussive	Subjunctive	Indicative	Perfect	
يُمَرُّ	مُرَّ		يَمُرَّ/يَمْرُرْ	يَمُرَّ	يَمُرُّ	مَرَّ	(هُوَ)
تُمَرُّ	مُرَّتْ		تَمُرَّ/تَمْرُرْ	تَمُرَّ	تَمُرُّ	مَرَّتْ	(هِيَ)
تُمَرُّ	مُرِرْتَ	مُرَّ/اُمْرُرْ	تَمُرَّ/تَمْرُرْ	تَمُرَّ	تَمُرُّ	مَرَرْتَ	(أَنْتَ)
تُمَرِّينَ	مُرِرْتِ	مُرِّي	تَمُرِّي	تَمُرِّي	تَمُرِّينَ	مَرَرْتِ	(أَنْتِ)
أُمَرُّ	مُرِرْتُ		أَمُرَّ/أَمْرُرْ	أَمُرَّ	أَمُرُّ	مَرَرْتُ	(أَنَا)
يُمَرُّونَ	مُرُّوا		يَمُرُّوا	يَمُرُّوا	يَمُرُّونَ	مَرُّوا	(هُمْ)
يُمْرَرْنَ	مُرِرْنَ		يَمْرُرْنَ	يَمْرُرْنَ	يَمْرُرْنَ	مَرَرْنَ	(هُنَّ)
تُمَرُّونَ	مُرِرْتُمْ	مُرُّوا	تَمُرُّوا	تَمُرُّوا	تَمُرُّونَ	مَرَرْتُمْ	(أَنْتُمْ)
تُمْرَرْنَ	مُرِرْتُنَّ	اُمْرُرْنَ	تَمْرُرْنَ	تَمْرُرْنَ	تَمْرُرْنَ	مَرَرْتُنَّ	(أَنْتُنَّ)
نُمَرُّ	مُرِرْنَا		نَمُرَّ/نَمْرُرْ	نَمُرَّ	نَمُرُّ	مَرَرْنَا	(نَحْنُ)
يُمَرَّانِ	مُرَّا		يَمُرَّا	يَمُرَّا	يَمُرَّانِ	مَرَّا	(هُمَا)
تُمَرَّانِ	مُرَّتَا		تَمُرَّا	تَمُرَّا	تَمُرَّانِ	مَرَّتَا	(هُمَا)
تُمَرَّانِ	مُرِرْتُمَا	مُرَّا	تَمُرَّا	تَمُرَّا	تَمُرَّانِ	مَرَرْتُمَا	(أَنْتُمَا)

Table 24 : DOUBLED VERBS R2 = R3 (مَرَّ): FORMS II - X

Passive		Active					
Imperfect	Perfect				Imperfect		Perfect
Indicative		Imperative	Jussive	Subjunctive	Indicative	Perfect	
يُمَرَّرُ	مُرِّرَ	مَرِّرْ	يُمَرِّرْ	يُمَرِّرَ	يُمَرِّرُ	مَرَّرَ	II
يُمَارُّ	مُورِرَ	مَارَّ / مَارِرْ	يُمَارَّ/ يُمَارِرْ	يُمَارَّ	يُمَارُّ	مَارَّ	III
يُمَرُّ	أُمِرَّ	أَمِرَّ/ أَمْرِرْ	يُمِرَّ / يُمْرِرْ	يُمِرَّ	يُمِرُّ	أَمَرَّ	IV
يُتَمَرَّرُ	تُمُرِّرَ	تَمَرَّرْ	يَتَمَرَّرْ	يَتَمَرَّرَ	يَتَمَرَّرُ	تَمَرَّرَ	V
يُتَمَارُّ	تُمُورِرَ	تَمَارَّ / تَمَارَرْ	يَتَمَارَّ/ يَتَمَارَرْ	يَتَمَارَّ	يَتَمَارُّ	تَمَارَّ	VI
يُنْمَرُّ	اُنْمُرَّ	اِنْمَرَّ / اِنْمَرِرْ	يَنْمَرَّ/ يَنْمَرِرْ	يَنْمَرَّ	يَنْمَرُّ	اِنْمَرَّ	VII
يُمْتَرُّ	اُمْتُرَّ	اِمْتَرَّ / اِمْتَرِرْ	يَمْتَرَّ/ يَمْتَرِرْ	يَمْتَرَّ	يَمْتَرُّ	اِمْتَرَّ	VIII
يُسْتَمَرُّ	اُسْتُمِرَّ	اِسْتَمِرَّ/ اِسْتَمْرِرْ	يَسْتَمِرَّ/يَسْتَمْرِرْ	يَسْتَمِرَّ	يَسْتَمِرُّ	اِسْتَمَرَّ	X

WEAK VERBS (أَلْفِعْلُ الْمُعْتَلُّ)

ASSIMILATED VERBS R1 = و or ى (أَلْفِعْلُ الْمِثَالِ)

There are certain peculiarities in the conjugation of the weak verbs in which the "weak" consonants و or ى occur as R1, R2 or R3. The perfect and imperfect tense of these verbs are shown here on the basis of model verbs. Their conjugational paradigms are to be applied analogously to verbs of the same structure.

Table 25 : ASSIMILATED VERBS R1 = و (وَصَلَ) : FORM I (أَلْفِعْلُ الْمِثَالُ الْوَاوِيُّ)

The perfect tense of verbs with R1 = و or ى is formed in the same way as the strong verbs. The imperfect tense of verbs with R1 = و is formed with R1 being omitted. The patterns for subjunctive, jussive and passive follow the rules of the sound verbs.

Passive		Active					
Imperfect	Perfect	Imperative	Imperfect			Perfect	
Indicative			Jussive	Subjunctive	Indicative		
يُوصَلُ	وُصِلَ		يَصِلْ	يَصِلَ	يَصِلُ	وَصَلَ	(هُوَ)
تُوصَلُ	وُصِلَتْ		تَصِلْ	تَصِلَ	تَصِلُ	وَصَلَتْ	(هِيَ)
تُوصَلُ	وُصِلْتَ	صِلْ	تَصِلْ	تَصِلَ	تَصِلُ	وَصَلْتَ	(أَنْتَ)
تُوصَلِينَ	وُصِلْتِ	صِلي	تَصِلي	تَصِلي	تَصِلِينَ	وَصَلْتِ	(أَنْتِ)
أُوصَلُ	وُصِلْتُ		أَصِلْ	أَصِلَ	أَصِلُ	وَصَلْتُ	(أَنَا)
يُوصَلُونَ	وُصِلُوا		يَصِلُوا	يَصِلُوا	يَصِلُونَ	وَصَلُوا	(هُمْ)
يُوصَلْنَ	وُصِلْنَ		يَصِلْنَ	يَصِلْنَ	يَصِلْنَ	وَصَلْنَ	(هُنَّ)
تُوصَلُونَ	وُصِلْتُمْ	صِلُوا	تَصِلُوا	تَصِلُوا	تَصِلُونَ	وَصَلْتُمْ	(أَنْتُمْ)
تُوصَلْنَ	وُصِلْتُنَّ	صِلْنَ	تَصِلْنَ	تَصِلْنَ	تَصِلْنَ	وَصَلْتُنَّ	(أَنْتُنَّ)
نُوصَلُ	وُصِلْنَا		نَصِلْ	نَصِلَ	نَصِلُ	وَصَلْنَا	(نَحْنُ)
يُوصَلَانِ	وُصِلَا		يَصِلَا	يَصِلَا	يَصِلَانِ	وَصَلَا	(هُمَا)
تُوصَلَانِ	وُصِلَتَا		تَصِلَا	تَصِلَا	تَصِلَانِ	وَصَلَتَا	(هُمَا)
تُوصَلَانِ	وُصِلْتُمَا	صِلَا	تَصِلَا	تَصِلَا	تَصِلَانِ	وَصَلْتُمَا	(أَنْتُمَا)

ASSIMILATED VERBS R1 = و : FORMS II - X (أَلْفِعْلُ الْمِثَالُ الْوَاوِيُّ)

The derived forms of the verbs with R1 = و or ى as first radical have the same characteristics as the derived forms of the strong verbs. Apparent peculiarities only arise from the fact that و or ى appear as consonants in some forms and as vowels in others. The latter are contracted in some jussive and imperative forms, and therefore do not appear in the typeface any more.

وَصَل is employed as the model verb for the derived forms as well. It serves the purpose of representing the respective patterns of all verbs starting with و, without actually being really in use in each individual form. Only Forms VIII and X have some peculiarities. R1 is assimilated to the infix *t-* in Form VIII.

	X	VIII
perfect tense	اسْتَوْصَلَ	اتَّصَلَ
imperfect tense	يَسْتَوْصِلُ	يَتَّصِلُ
imperative	اسْتَوْصِلْ	اتَّصِلْ

There are no verbs starting with و or ى in Form VII. ☞ following table.

Table 26 : ASSIMILATED VERBS R1 = و : FORMS II - X (أَلْفِعْلُ الْمِثَالُ الْوَاوِيُّ)

Passive		Active					
Imperfect	Perfect	Imperative	Imperfect			Perfect	
Indicative			Jussive	Subjunctive	Indicative		
يُوَصَّلُ	وُصِّلَ	وَصِّلْ	يُوَصِّلْ	يُوَصِّلَ	يُوَصِّلُ	وَصَّلَ	II
يُوَاصَلُ	وُوصِلَ	وَاصِلْ	يُوَاصِلْ	يُوَاصِلَ	يُوَاصِلُ	وَاصَلَ	III
يُوصَلُ	أُوصِلَ	أَوْصِلْ	يُوصِلْ	يُوصِلَ	يُوصِلُ	أَوْصَلَ	IV
يُتَوَصَّلُ	تُوُصِّلَ	تَوَصَّلْ	يَتَوَصَّلْ	يَتَوَصَّلَ	يَتَوَصَّلُ	تَوَصَّلَ	V
يُتَوَاصَلُ	تُوُوصِلَ	تَوَاصَلْ	يَتَوَاصَلْ	يَتَوَاصَلَ	يَتَوَاصَلُ	تَوَاصَلَ	VI
no forms							VII
يُتَّصَلُ	اتُّصِلَ	اتَّصِلْ	يَتَّصِلْ	يَتَّصِلَ	يَتَّصِلُ	اتَّصَلَ	VIII
يُسْتَوْصَلُ	اسْتُوصِلَ	اسْتَوْصِلْ	يَسْتَوْصِلْ	يَسْتَوْصِلَ	يَسْتَوْصِلُ	اسْتَوْصَلَ	X

Table 27 : ASSIMILATED VERBS R1 = ي (يَبِسَ) : FORMS I - X (أَلْفِعْلُ الْمِثَالُ الْيَائِيُّ)

There are only about a dozen verbs having ي as first radical in modern Arabic. They occur nearly exclusively in the derived forms and follow the same conjugational patterns of the sound verbs as seen in the following table. Their imperfect tense is formed according to the strong verbs, i.e. R1 is not omitted.

Passive		Active					
Imperfect	Perfect	Imperative	Imperfect			Perfect	
Indicative			Jussive	Subjunctive	Indicative		
يُوبَسُ	يُبِسَ	ايبَسْ	يَيْبَسْ	يَيْبَسَ	يَيْبَسُ	يَبِسَ	I
يُيَبَّسُ	يُبِّسَ	يَبِّسْ	يُيَبِّسْ	يُيَبِّسَ	يُيَبِّسُ	يَبَّسَ	II
يُيَابَسُ	يُوبِسَ	يَابِسْ	يُيَابِسْ	يُيَابِسَ	يُيَابِسُ	يَابَسَ	III
يُوبَسُ	أُوبِسَ	أَيْبِسْ	يُوبِسْ	يُوبِسَ	يُوبِسُ	أَيْبَسَ	IV

يُتَيَّسُ	نَيَّسْ	نَيَّسْ	يَتَيَّسْ	يَتَيَّسْ	يَتَيَّسُ	تَيَّسَ	V
يُتَيَابَسُ	تَيَابَسْ	تَيَابَسْ	يَتَيَابَسْ	يَتَيَابَسْ	يَتَيَابَسُ	تَيَابَسَ	VI
no forms							VII
يُتَّبَسُ	اتَّبِسْ	اتَّبِسْ	يَتَّبِسْ	يَتَّبِسْ	يَتَّبِسُ	اتَّبَسَ	VIII
يُسْتَيَبَسُ	اسْتَوْبِسْ	اسْتَيْبِسْ	يَسْتَيْبِسْ	يَسْتَيْبِسْ	يَسْتَيْبِسُ	اسْتَيْبَسَ	X

HOLLOW VERBS R2 = و OR ى: FORM I (الْفِعْلُ الْأَجْوَفُ)

The following explanations and tables are based on three model verbs:

      C   **B**   **A**

     خَافَ   بَاعَ   قَامَ

Their conjugational patterns are to be applied analogously to all other verbs of the same structure.

THE PERFECT TENSE OF HOLLOW VERBS R2 = و OR ى

R1 has the long vowel *ā* in the perfect tense in verbs in which R2 = و or ى if a vowel follows R3:

A قَامَ "to get up" (فَعَلَ = قَوَمَ) R2 = و	(هم) قَامُوا	(هي) قَامَتْ	(هو) قَامَ
B بَاعَ "to sell" (فَعَلَ = بَيَعَ) R2 = ى	(هم) بَاعُوا	(هي) بَاعَتْ	(هو) بَاعَ
C خَافَ "to fear" (فَعِلَ = خَوِفَ) R2 = و	(هم) خَافُوا	(هي) خَافَتْ	(هو) خَافَ

Consequently, in these forms it is not clear in unpointed typeface whether it is a verb R_2 = و or a verb R_2 = ى. It is possible to discern the group the respective verb belongs to from the imperfect tense. R1 has the short vowel *u* or *i* in the perfect tense in verbs with R2 = و or ى if R3 is not followed by a vowel:

C	B	A	
خِفْتَ	بِعْتَ	قُمْتَ	(أنتَ)
خِفْتِ	بِعْتِ	قُمْتِ	(أنتِ)
خِفْتُ	بِعْتُ	قُمْتُ	(أنا)
خِفْنَ	بِعْنَ	قُمْنَ	(هنَّ)
خِفْتُمْ	بِعْتُمْ	قُمْتُمْ	(أنتمْ)
خِفْتُنَّ	بِعْتُنَّ	قُمْتُنَّ	(أنتنَّ)
خِفْنا	بِعْنا	قُمْنا	(نحنُ)

Accordingly, the verbs which belong to group A have the short vowel *u*, the verbs which belong to groups B and C have the short vowel *i* .

The same rules apply to the dual forms. Since they are relatively rare in use, they are not expressly mentioned here. They are listed in full in the respective table.

THE IMPERFECT TENSE OF HOLLOW VERBS R2 = و OR ى

TheVerbs with R2 = و or ى have the long vowel *ū* in the imperfect tense if they belong to group A, and the long vowel *ī* if they belong to group B. Verbs belonging to group C have the long vowel *ā* , when a vowel follows R3.
Examples with the model verbs:

A قَامَ "*to get up*" (فَعَلَ = قَوَمَ) R2 = و	(هو) يَقُومُ	(هي) تَقُومُ	(نحن) نَقُومُ
B بَاعَ "*to sell*" (فَعَلَ = بَيَعَ) R2= ى	(هو) يَبِيعُ	(هي) تَبِيعُ	(نحن) نَبِيعُ
C خَافَ "*to fear*" (فعِلَ = خَوِفَ) R2 = و	(هو) يَخَافُ	(هي) تَخَافُ	(نحن) نَخَافُ

Verbs with R2 = ى, e.g. نَالَ (نَيِلَ) يَنَالُ "*to obtain*", have the same forms as well.
R1 has the short vowel *u* in the imperfect tense of verbs with R2 = و or ى if they belong to group A, the short vowel *i* if they belong to group B, and the short vowel *a* if they belong to group C, when R3 is vowelless.
Examples with the model verbs:

C	B	A	
يَخَفْنَ	يَبِعْنَ	يَقُمْنَ	(هنَّ)
تَخَفْنَ	تَبِعْنَ	تَقُمْنَ	(أنتنَّ)

SUBJUNCTIVE AND JUSSIVE OF HOLLOW VERBS R2 = و OR ى

The subjunctive and the jussive of the defective verbs are formed according to the principles of the strong verbs. It is often difficult to find out which root the respective form is based on. The typeface does not provide any information whether the last consonant is R2 (دَعَا ⇦ يَدْعُ) or R3 (قَامَ ⇦ يَقُمْ).

IMPERATIVE OF HOLLOW VERBS R2 = و OR ى

The imperative is formed according to the principles of the strong verbs. The jussive is the form the imperative is derived from. (☞ Tables 28 - 33)

DERIVED FORMS OF HOLLOW VERBS R2 = و OR ى

The derived forms of the verbs R2 with و or ى have the same characteristics as the derived forms of the strong verbs. Apparent peculiarities only arise from the fact that و or ى appear as consonants in some forms and as vowels in others. The latter are contracted in some jussive and imperative forms, and therefore, do not appear in the typeface any more. خَافَ and قَامَ، بَاعَ are employed as model verbs in the derived forms as well. They serve the purpose of representing the respective pattern, without actually being really in use in each individual form. Thus e.g. قَامَ only occurs in Forms I - IV and X, but not in Forms V - IX.

Forms II and III of verbs R2 = و or ى are formed like those of the strong verbs, because و and ى are regarded as full consonants here. R1 is followed by a vowel in Form IV. In Form IV, the verbs R2 = و or ى have the same forms. Therefore, we give only one model verb here.

Form II

perfect tense:	بَيَّعَ	(pronounced: *qawwama*)	قَوَّمَ
imperfect tense:	يُبَيِّعُ	(pronounced: *yuqawwimu*)	يُقَوِّمُ
imperative:	بَيِّعْ	(pronounced: *qawwim*)	قَوِّمْ

Form III

perfect tense:	بَايَعَ		قَاوَمَ
imperfect tense:	يُبَايِعُ		يُقَاوِمُ
imperative:	بَايِعْ		قَاوِمْ

Form IV

perfect tense:			أَقَامَ
2nd p.sg.m.			أَقَمْتَ
imperfect tense indicative:			يُقِيمُ
imperfect tense jussive:			يُقِمْ
imperative:			أَقِمْ

Most imperfect tenses of Form II (R2 = ى) and IV (R2 = و or ى) cannot be differentiated without auxiliary signs. The same is the case regarding Form I and II of the verbs R2 = و.

Form V

| perfect tense | تَبَيَّعَ | | تَقَوَّمَ |
| imperfect tense | يَتَبَيَّعُ | | يَتَقَوَّمُ |

و and ى are full consonants as is the case with Forms II and III.

Form VI

perfect tense	تَبَايَعَ	تَقَاوَمَ
imperfect tense	يَتَبَايَعُ	يَتَقَاوَمُ

و and ى are full consonants as is the case with Forms II and III.

Form VII

perfect tense	اْنْقَامَ
imperfect indicative	يَنْقَامُ
imperfect jussive	يَنْقَمْ
imperative	اْنْقَمْ

Form VIII

perfect tense	اقْتَامَ
imperfect indicative	يَقْتَامُ
imperfect jussive	يَقْتَمْ
imperative	اقْتَمْ

Form X

perfect tense	اسْتَقَامَ
imperfect indicative	يَسْتَقِيمُ
imperfect jussive	يَسْتَقَمْ
imperative	اسْتَقِمْ

As is the case in Form IV, the verbs R2 = و or ى also have the same forms in Forms VII, VIII and X. Therefore, only قَامَ is used as a model verb here as well.

Table 28 : HOLLOW VERBS R2 = و (قَامَ) : FORM I   (أَلْفِعْلُ الأَجْوَفُ الْوَاوِيُّ)

Passive Imperfect Indicative	Passive Perfect	Active Imperative	Active Jussive	Active Subjunctive	Active Indicative	Active Perfect	
يُقَامُ	قِيمَ		يَقُمْ	يَقُومَ	يَقُومُ	قَامَ	(هُوَ)
تُقَامُ	قِيمَتْ		تَقُمْ	تَقُومَ	تَقُومُ	قَامَتْ	(هِيَ)
تُقَامُ	قِمْتَ	قُمْ	تَقُمْ	تَقُومَ	تَقُومُ	قُمْتَ	(أَنْتَ)
تُقَامِينَ	قِمْتِ	قُومِي	تَقُومِي	تَقُومِي	تَقُومِينَ	قُمْتِ	(أَنْتِ)
أُقَامُ	قِمْتُ		أُقَمْ	أَقُومَ	أَقُومُ	قُمْتُ	(أَنَا)
يُقَامُونَ	قِيمُوا		يَقُومُوا	يَقُومُوا	يَقُومُونَ	قَامُوا	(هُمْ)
يُقَمْنَ	قِمْنَ		يَقُمْنَ	يَقُمْنَ	يَقُمْنَ	قُمْنَ	(هُنَّ)
تُقَامُونَ	قِمْتُمْ	قُومُوا	تَقُومُوا	تَقُومُوا	تَقُومُونَ	قُمْتُمْ	(أَنْتُمْ)
تُقَمْنَ	قِمْتُنَّ	قُمْنَ	تَقُمْنَ	تَقُمْنَ	تَقُمْنَ	قُمْتُنَّ	(أَنْتُنَّ)
نُقَامُ	قِمْنَا		نَقُمْ	نَقُومَ	نَقُومُ	قُمْنَا	(نَحْنُ)
يُقَامَان	قِيمَا		يَقُومَا	يَقُومَا	يَقُومَان	قَامَا	(هُمَا)
تُقَامَان	قِيمَتَا		تَقُومَا	تَقُومَا	تَقُومَان	قَامَتَا	(هُمَا)
تُقَامَان	قُمْتُمَا	قُومَا	تَقُومَا	تَقُومَا	تَقُومَان	قُمْتُمَا	(أَنْتُمَا)

Table 29 : HOLLOW VERBS R2 = و (قَامَ) : FORMS II - X   (أَلْفِعْلُ الأَجْوَفُ الْوَاوِيُّ)

Passive Imperfect Indicative	Passive Perfect	Active Imperative	Active Jussive	Active Subjunctive	Active Indicative	Active Perfect	
يُقَوَّمُ	قُوِّمَ	قَوِّمْ	يُقَوِّمْ	يُقَوِّمَ	يُقَوِّمُ	قَوَّمَ	II
يُقَاوَمُ	قُووِمَ	قَاوِمْ	يُقَاوِمْ	يُقَاوِمَ	يُقَاوِمُ	قَاوَمَ	III
يُقَامُ	أُقِيمَ	أَقِمْ	يُقِمْ	يُقِيمَ	يُقِيمُ	أَقَامَ	IV
يَتَقَوَّمُ	تُقُوِّمَ	تَقَوَّمْ	يَتَقَوَّمْ	يَتَقَوَّمَ	يَتَقَوَّمُ	تَقَوَّمَ	V
يُتَقَاوَمُ	تُقُووِمَ	تَقَاوَمْ	يَتَقَاوَمْ	يَتَقَاوَمَ	يَتَقَاوَمُ	تَقَاوَمَ	VI
يُنْقَامُ	أُنْقِيمَ	اِنْقَمْ	يَنْقَمْ	يَنْقَامَ	يَنْقَامُ	اِنْقَامَ	VII
يُقْتَامُ	اقتِيمَ	اقْتَمْ	يَقْتَمْ	يَقْتَامَ	يَقْتَامُ	اقْتَامَ	VIII
يُسْتَقَامُ	أُسْتُقِيمَ	اِسْتَقِمْ	يَسْتَقِمْ	يَسْتَقِيمَ	يَسْتَقِيمُ	اِسْتَقَامَ	X

Table 30 : HOLLOW VERBS R2 = ى (بَاعَ) : FORM I (أَلْفِعْلُ الأَجْوَفُ الْيَائِيُّ)

Passive		Active					
Imperfect	Perfect	Imperative	Imperfect			Perfect	
Indicative			Jussive	Subjunctive	Indicative		
يُبَاعُ	بِيعَ		يَبِعْ	يَبِيعَ	يَبِيعُ	بَاعَ	(هُوَ)
تُبَاعُ	بِيعَتْ		تَبِعْ	تَبِيعَ	تَبِيعُ	بَاعَتْ	(هِيَ)
تُبَاعُ	بِعْتَ	بِعْ	تَبِعْ	تَبِيعَ	تَبِيعُ	بِعْتَ	(أَنْتَ)
تُبَاعِينَ	بِعْتِ	بِيعِي	تَبِيعِي	تَبِيعِي	تَبِيعِينَ	بِعْتِ	(أَنْتِ)
أُبَاعُ	بِعْتُ		أَبِعْ	أَبِيعَ	أَبِيعُ	بِعْتُ	(أَنَا)
يُبَاعُونَ	بِيعُوا		يَبِيعُوا	يَبِيعُوا	يَبِيعُونَ	بَاعُوا	(هُمْ)
يُبَعْنَ	بِعْنَ		يَبِعْنَ	يَبِعْنَ	يَبِعْنَ	بِعْنَ	(هُنَّ)
تُبَاعُونَ	بِعْتُمْ	بِيعُوا	تَبِيعُوا	تَبِيعُوا	تَبِيعُونَ	بِعْتُمْ	(أَنْتُمْ)
تُبَعْنَ	بِعْتُنَّ	بِعْنَ	تَبِعْنَ	تَبِعْنَ	تَبِعْنَ	بِعْتُنَّ	(أَنْتُنَّ)
نُبَاعُ	بِعْنَا		نَبِعْ	نَبِيعَ	نَبِيعُ	بِعْنَا	(نَحْنُ)
يُبَاعَانِ	بِيعَا		يَبِيعَا	يَبِيعَا	يَبِيعَانِ	بَاعَا	(هُمَا)
تُبَاعَانِ	بِيعَتَا		تَبِيعَا	تَبِيعَا	تَبِيعَانِ	بَاعَتَا	(هُمَا)
تُبَاعَانِ	بِعْتُمَا	بِيعَا	تَبِيعَا	تَبِيعَا	تَبِيعَانِ	بِعْتُمَا	(أَنْتُمَا)

Table 31 : HOLLOW VERBS R2 = ى (بَاعَ) : FORMS II - X (أَلْفِعْلُ الأَجْوَفُ الْيَائِيُّ)

Passive		Active					
Imperfect	Perfect					Perfect	
Indicative		Imperative	Jussive	Subjunctive	Indicative		
يُبَيَّعُ	بُيِّعَ	بَيِّعْ	يُبَيِّعْ	يُبَيِّعَ	يُبَيِّعُ	بَيَّعَ	II
يُبَايَعُ	بُويِعَ	بَايِعْ	يُبَايِعْ	يُبَايِعَ	يُبَايِعُ	بَايَعَ	III
يُبَاعُ	أُبِيعَ	أَبِعْ	يُبِعْ	يُبِيعَ	يُبِيعُ	أَبَاعَ	IV
يُتَبَيَّعُ	تُبُيِّعَ	تَبَيَّعْ	يَتَبَيَّعْ	يَتَبَيَّعَ	يَتَبَيَّعُ	تَبَيَّعَ	V
يُتَبَايَعُ	تُبُويِعَ	تَبَايَعْ	يَتَبَايَعْ	يَتَبَايَعَ	يَتَبَايَعُ	تَبَايَعَ	VI
يُنْبَاعُ	اُنْبِيعَ	اِنْبَعْ	يَنْبَعْ	يَنْبَاعَ	يَنْبَاعُ	اِنْبَاعَ	VII
يُبْتَاعُ	اُبْتِيعَ	اِبْتَعْ	يَبْتَعْ	يَبْتَاعَ	يَبْتَاعُ	اِبْتَاعَ	VIII
يُسْتَبَاعُ	اُسْتُبِيعَ	اِسْتَبِعْ	يَسْتَبِعْ	يَسْتَبِيعَ	يَسْتَبِيعُ	اِسْتَبَاعَ	X

Table 32 : HOLLOW VERBS R2 = و (خَافَ) : FORM I (أَلْفِعْلُ الأَجْوَفُ الْوَاوِيُّ)

Passive		Active					
Imperfect	Perfect				Imperfect	Perfect	
Indicative		Imperative	Jussive	Subjunctive	Indicative		
يُخَافُ	خِيفَ		يَخَفْ	يَخَافَ	يَخَافُ	خَافَ	(هُوَ)
تُخَافُ	خِيفَتْ		تَخَفْ	تَخَافَ	تَخَافُ	خَافَتْ	(هِيَ)
تُخَافُ	خِفْتَ	خَفْ	تَخَفْ	تَخَافَ	تَخَافُ	خِفْتَ	(أَنْتَ)
تُخَافِينَ	خِفْتِ	خَافِي	تَخَافِي	تَخَافِي	تَخَافِينَ	خِفْتِ	(أَنْتِ)
أُخَافُ	خِفْتُ		أَخَفْ	أَخَافَ	أَخَافُ	خِفْتُ	(أَنَا)
يُخَافُونَ	خِيفُوا		يَخَافُوا	يَخَافُوا	يَخَافُونَ	خَافُوا	(هُمْ)
يُخَفْنَ	خِفْنَ		يَخَفْنَ	يَخَفْنَ	يَخَفْنَ	خِفْنَ	(هُنَّ)
تُخَافُونَ	خُفْتُمْ	خَافُوا	تَخَافُوا	تَخَافُوا	تَخَافُونَ	خِفْتُمْ	(أَنْتُمْ)
تُخَفْنَ	خِفْتُنَّ	خَفْنَ	تَخَفْنَ	تَخَفْنَ	تَخَفْنَ	خِفْتُنَّ	(أَنْتُنَّ)
نُخَافُ	خِفْنَا		نَخَفْ	نَخَافَ	نَخَافُ	خِفْنَا	(نَحْنُ)
يُخَافَانِ	خِيفَا		يَخَافَا	يَخَافَا	يَخَافَانِ	خَافَا	(هُمَا)
تُخَافَانِ	خِيفَتَا		تَخَافَا	تَخَافَا	تَخَافَانِ	خَافَتَا	(هُمَا)
تُخَافَانِ	خِفْتُمَا	خَافَا	تَخَافَا	تَخَافَا	تَخَافَانِ	خِفْتُمَا	(أَنْتُمَا)

Table 33 : HOLLOW VERBS R2 = و (خَافَ) : FORMS II-X (أَلْفِعْلُ الأَجْوَفُ الْوَاوِيُّ)

Passive		Active					
Imperfect	Perfect				Imperfect	Perfect	
Indicative		Imperative	Jussive	Subjunctive	Indicative		
يُخَوَّفُ	خُوِّفَ	خَوِّفْ	يُخَوِّفْ	يُخَوِّفَ	يُخَوِّفُ	خَوَّفَ	II
يُخَاوَفُ	خُووِفَ	خَاوِفْ	يُخَاوِفْ	يُخَاوِفَ	يُخَاوِفُ	خَاوَفَ	III
يُخَافُ	أُخِيفَ	أَخِفْ	يُخِفْ	يُخِيفَ	يُخِيفُ	أَخَافَ	IV
يُتَخَوَّفُ	تُخُوِّفَ	تَخَوَّفْ	يَتَخَوَّفْ	يَتَخَوَّفَ	يَتَخَوَّفُ	تَخَوَّفَ	V
يُتَخَاوَفُ	تُخُووِفَ	تَخَاوَفْ	يَتَخَاوَفْ	يَتَخَاوَفَ	يَتَخَاوَفُ	تَخَاوَفَ	VI
يُنْخَافُ	أُنْخِيفَ	انْخَفْ	يَنْخَفْ	يَنْخَافَ	يَنْخَافُ	انْخَافَ	VII
يُخْتَافُ	اُخْتِيفَ	اخْتَفْ	يَخْتَفْ	يَخْتَافَ	يَخْتَافُ	اخْتَافَ	VIII
يُسْتَخَافُ	اُسْتُخِيفَ	اسْتَخِفْ	يَسْتَخِفْ	يَسْتَخِيفَ	يَسْتَخِيفُ	اسْتَخَافَ	X

DEFECTIVE VERBS R3 = و OR ى (أَلْفِعْلُ النَّاقِصُ)

PERFECT TENSE

R3 is omitted in the 3rd p.sg. f. (groups **D** and **E**).

Examples with the model verbs:

D دَعَا *"to invite"* (فَعَلَ = دَعَوَ) R3 = و	(هِيَ) دَعَتْ	(هُوَ) دَعَا
E مَشَى *"to walk"* (فَعَلَ = مَشَيَ) R3 = ى	(هِيَ) مَشَتْ	(هُوَ) مَشَى
F لَقِيَ *"to meet"* (فعِل = لَقِيَ) R3 = ى	(هِيَ) لَقِيَتْ	(هُوَ) لَقِيَ

ى which represents R3 has the phonetic value *ā* when identified in the verbs of group E (model verb مَشَى). *Alif maqsūra* in words like أَلْمَقْهَى and أَلْمُسْتَوَى becomes visible as *Alif* (ا) if an affixed pronoun is added to these words: مَقْهَاهُ, *"his café"*, تَرَانِي *"you see me"*.

All other forms are characterized by a diphthong after R2 in verbs belonging to groups D and E, and by a long vowel after R2 in verbs of the group F. This produces the following paradigm:

F	E	D	
لَقِيَ	مَشَى	دَعَا	(هُوَ)
لَقِيَتْ	مَشَتْ	دَعَتْ	(هِيَ)
لَقِيتَ	مَشَيْتَ	دَعَوْتَ	(أَنْتَ)
لَقِيتِ	مَشَيْتِ	دَعَوْتِ	(أَنْتِ)
لَقِيتُ	مَشَيْتُ	دَعَوْتُ	(أَنَا)
لَقُوا	مَشَوْا	دَعَوْا	(هُمْ)
لَقِينَ	مَشَيْنَ	دَعَوْنَ	(هُنَّ)
لَقِيتُمْ	مَشَيْتُم	دَعَوْتُمْ	(أَنْتُمْ)
لَقِيتُنَّ	مَشَيْتُنَّ	دَعَوْتُنَّ	(أَنْتُنَّ)
لَقِينا	مَشَيْنا	دَعَوْنا	(نَحْنُ)

IMPERFECT TENSE

In the imperfect tense R2 has the long vowel $\bar{u}$ in verbs with R3 = و or ى if they belong to group D, the long vowel $\bar{\imath}$ if they are verbs of group E and the long vowel $\bar{a}$ (*Alif maqṣūra*) if they belong to group F.

Examples with the model verbs:

D دَعَا "to invite" (فَعَلَ = دَعَوَ) R3 = و	(نَحْنُ) نَدْعُو	(هِيَ) تَدْعُو	(هُوَ) يَدْعُو
E مَشَى "to walk" (فَعَلَ = مَشَيَ) R3 = ى	(نَحْنُ) نَمْشِي	(هِيَ) تَمْشِي	(هُوَ) يَمْشِي
F لَقِيَ "to meet" (= فَعِلَ) R3 = ى	(نَحْنُ) نَلْقَى	(هِيَ) تَلْقَى	(هُوَ) يَلْقَى

Occasionally, we find verbs in group E, model verb مَشَى, which are inflected in the imperfect tense like the verbs in group F, model verb لَقِيَ, e.g. سَعَى "to endeavour, to strive" يَسْعَى، تَسْعَى etc. (☞ Table 42)

The forms which have a suffix are characterized by a long vowel following R2 if the respective verb belongs to the groups D and E, and by a diphthong following R2 in the verbs which belong to group F.

F	E	D	
تَلْقَيْنَ	تَمْشِينَ	تَدْعِينَ	(أَنْتِ)
تَلْقَوْنَ	تَمْشُونَ	تَدْعُونَ	(أَنْتُمْ)

Thus the following conjugational paradigms ensue:

F	E	D	
يَلْقَى	يَمْشِي	يَدْعُو	(هُوَ)
تَلْقَى	تَمْشِي	تَدْعُو	(هِيَ)
تَلْقَى	تَمْشِي	تَدْعُو	(أَنْتَ)
تَلْقَيْنَ	تَمْشِينَ	تَدْعِينَ	(أَنْتِ)
أَلْقَى	أَمْشِي	أَدْعُو	(أَنَا)
يَلْقَوْنَ	يَمْشُونَ	يَدْعُونَ	(هُمْ)
يَلْقَيْنَ	يَمْشِينَ	يَدْعُونَ	(هُنَّ)
تَلْقَوْنَ	تَمْشُونَ	تَدْعُونَ	(أَنْتُمْ)
تَلْقَيْنَ	تَمْشِينَ	تَدْعُونَ	(أَنْتُنَّ)
نَلْقَى	نَمْشِي	نَدْعُو	(نَحْنُ)

DERIVED FORMS OF DEFECTIVE VERBS R3 = و OR ى (أَلْفِعْلُ النَّاقِصُ)

The derived forms of verbs R3 = و or ى are the same, therefore we give only one model verb for the individual forms.

Form II

perfect tense:	لَقَّى
imperfect tense indicative:	يُلَقِّي
imperfect tense jussive:	يُلَقِّ
imperative:	لَقِّ

Form III

perfect tense:	لاَقَى
imperfect tense indicative:	يُلاَقِي
imperfect tense jussive:	يُلاَقِ
imperative:	لاَقِ

Form IV

perfect tense:	أَلْقَى
imperfect tense indicative:	يُلْقِي
imperfect tense jussive:	يُلْقِ
imperative:	أَلْقِ

Forms II, III and IV of the verbs R3 = و or ى are conjugated like Form I of the model verb مَشَى. The imperfect tense of Forms II and IV can neither be differentiated from each other nor from Form I (R3 = ى, in some forms also R3 = و) without auxiliary signs.

Form V

perfect tense	تَلَقَّى
imperfect tense indicative	يَتَلَقَّى
imperfect tense subjunctive	يَتَلَقَّى
imperfect tense jussive	يَتَلَقَّ

Form VI

perfect tense	تَلاَقَى
imperfect tense indicative	يَتَلاَقَى
imperfect tense subjunctive	يَتَلاَقَى
imperfect tense jussive	يَتَلاَقَ

The verbs R3 = و or ى are conjugated in the perfect tense of Forms V and VI like the model verb مَشَى, and in the imperfect tense like Form I of the model verb لَقِيَ.

Form VII

perfect tense	اِنْلَقَى
imperfect indicative	يَنْلَقِي
imperfect jussive	يَنْلَقِ
imperative	اِنْلَقِ

Form VIII

perfect tense	اِلْتَقَى
imperfect indicative	يَلْتَقِي
imperfect jussive	يَلْتَقِ
imperative	اِلْتَقِ

Form X

perfect tense	اِسْتَلْقَى
imperfect indicative	يَسْتَلْقِي
imperfect jussive	يَسْتَلْقِ
imperative	اِسْتَلْقِ

Forms VII, VIII and X of these verbs are conjugated like Form I of the model verb مَشَى .

The following tables provide a full survey of all forms.

Table 34 : DEFECTIVE VERBS R3 = و (دَعَا): FORM I (أَلْفِعْلُ النَّاقِصُ)

Passive			Active				
Imperfect	Perfect			Imperfect		Perfect	
Indicative		Imperative	Jussive	Subjunctive	Indicative		
يُدْعَى	دُعِيَ		يَدْعُ	يَدْعُوَ	يَدْعُو	دَعَا	(هُوَ)
تُدْعَى	دُعِيَتْ		تَدْعُ	تَدْعُوَ	تَدْعُو	دَعَتْ	(هِيَ)
تُدْعَى	دُعِيتَ	أُدْعُ	تَدْعُ	تَدْعُوَ	تَدْعُو	دَعَوْتَ	(أَنْتَ)
تُدْعَيْنَ	دُعِيتِ	أُدْعِي	تَدْعِي	تَدْعِي	تَدْعِينَ	دَعَوْتِ	(أَنْتِ)
أُدْعَى	دُعِيتُ		أَدْعُ	أَدْعُوَ	أَدْعُو	دَعَوْتُ	(أَنَا)
يُدْعَوْنَ	دُعُوا		يَدْعُوا	يَدْعُوا	يَدْعُونَ	دَعَوْا	(هُمْ)
يُدْعَيْنَ	دُعِينَ		يَدْعُونَ	يَدْعُونَ	يَدْعُونَ	دَعَوْنَ	(هُنَّ)
تُدْعَوْنَ	دُعِيتُمْ	أُدْعُوا	تَدْعُوا	تَدْعُوا	تَدْعُونَ	دَعَوْتُمْ	(أَنْتُمْ)
تُدْعَيْنَ	دُعِيتُنَّ	أُدْعُونَ	تَدْعُونَ	تَدْعُونَ	تَدْعُونَ	دَعَوْتُنَّ	(أَنْتُنَّ)
نُدْعَى	دُعِينَا		نَدْعُ	نَدْعُوَ	نَدْعُو	دَعَوْنَا	(نَحْنُ)
يُدْعَيَانِ	دُعِيَا		يَدْعُوَا	يَدْعُوَا	يَدْعُوَانِ	دَعَوَا	(هُمَا)
تُدْعَيَانِ	دُعِيَتَا		تَدْعُوَا	تَدْعُوَا	تَدْعُوَانِ	دَعَتَا	(هُمَا)
تُدْعَيَانِ	دُعِيتُمَا	أُدْعُوَا	تَدْعُوَا	تَدْعُوَا	تَدْعُوَانِ	دَعَوْتُمَا	(أَنْتُمَا)

Table 35 : DEFECTIVE VERBS R3 = و (دَعَا) : FORMS II - X

Passive			Active				
Imperfect	Perfect			Imperfect		Perfect	
Indicative		Imperative	Jussive	Subjunctive	Indicative		
يُدَعَّى	دُعِّيَ	دَعِّ	يُدَعِّ	يُدَعِّيَ	يُدَعِّي	دَعَّى	II
يُدَاعَى	دُوعِيَ	دَاعِ	يُدَاعِ	يُدَاعِيَ	يُدَاعِي	دَاعَى	III
يُدْعَى	أُدْعِيَ	أَدْعِ	يُدْعِ	يُدْعِيَ	يُدْعِي	أَدْعَى	IV
يُتَدَعَّى	تُدُعِّيَ	تَدَعَّ	يَتَدَعَّ	يَتَدَعَّى	يَتَدَعَّى	تَدَعَّى	V
يُتَدَاعَى	تُدُوعِيَ	تَدَاعَ	يَتَدَاعَ	يَتَدَاعَى	يَتَدَاعَى	تَدَاعَى	VI
يُنْدَعَى	أُنْدُعِيَ	انْدَعِ	يَنْدَعِ	يَنْدَعِيَ	يَنْدَعِي	انْدَعَى	VII
يُدَّعَى	أُدُّعِيَ	ادَّعِ	يَدَّعِ	يَدَّعِيَ	يَدَّعِي	ادَّعَى	VIII
يُسْتَدْعَى	اُسْتُدْعِيَ	اسْتَدْعِ	يَسْتَدْعِ	يَسْتَدْعِيَ	يَسْتَدْعِي	اسْتَدْعَى	X

Table 36 : DEFECTIVE VERBS R3 = ى (مَشَى) : FORM I : (أَلْفِعْلُ النَّاقِصُ)

Passive					Active		
Imperfect	Perfect				Imperfect		Perfect
Indicative		Imperative	Jussive	Subjunctive	Indicative		
يُمْشَى	مُشِيَ		يَمْشِ	يَمْشِيَ	يَمْشِي	مَشَى	(هُوَ)
تُمْشَى	مُشِيَتْ		تَمْشِ	تَمْشِيَ	تَمْشِي	مَشَتْ	(هِيَ)
تُمْشَى	مُشِيتَ	امْشِ	تَمْشِ	تَمْشِيَ	تَمْشِي	مَشَيْتَ	(أَنْتَ)
تُمْشَيْنَ	مُشِيتِ	امْشِي	تَمْشِي	تَمْشِي	تَمْشِينَ	مَشَيْتِ	(أَنْتِ)
أُمْشَى	مُشِيتُ		أَمْشِ	أَمْشِيَ	أَمْشِي	مَشَيْتُ	(أَنَا)
يُمْشَوْنَ	مُشُوا		يَمْشُوا	يَمْشُوا	يَمْشُونَ	مَشَوْا	(هُمْ)
يُمْشَيْنَ	مُشِينَ		يَمْشِينَ	يَمْشِينَ	يَمْشِينَ	مَشَيْنَ	(هُنَّ)
تُمْشَوْنَ	مُشِيتُمْ	امْشُوا	تَمْشُوا	تَمْشُوا	تَمْشُونَ	مَشَيْتُمْ	(أَنْتُمْ)
تُمْشَيْنَ	مُشِيتُنَّ	امْشِينَ	تَمْشِينَ	تَمْشِينَ	تَمْشِينَ	مَشَيْتُنَّ	(أَنْتُنَّ)
نُمْشَى	مُشِينَا		نَمْشِ	نَمْشِيَ	نَمْشِي	مَشَيْنَا	(نَحْنُ)
يُمْشَيَانِ	مُشِيَا		يَمْشِيَا	يَمْشِيَا	يَمْشِيَانِ	مَشَيَا	(هُمَا)
تُمْشَيَانِ	مُشِيَتَا		تَمْشِيَا	تَمْشِيَا	تَمْشِيَانِ	مَشَتَا	(هُمَا)
تُمْشَيَانِ	مُشِيتُمَا	امْشِيَا	تَمْشِيَا	تَمْشِيَا	تَمْشِيَانِ	مَشَيْتُمَا	(أَنْتُمَا)

Table 37 : DEFECTIVE VERBS R3 = ى (مَشَى) : FORMS II – X

Passive					Active		
Imperfect	Perfect				Imperfect		Perfect
Indicative		Imperative	Jussive	Subjunctive	Indicative		
يُمَشَّى	مُشِّيَ	مَشِّ	يُمَشِّ	يُمَشِّيَ	يُمَشِّي	مَشَّى	II
يُمَاشَى	مُوشِيَ	مَاشِ	يُمَاشِ	يُمَاشِيَ	يُمَاشِي	مَاشَى	III
يُمْشَى	أُمْشِيَ	أَمْشِ	يُمْشِ	يُمْشِيَ	يُمْشِي	أَمْشَى	IV
يُتَمَشَّى	تُمُشِّيَ	تَمَشَّ	يَتَمَشَّ	يَتَمَشَّى	يَتَمَشَّى	تَمَشَّى	V
يُتَمَاشَى	تُمُوشِيَ	تَمَاشَ	يَتَمَاشَ	يَتَمَاشَى	يَتَمَاشَى	تَمَاشَى	VI
يُنْمَشَى	أُنْمُشِيَ	انْمَشِ	يَنْمَشِ	يَنْمَشِيَ	يَنْمَشِي	انْمَشَى	VII
يُمْتَشَى	أُمْتُشِيَ	امْتَشِ	يَمْتَشِ	يَمْتَشِيَ	يَمْتَشِي	امْتَشَى	VIII
يُسْتَمْشَى	أُسْتُمْشِيَ	اسْتَمْشِ	يَسْتَمْشِ	يَسْتَمْشِيَ	يَسْتَمْشِي	اسْتَمْشَى	X

Table 38 : DEFECTIVE VERBS R3 = ى (لَقِيَ) : FORM I (أَلْفِعْلُ النَّاقِصُ)

Passive		Active					
Imperfect	Perfect				Imperfect		Perfect
Indicative		Imperative	Jussive	Subjunctive	Indicative		
يُلْقَى	لُقِيَ		يَلْقَ	يَلْقَى	يَلْقَى	لَقِيَ	(هُوَ)
تُلْقَى	لُقِيَتْ		تَلْقَ	تَلْقَى	تَلْقَى	لَقِيَتْ	(هِيَ)
تُلْقَى	لُقِيتَ	اِلْقَ	تَلْقَ	تَلْقَى	تَلْقَى	لَقِيتَ	(أَنْتَ)
تُلْقَيْنَ	لُقِيتِ	اِلْقَيْ	تَلْقَيْ	تَلْقَيْ	تَلْقَيْنَ	لَقِيتِ	(أَنْتِ)
أُلْقَى	لُقِيتُ		أَلْقَ	أَلْقَى	أَلْقَى	لَقِيتُ	(أَنَا)
يُلْقَوْنَ	لُقُوا		يَلْقَوْا	يَلْقَوْا	يَلْقَوْنَ	لَقُوا	(هُمْ)
يُلْقَيْنَ	لُقِينَ		يَلْقَيْنَ	يَلْقَيْنَ	يَلْقَيْنَ	لَقِينَ	(هُنَّ)
تُلْقَوْنَ	لُقِيتُمْ	اِلْقَوْا	تَلْقَوْا	تَلْقَوْا	تَلْقَوْنَ	لَقِيتُمْ	(أَنْتُمْ)
تُلْقَيْنَ	لُقِيتُنَّ	اِلْقَيْنَ	تَلْقَيْنَ	تَلْقَيْنَ	تَلْقَيْنَ	لَقِيتُنَّ	(أَنْتُنَّ)
نُلْقَى	لُقِينَا		نَلْقَ	نَلْقَى	نَلْقَى	لَقِينَا	(نَحْنُ)
يُلْقَيَان	لُقِيَا		يَلْقَيَا	يَلْقَيَان	يَلْقَيَان	لَقِيَا	(هُمَا)
تُلْقَيَان	لُقِيَتَا		تَلْقَيَا	تَلْقَيَان	تَلْقَيَان	لَقِيَتَا	(هُمَا)
تُلْقَيَان	لُقِيتُمَا	اِلْقَيَا	تَلْقَيَا	تَلْقَيَان	تَلْقَيَان	لَقِيتُمَا	(أَنْتُمَا)

Table 39 : DEFECTIVE VERBS R3 = ى (لَقِيَ) : FORMS II - X

Passive		Active				
Imperfect	Perfect				Imperfect	Perfect
Indicative		Imperative	Jussive	Subjunctive	Indicative	
يُلَقَّى	لُقِّيَ	لَقِّ	يُلَقِّ	يُلَقِّيَ	يُلَقِّي	لَقَّى	II
يُلَاقَى	لُوقِيَ	لَاقِ	يُلَاقِ	يُلَاقِيَ	يُلَاقِي	لَاقَى	III
يُلْقَى	أُلْقِيَ	أَلْقِ	يُلْقِ	يُلْقِيَ	يُلْقِي	أَلْقَى	IV
يُتَلَقَّى	تُلُقِّيَ	تَلَقَّ	يَتَلَقَّ	يَتَلَقَّى	يَتَلَقَّى	تَلَقَّى	V
يُتَلَاقَى	تُلُوقِيَ	تَلَاقَ	يَتَلَاقَ	يَتَلَاقَى	يَتَلَاقَى	تَلَاقَى	VI
يُنْلَقَى	اُنْلُقِيَ	اِنْلَقِ	يَنْلَقِ	يَنْلَقِيَ	يَنْلَقِي	اِنْلَقَى	VII
يُلْتَقَى	اُلْتُقِيَ	اِلْتَقِ	يَلْتَقِ	يَلْتَقِيَ	يَلْتَقِي	اِلْتَقَى	VIII
يُسْتَلْقَى	اُسْتُلْقِيَ	اِسْتَلْقِ	يَسْتَلْقِ	يَسْتَلْقِيَ	يَسْتَلْقِي	اِسْتَلْقَى	X

Table 40 : QUADRILITERAL VERBS: دَحْرَجَ تَدَحْرَجَ إطْمَأَنَّ (أَلْفِعْلُ الرُّبَاعِيُّ)

Passive Imperfect	Passive Perfect	Imperative	Jussive	Subjunctive	Indicative	Perfect		
يُدَحْرَجُ	دُحْرِجَ		يُدَحْرِجْ	يُدَحْرِجَ	يُدَحْرِجُ	دَحْرَجَ	هو	I
تُدَحْرَجُ	دُحْرِجْتَ	دَحْرِجْ	تُدَحْرِجْ	تُدَحْرِجَ	تُدَحْرِجُ	دَحْرَجْتَ	أنتَ	
أُدَحْرَجُ	دُحْرِجْتُ		أُدَحْرِجْ	أُدَحْرِجَ	أُدَحْرِجُ	دَحْرَجْتُ	أنا	
يُدَحْرَجُونَ	دُحْرِجُوا		يُدَحْرِجُوا	يُدَحْرِجُوا	يُدَحْرِجُونَ	دَحْرَجُوا	هم	
تُدَحْرَجُونَ	دُحْرِجْتُم	دَحْرِجُوا	تُدَحْرِجُوا	تُدَحْرِجُوا	تُدَحْرِجُونَ	دَحْرَجْتُم	أنتم	
نُدَحْرَجُ	دُحْرِجْنَا		نُدَحْرِجْ	نُدَحْرِجَ	نُدَحْرِجُ	دَحْرَجْنَا	نحن	
يُتَدَحْرَجُ	تُدُحْرِجَ		يَتَدَحْرَجْ	يَتَدَحْرَجَ	يَتَدَحْرَجُ	تَدَحْرَجَ	هو	II
تُتَدَحْرَجُ	تُدُحْرِجْتَ	تَدَحْرَجْ	تَتَدَحْرَجْ	تَتَدَحْرَجَ	تَتَدَحْرَجُ	تَدَحْرَجْتَ	أنتَ	
أُتَدَحْرَجُ	تُدُحْرِجْتُ		أَتَدَحْرَجْ	أَتَدَحْرَجَ	أَتَدَحْرَجُ	تَدَحْرَجْتُ	أنا	
يُتَدَحْرَجُونَ	تُدُحْرِجُوا		يَتَدَحْرَجُوا	يَتَدَحْرَجُوا	يَتَدَحْرَجُونَ	تَدَحْرَجُوا	هم	
تُتَدَحْرَجُونَ	تُدُحْرِجْتُم	تَدَحْرَجُوا	تَتَدَحْرَجُوا	تَتَدَحْرَجُوا	تَتَدَحْرَجُونَ	تَدَحْرَجْتُم	أنتم	
نُتَدَحْرَجُ	تُدُحْرِجْنَا		نَتَدَحْرَجْ	نَتَدَحْرَجَ	نَتَدَحْرَجُ	تَدَحْرَجْنَا	نحن	
			يَطْمَئِنَّ	يَطْمَئِنَّ	يَطْمَئِنُّ	اطْمَأَنَّ	هو	IV
		اطْمَئِنَّ	تَطْمَئِنَّ	تَطْمَئِنَّ	تَطْمَئِنُّ	اطْمَأْنَنْتَ	أنتَ	
			أَطْمَئِنَّ	أَطْمَئِنَّ	أَطْمَئِنُّ	اطْمَأْنَنْتُ	أنا	
			يَطْمَئِنُّوا	يَطْمَئِنُّوا	يَطْمَئِنُّونَ	اطْمَأَنُّوا	هم	
		اطْمَئِنُّوا	تَطْمَئِنُّوا	تَطْمَئِنُّوا	تَطْمَئِنُّونَ	اطْمَأْنَنْتُم	أنتم	
			نَطْمَئِنَّ	نَطْمَئِنَّ	نَطْمَئِنُّ	اطْمَأْنَنَّا	نحن	

The consecution of the vowels of the quadriliteral verbs in Forms I, II and IV is the same as in Forms II, V, VIII of the triliteral verb. The jussive has also a long form: يَطْمَأْنِنْ etc.

Table 41 : DOUBLY WEAK VERBS: جَاءَ (أَلْفِعْلُ الْمُعْتَلُّ بِحَرْفَيْنِ)

Passive		Active					
Imperfect	Perfect			Imperfect		Perfect	
Indicative		Imperative	Jussive	Subjunctive	Indicative		
			يَجِئْ	يَجِيءَ	يَجِيءُ	جَاءَ	(هُوَ)
			تَجِئْ	تَجِيءَ	تَجِيءُ	جَاءَتْ	(هِيَ)
		*جِئْ	تَجِئْ	تَجِيءَ	تَجِيءُ	جِئْتَ	(أَنْتَ)
		*جِيئِى	تَجِيئِى	تَجِيئِى	تَجِيئِينَ	جِئْتِ	(أَنْتِ)
			أَجِئْ	أَجِيءَ	أَجِيءُ	جِئْتُ	(أَنَا)
Not in use			يَجِيئُوا	يَجِيئُوا	يَجِيئُونَ	جَاؤُوا	(هُمْ)
			يَجِئْنَ	يَجِئْنَ	يَجِئْنَ	جِئْنَ	(هُنَّ)
		*جِيئُوا	تَجِيئُوا	تَجِيئُوا	تَجِيئُونَ	جِئْتُمْ	(أَنْتُمْ)
		*جِئْنَ	تَجِئْنَ	تَجِئْنَ	تَجِئْنَ	جِئْتُنَّ	(أَنْتُنَّ)
			نَجِئْ	نَجِيءَ	نَجِيءُ	جِئْنَا	(نَحْنُ)
			يَجِيئَا	يَجِيئَا	يَجِيئَانِ	جَاءَا	(هُمَا)
			تَجِيئَا	تَجِيئَا	تَجِيئَانِ	جَاءَتَا	(هُمَا)
		*جِيئَا	تَجِيئَا	تَجِيئَا	تَجِيئَانِ	جِئْتُمَا	(أَنْتُمَا)

* All these imperatives are practically not used. Native speakers prefer:

تَعَالْ	أَنْتَ
تَعَالِي	أَنْتِ
تَعَالُوا	أَنْتُمْ / أَنْتُنَّ

active participle:	جَاءٍ / الْجَائِيُّ
passive participle:	مَجِيءٌ
infinitive :	مَجِيءٌ

Table 42 : DOUBLY WEAK VERBS: رَأَى (أَلْفِعْلُ الْمُعْتَلُّ بِحَرْفَيْنِ)

	Passive			Active			
	Imperfect	Perfect			Imperfect		Perfect
	Indicative		Imperative	Jussive	Subjunctive	Indicative	
(هُوَ)	رَأَى	يَرَى	يَرَى	يَرَ		رُئِيَ	يُرَى
(هِيَ)	رَأَتْ	تَرَى	تَرَى	تَرَ		رُئِيَتْ	تُرَى
(أَنْتَ)	رَأَيْتَ	تَرَى	تَرَى	تَرَ	رَهْ*	رُئِيْتَ	تُرَى
(أَنْتِ)	رَأَيْتِ	تَرَيْنَ	تَرَيْ	تَرَيْ	رَيْ*	رُئِيْتِ	تُرَيْنَ
(أَنَا)	رَأَيْتُ	أَرَى	أَرَى	أَرَى		رُئِيْتُ	أُرَى
(هُمْ)	رَأَوْا	يَرَوْنَ	يَرَوْا	يَرَوْا		رُئِيُوا	يُرَوْنَ
(هُنَّ)	رَأَيْنَ	يَرَيْنَ	يَرَيْنَ	يَرَيْنَ		رُئِيْنَ	يُرَيْنَ
(أَنْتُمْ)	رَأَيْتُمْ	تَرَوْنَ	تَرَوْا	تَرَوْا	رَوْا*	رُئِيْتُمْ	تُرَوْنَ
(أَنْتُنَّ)	رَأَيْتُنَّ	تَرَيْنَ	تَرَيْنَ	تَرَيْنَ	رَيْنَ*	رُئِيْتُنَّ	تُرَيْنَ
(نَحْنُ)	رَأَيْنَا	نَرَى	نَرَى	نَرَ		رُئِيْنَا	نُرَى
(هُمَا)	رَأَيَا	يَرَيَانِ	يَرَيَا	يَرَيَا		رُئِيَا	يُرَيَانِ
(هُمَا)	رَأَتَا	تَرَيَانِ	تَرَيَا	تَرَيَا		رُئِيَتَا	تُرَيَانِ
(أَنْتُمَا)	رَأَيْتُمَا	تَرَيَانِ	تَرَيَا	تَرَيَا	رَيَا*	رُئِيْتُمَا	تُرَيَانِ

* All these imperatives are practically not used. Native speakers prefer:

شُوفْ	أَنْتَ
شُوفِي	أَنْتِ
شُوفُوا	أَنْتُمْ / أَنْتُنَّ

active participle:	رَاءٍ / الرَّائِيُّ
passive participle:	مَرْئِيٌّ
infinitive :	رَأْيٌ / رُؤْيَةٌ

Table 43 : DOUBLY WEAK VERBS: أَتَى (اَلْفِعْلُ الْمُعْتَلُّ بِحَرْفَيْنِ)

	Passive				Active			
	Imperfect	Perfect				Imperfect		Perfect	
	Indicative		Imperative	Jussive	Subjunctive	Indicative		Perfect	
	يُؤْتَى	أُتِيَ		يَأْتِ	يَأْتِيَ	يَأْتِي	أَتَى	(هُوَ)
	تُؤْتَى	أُتِيَتْ		تَأْتِ	تَأْتِيَ	تَأْتِي	أَتَتْ	(هِيَ)
	تُؤْتَى	أُتِيتَ	not used*	تَأْتِ	تَأْتِيَ	تَأْتِي	أَتَيْتَ	(أَنْتَ)
	تُؤْتَيْنَ	أُتِيتِ		تَأْتِي	تَأْتِيَ	تَأْتِينَ	أَتَيْتِ	(أَنْتِ)
	أُوتَى	أُتِيتُ		آتِ	آتِيَ	آتِي	أَتَيْتُ	(أَنَا)
	يُؤْتَوْنَ	أُتُوا		يَأْتُوا	يَأْتُوا	يَأْتُونَ	أَتَوْا	(هُمْ)
	يُؤْتَيْنَ	أُتِينَ		يَأْتِينَ	يَأْتِينَ	يَأْتِينَ	أَتَيْنَ	(هُنَّ)
	تُؤْتَوْنَ	أُتِيتُمْ		تَأْتُوا	تَأْتُوا	تَأْتُونَ	أَتَيْتُمْ	(أَنْتُمْ)
	تُؤْتَيْنَ	أُتِيتُنَّ		تَأْتِينَ	تَأْتِينَ	تَأْتِينَ	أَتَيْتُنَّ	(أَنْتُنَّ)
	نُؤْتَى	أُتِينَا		نَأْتِ	نَأْتِيَ	نَأْتِي	أَتَيْنَا	(نَحْنُ)
	يُؤْتَيَان	أُتِيَا		يَأْتِيَا	يَأْتِيَا	يَأْتِيَان	أَتَيَا	(هُمَا)
	تُؤْتَيَان	أُتِيَتَا		تَأْتِيَا	تَأْتِيَا	تَأْتِيَان	أَتَتَا	(هُمَا)
	تُؤْتَيَان	أُتِيتُمَا		تَأْتِيَا	تَأْتِيَا	تَأْتِيَان	أَتَيْتُمَا	(أَنْتُمَا)

* ☞ جَاءَ

active participle:	آتٍ / الْآتِيُّ
passive participle:	مَأْتِيٌّ
infinitive :	إِتْيَانٌ

Table 44 : DOUBLY WEAK VERBS: وَفَى (ألْفِعْلُ الْمُعْتَلُّ بِحَرْفَيْن)

Passive			Active				
Imperfect	Perfect			Imperfect		Perfect	
Indicative		Imperative	Jussive	Subjunctive	Indicative		
يُوفَى	وُفِيَ		يَفِ	يَفِيَ	يَفِي	وَفَى	(هُوَ)
تُوفَى	وُفِيَتْ		تَفِ	تَفِيَ	تَفِي	وَفَتْ	(هِيَ)
تُوفَى	وُفِيتَ	فِهِ	تَفِ	تَفِيَ	تَفِي	وَفَيْتَ	(أَنْتَ)
تُوفَيْنَ	وُفِيتِ	فِي	تَفِي	تَفِي	تَفِينَ	وَفَيْتِ	(أَنْتِ)
أُوفَى	وُفِيتُ		أَفِ	أَفِيَ	أَفِي	وَفَيْتُ	(أَنَا)
يُوفَوْنَ	وُفُوا		يَفُوا	يَفُوا	يَفُونَ	وَفُوْا	(هُمْ)
يُوفَيْنَ	وُفِينَ		يَفِينَ	يَفِينَ	يَفِينَ	وَفَيْنَ	(هُنَّ)
تُوفَوْنَ	وُفِيتُمْ	فُوا	تَفُوا	تَفُوا	تَفُونَ	وَفَيْتُمْ	(أَنْتُم)
تُوفَيْنَ	وُفِيتُنَّ	فِينَ	تَفِينَ	تَفِينَ	تَفِينَ	وَفَيْتُنَّ	(أَنْتُنَّ)
تُوفَى	وُفِينَا		نَفِ	نَفِيَ	نَفِي	وَفَيْنَا	(نَحْنُ)
يُوفَيَان	وُفِيَا		يَفِيَا	يَفِيَا	يَفِيَان	وَفَيَا	(هُمَا)
تُوفَيَان	وُفِيَتَا		تَفِيَا	تَفِيَا	تَفِيَان	وَفَتَا	(هُمَا)
تُوفَيَان	وُفِيتُمَا	فِيَا	تَفِيَا	تَفِيَا	تَفِيَان	وَفَيْتُمَا	(أَنْتُمَا)

active participle:	وَافٍ / الْوَافِيُّ
passive participle:	مَوْفِيٌّ
infinitive :	وَفَاءٌ

NOUNS (أَلأَسْمَاءُ)

PRIMARY (أَلاسْمُ الْجَامِدُ) AND DERIVED NOUNS (أَلاسْمُ الْمُشْتَقُّ)

The noun (اسْمٌ) is besides the verbs (فِعْلٌ) and the particles (حَرْفٌ) one of the three classes of words according to traditional Arabic grammar. Arabic has basically two types of nouns: Primary and derived nouns.

Primary nouns are nouns which are not derived from verbs, e.g.:

tiger	نَمِرٌ	man	رَجُلٌ
rabbit	أَرْنَبٌ	woman	إمْرَأَةٌ

In Arabic grammars **primary nouns** are subdivided as follows:

Table 45: PRIMARY NOUNS (أَلاسْمُ الْجَامِدُ)

Infinitives of Form I (☞ Infinitives)	مَصَادِرُ الْفِعْلِ الثَّلاثِيُّ
Infinitives of the derived Forms (☞ Infinitives)	مَصَادِرُ غَيْرُ الثَّلاثِيِّ
Infinitives starting with *Mīm* (☞ Infinitives)	أَلْمَصْدَرُ الْمِيمِيُّ
"artificial" infinitives (☞ Feminine *Nisba*)	أَلْمَصْدَرُ الصِّنَاعِيُّ
Nouns denoting a single action (☞ Accusative)	اسْمُ الْمَرَّة
Nouns denoting circumstances of an action (☞ Accusative)	اسْمُ الْهَيْئَة / النَّوْع

Derived nouns are subdivided as follows:

Table 46: DERIVED NOUNS (أَلاسْمُ الْمُشْتَقُّ)

☞ Active Participle	اِسْمُ الْفَاعِلِ
☞ Passive Participle	اِسْمُ الْمَفْعُول
☞ Nouns of Intensity	اِسْمُ الْمُبَالَغَة
☞ Adjectives	أَلصِّفَةُ الْمُشَبَّهَةُ
☞ *Elative*	اِسْمُ التَّفْضِيل
☞ Nouns of Place and Time	اِسْمُ الزَّمَانِ وَالْمَكَانِ
☞ Nouns of Instruments and Vessels	اِسْمُ الآلَةِ وَالْوِعَاءِ

All the other nouns are derived from verbs or other nouns and may have the following structural patterns:

entering	فُعُولٌ: دُخُولٌ	spending	فَعْلٌ: صَرْفٌ
ease	فُعُولَةٌ: سُهُولَةٌ	mercy	فَعْلَةٌ: رَحْمَةٌ
cough	فُعَالٌ: سُعَالٌ	quest	فَعَلٌ: طَلَبٌ
bran, waste	فُعَالَةٌ : نُخَالَةٌ	generosity	فَعَلَةٌ: كَرَمَةٌ
spy	فَاعُولٌ: جَاسُوسٌ	memory	فِعْلٌ: ذِكْرٌ
omnipotence	فَعَلُوتٌ: جَبَرُوتٌ	writing	فِعْلَةٌ: كِتْبَةٌ
collaborator	فَعِيلٌ: عَمِيلٌ	camels	فِعِلٌ: إِبِلٌ
heartbeat	فَعَلَانٌ: خَفَقَانٌ	graduate	فِعِّيلٌ: خِرِّيجٌ
story	أُفْعُولَةٌ: أُحْدُوثَةٌ	bigness	فِعَلٌ: كِبَرٌ
bolting (horse)	فِعَالٌ: شِرَادٌ	thank	فُعْلٌ: شُكْرٌ
writing	فِعَالَةٌ: كِتَابَةٌ	pleasure	فُعْلَةٌ: مُتْعَةٌ
density	فَعَالَةٌ: كَثَافَةٌ	man	فَعُلٌ: رَجُلٌ
going	فَعَالٌ: ذَهَابٌ	hedgehog	فُعْلُلٌ : قُنْفُذٌ
chick-pea	فِعِّلٌ: حِمِّصٌ	bishop	أُفْعُلٌ : أُسْقُفٌ
box	فُعْلُولٌ : صُنْدُوق	scarab	فُعْلَلَاءُ : خُنْفَسَاءُ

INFINITIVES (أَلْمَصْدَرُ)

The infinitive (verbal noun) is one of the two nominal forms of the Arabic verb.

The Form

In Form I, there are more than 40 patterns of the infinitive, of which one or several can belong to a verb. The two infinitives which occur most frequently are:

فَعْلٌ (فَعَلَ) : بَاعَ ⇦ بَيْعٌ، نَامَ ⇦ نَوْمٌ، شَرَحَ ⇦ شَرْحٌ، عَرَضَ ⇦ عَرْضٌ

فُعُولٌ (فَعَلَ/فَعِلَ): حَصَلَ ⇦ حُصُولٌ، صَعِدَ ⇦ صُعُودٌ، دَخَلَ ⇦ دُخُولٌ

The derived Forms have only one infinitive with few exceptions.

Table 47: PATTERNS OF THE INFINITIVE (SOUND VERBS)

II	III	IV	V	VI	VII	VIII	IX	X
تَفْعِيلٌ	مُفَاعَلَةٌ / فِعَالٌ	إِفْعَالٌ	تَفَعُّلٌ	تَفَاعُلٌ	اِنْفِعَالٌ	اِفْتِعَالٌ	اِفْعِلَالٌ	اِسْتِفْعَالٌ

The quadriliteral verbs have the following infinitives:

I (q)		II (q)	
فَعْلَلَ ⇦ فَعْلَلَةٌ / فِعْلَالٌ		تَفَعْلَلَ ⇦ تَفَعْلُلٌ	
translation	تَرْجَمَةٌ	*rolling*	تَدَحْرُجٌ
earthquake	زِلْزَالٌ	*fall, decline*	تَدَهْوُرٌ

The initial *Hamza* of the Forms VII, VIII, IX and X is a *Hamzat waṣl*, of Form IV a *Hamzat qaṭ'*. In Form III, مُفَاعَلَةٌ occurs more frequently than فِعَالٌ. If both infinitives are in use, they almost always differ in meaning:

fight (for)	كِفَاحٌ	*struggle*	صِرَاعٌ
fighting (against)	مُكَافَحَةٌ	*wrestling*	مُصَارَعَةٌ

There are some peculiarities with regard to the infinitives of the defective verbs:

Verbs R1 = و or ى : **Forms IV** and **X** have the long vowel *ī* (R1 = و⇦ى):	اِسْتَوْصَلَ ⇦ اِسْتِيصَالٌ، أَوْصَلَ ⇦ إِيصَالٌ
Verbs R2 = و or ى : **Forms IV** and **X** have a final *Tā' marbūṭa*	اِسْتَقَامَ ⇦ اِسْتِقَامَةٌ، أَقَامَ ⇦ إِقَامَةٌ
Verbs R3 = و or ى : Forms **IV**, **VII**, **VIII** and **X** have a final *Hamza*:	أَلْقَى ⇦ إِلْقَاءٌ، اِنْلَقَى ⇦ اِنْلِقَاءٌ، اِلْتَقَى ⇦ الْتِقَاءٌ، اِسْتَلْقَى ⇦ اِسْتِلْقَاءٌ
Forms II and **III**:	تَفْعَلَةٌ : لَقَّى ⇦ تَلْقِيةٌ، لاقَى ⇦ مُلاقَاةٌ
Forms V and **VI**:	تَلَقَّى ⇦ تَلَقٍّ/التَّلَقِّي، تَلاقَى ⇦ تَلاقٍ/التَّلاقِي

The following table provides a full survey of all infinitives.

Table 48: PATTERNS OF THE INFINITIVE (ALL VERBS, FORMS II - X)

R3 و	R2 و	R2 ى	R2 و	R1 ى	R1 و	*fa'ala*	
تَدْعِيَةٌ	تَخْوِيفٌ	تَبْيِيعٌ	تَقْوِيمٌ	تَيْبِيسٌ	تَوْصِيلٌ	تَفْعِيلٌ	II
مُدَاعَاةٌ	مُخَاوَفَةٌ	مُبَايَعَةٌ	مُقَاوَمَةٌ	مُيَابَسَةٌ	مُوَاصَلَةٌ	مُفَاعَلَةٌ	III
دُعَاءٌ	خِوَافٌ	بِيَاعٌ	قِوَامٌ	يِيَاسٌ	وِصَالٌ	فِعَالٌ	

إدْعَاءٌ	إخَافَةٌ	إبَاعَةٌ	إقَامَةٌ	إيبَاسٌ	إيصَالٌ	إفْعَالٌ	IV
تَدَعٍّ	تَخَوُّفٌ	تَبَيُّعٌ	تَقَوُّمٌ	تَيَبُّسٌ	تَوَصُّلٌ	تَفَعُّلٌ	V
تَدَاعٍ	تَخَاوُفٌ	تَبَايُعٌ	تَقَاوُمٌ	تَيَابُسٌ	تَوَاصُلٌ	تَفَاعُلٌ	VI
انْدِعَاءٌ	انْخِيَافٌ	انْبِيَاعٌ	انْقِيَامٌ	-	-	انْفِعَالٌ	VII
ادِّعَاءٌ	اخْتِيَافٌ	ابْتِيَاعٌ	اقْتِيَامٌ	اتِّبَاسٌ	اتِّصَالٌ	افْتِعَالٌ	VIII
اسْتِدْعَاءٌ	اسْتِخَافَةٌ	اسْتِبَاعَةٌ	اسْتِقَامَةٌ	اسْتِيبَاسٌ	اسْتِيصَالٌ	اسْتِفْعَالٌ	X

R₃ ء	R₂ ء	R₁ ء	R₂=R₃	R₃ ى	R₃ ى	
تَقْرِئَةٌ	تَسْئِيلٌ	تَأْخِيذٌ	تَمْرِيرٌ	تَلْقِيَةٌ	تَمْشِيَةٌ	II
مُقَارَأَةٌ	مُسَاءَلَةٌ	مُؤَاخَذَةٌ	مُمَارَّةٌ	مُلَاقَاةٌ	مُمَاشَاةٌ	III
قِرَاءٌ	سِئَالٌ	إخَاذٌ	مِرَارٌ	لِقَاءٌ	مِشَاءٌ	
إقْرَاءٌ	إسْآلٌ	إيخَاذٌ	إمْرَارٌ	إلْقَاءٌ	إمْشَاءٌ	IV
تَقَرُّؤٌ	تَسَؤُّلٌ	تَأَخُّذٌ	تَمَرُّرٌ	تَلَقٍّ	تَمَشٍّ	V
تَقَارُؤٌ	تَسَاؤُلٌ	تَآخُذٌ	تَمَارٌّ	تَلَاقٍ	تَمَاشٍ	VI
انْقِرَاءٌ	انْسِئَالٌ	-	انْمِرَارٌ	الْلِقَاءُ	انْمِشَاءُ	VII
اقْتِرَاءٌ	اسْتِئَالٌ	اتِّخَاذٌ	امْتِرَارٌ	الْتِقَاءُ	امْتِشَاءُ	VIII
اسْتِقْرَاءٌ	اسْتِسْآلٌ	اسْتِئْخَاذٌ	اسْتِمْرَارٌ	اسْتِلْقَاءُ	اسْتِمْشَاءُ	X

Other rare patterns of the infinitive are the following:

to be deep black	افْعِيلَالٌ (افْعَوْعَلَ): إحْلِيلَاكٌ (إحْلَوْلَكَ)
disappearance	افْعِلَالٌّ (افْعَلَلَّ): اضْمِحْلَالٌ (اضْمَحَلَّ)
to become poor	تَمَفْعَلَةٌ (تَمَفْعَلَ) : تَمَسْكُنٌ (تَمَسْكَنَ)
to behave like a devil	تَفْيعُلٌ (تَفْيعَلَ) : تَشَيْطُنٌ (تَشَيْطَنَ)
to dominate	فَيْعَلَةٌ (فَيْعَلَ) : سَيْطَرَةٌ (سَيْطَرَ)
to walk fast	فَعْوَلَةٌ (فَعْوَلَ) : هَرْوَلَةٌ (هَرْوَلَ)

| decline | تَفَعْوُلٌ (تَفَعْوَلَ) : تَدَهْوُرٌ (تَدَهْوَرَ) |
| to go away | افْعِنْلالٌ (افْعَنْلَلَ) : افْرِنْقَاعٌ (افْرَنْقَعَ) |

Another rare pattern of the infinitive is the so-called أَلْمَصْدَرُ الْمِيمِيُّ which does not differ in meaning from the regular infinitive:

| place where s.th. falls down | مَفْعِلٌ: مَوْقِعٌ |
| sight | مَفْعَلٌ: مَنْظَرٌ |

The feminine *Nisba*, also called أَلْمَصْدَرُ الصِّنَاعِيُّ , is another type of a derived noun forming numerous abstract nouns:

He is a supporter of nationalism.	هُوَ مِنْ أَنْصَارِ الْقَوْمِيَّةِ.
He defends the continuity of teaching.	يُدَافِعُ عَنِ اسْتِمْرَارِيَّةِ التَّدْرِيسِ.
He bears the responsibility for this resolution.	يَتَحَمَّلُ الْمَسْؤُولِيَّةَ عَنْ هَذَا الْقَرَارِ.
He lost his credibility.	فَقَدَ مِصْدَاقِيَّتَهُ.
He knows the attractiveness of the fair.	يَعْرِفُ جَاذِبِيَّةَ الْمَعْرِضِ.
He spoke about the readiness of the army.	تَكَلَّمَ عَنْ جَاهِزِيَّةِ الْجَيْشِ.

PLURAL OF THE INFINITIVES

The infinitives of Form I have various plural forms. The infinitives of **Form II** have either the sound feminine plural (ـــَات) or the broken plural تَفَاعِيلُ. The infinitives of **Forms III - X** have the sound feminine plural (ـــَات), Form **IV** occasionally has the broken plural أَفَاعِيلُ.

THE USE

The infinitive combines the verbal meaning with the formal characteristics of the noun. Its nominal structure also determines its syntactic use as a subject, an object and a predicate complement. It can take on all cases and can take suffixes and attributive adjuncts.

1. Most infinitives are lexicalized as nouns, i.e. they do not only express the verbal action as an event, but also have an individual meaning comprehensible, in the sense of the result of this event:

كَذْبٌ *"(the) denying"* and *"lie"* (with the plural أَكْذَابٌ),

سُؤَالٌ *"(the) asking"* and *"question"* (with the plural أَسْئِلَةٌ).

The infinitive is lexicalized in these   cases like the *Nomen vicis* (اِسْمُ الْمَرَّةِ,
infinitive + *Ta' marbūṭa*), which denotes the single execution of the verbal action
expressed by the infinitive: ضَرْبَة (single beating) = "*blow*" (ضَرَبَ> "*to beat*",
أَلضَّرْبُ "*the beating*").

2. The infinitive can take the place of a subordinate clause. An infinitive
construction can replace the objective or nominal clause introduced by أَنْ and أَنَّ
as well as adverbial clauses.

a) Objective clause: Infinitive instead of أَنْ + verb

He can do this job.	يَسْتَطِيعُ أَنْ يُنْجِزَ هَذَا الْعَمَلَ. = يَسْتَطِيعُ إِنْجَازَ هَذَا الْعَمَلِ.

b) Nominative clause: Infinitive instead of أَنْ + verb

It is possible for him to do this job.	يُمْكِنُهُ أَنْ يُنْجِزَ هَذَا الْعَمَلَ. = يُمْكِنُهُ إِنْجَازُ هَذَا الْعَمَلِ.

c) Adverbial clauses: Preposition + infinitive instead of conjunction + verb

a) قَبْلَ

I will visit him before he returns/his return.	سَأَزُورُهُ قَبْلَ أَنْ يَعُودَ. = سَأَزُورُهُ قَبْلَ عَوْدته.

b) بَعْدَ

He visited me after he had returned / after his return.	زَارَنِي بَعْدَ أَنْ عَادَ. = زَارَنِي بَعْدَ عَوْدته.

c) مُنْذُ

He has visited me twice since he returned / since his return.	زَارَنِي مَرَّتَيْنِ مُنْذُ أَنْ عَادَ. = زَارَنِي مَرَّتَيْنِ مُنْذُ عَوْدته.

d) حَتَّى

He stayed until the event ended / until the end of the event.	بَقِيَ حَتَّى انْتهتِ الحفلةُ. = بَقِيَ حَتَّى انْتهاءِ الحفلةِ.

e) لِ

He came in order to study Arabic.	جَاءَ لِيَدْرُسَ اللُّغَةَ الْعَرَبِيَّة. = جَاءَ لِدرَاسَة اللُّغَةِ الْعَرَبِيَّةِ.

3. The infinitive has the same power of governing a case that the verb has. It can
take an object dependent on a preposition analog to the government of the
respective verb.

the welcoming of the guests	أَلتَّرْحِيبُ بالضُّيُوف
the answering of the questions	أَلإِجَابَةُ عَلَى الأَسْئِلَة

| the need for drinks | أَلْاِحْتِيَاجُ إِلَى الْمَشْرُوبَاتِ |
| the expression of one's views | أَلتَّعْبِيرُ عَنِ الآرَاءِ |

In general, the accusative object of a transitive verb will not be employed as a direct object related to an infinitive, but is connected with a genitive.

to study the Arabic language	دَرَسَ اللُّغَةَ الْعَرَبِيّةَ
the study of the Arabic language	دِرَاسَةُ اللُّغَةِ الْعَرَبِيّةِ
to do the jobs	أَنْجَزَ الأَعْمَالَ
the doing of the jobs	إِنْجَازُ الأَعْمَالِ

Formally, the 2nd term of the genitive construction takes the genitive, but it is the logical object of the infinitive.

There are also cases, however, in which the infinitive of a transitive verb takes on an **accusative object.** This type of construction occurs when the infinitive is already in the construct state and adding the object to the infinitive as the 2nd term of a genitive construction is not possible:

| lit.: their studying of the Arabic language = their study of the Arabic language, (the circumstance, the fact) that they study Arabic | دِرَاسَتُهُمُ اللُّغَةَ الْعَرَبِيّةَ |

The following sentence:

| He asks before he writes the letter. | يَسْأَلُ قَبْلَ أَنْ يَكْتُبَ الرِّسَالَةَ. |

can be transformed into an infinitive construction as follows:

| He asks before (his) writing the letter. | يَسْأَلُ قَبْلَ كِتَابَتِهِ الرِّسَالَةَ. / يَسْأَلُ قَبْلَ كِتَابَتِهِ لِلرِّسَالَةِ. |

4. Another method to nominalize a predicate is connecting the infinitive with **prepositional verbs.** In these patterns, the actual predicate is rendered by the infinitive.

قَامَ + preposition بِ is the verb used most frequently in this connection:

Aḥmad visited the capital city.	زَارَ أَحْمَدُ الْعَاصِمَةَ.
~ (lit.: Aḥmad carried out a visit to the capital city.)	قَامَ أَحْمَدُ بِزِيَارَةِ الْعَاصِمَةِ.
A Lebanese student has accompanied the delegation.	رَافَقَ الْوَفْدَ طَالِبٌ لُبْنَانِيّ.
~ (lit.: A Leb. student has carried out the accompanying of the delegation.)	قَامَ بِمُرَافَقَةِ الْوَفْدِ طَالِبٌ لُبْنَانِيّ.

The periphrasis of the passive voice is a special variety of this usage of the infinitive as a noun. The perfect or imperfect tense of تَمَّ / يَتِمُّ "to come about, to be performed, to be accomplished, to take place, to happen" or جَرَى / يَجْرِي " to occur, to come to pass, to take place, to happen" + infinitive is employed instead of the passive voice:

The papers were delivered yesterday. ~ (lit.: The delivery of the papers came about yesterday, took place yesterday.)	سُلِّمَت الأوْرَاقُ أمْس. تَمَّ / جَرَى تَسْلِيمُ الأوْرَاقِ أمْس.

The project is considered quickly. ~ (lit.: The considering of the project is done with speed / speedily.)	يُدرَسُ الْمَشْرُوعُ بِسُرْعَة. تَتِمُّ / تَجْرِي دِرَاسَةُ الْمَشْرُوعِ بِسُرْعَةٍ.

However, it is to be observed in colloquial and written usage that تَمَّ is often used in its masculine form although it is followed by a feminine noun:

The project was / is studied.	تَمَّ / يَتِمُّ دِرَاسَةُ الْمَشْرُوعِ.

PARTICIPLES (اسْمُ الْفَاعِل): FORM, PLURAL, USE OF THE PARTICIPLE

The participle and the infinitive are the two nominal forms of the Arabic verb. Arabic has active participles (اسْمُ الْفَاعِل) and passive participles (اسْمُ الْمَفْعُول).

The participles are also used as nouns, some of them with a special meaning.

Form I:

passive participle	active participle
مَفْعُولٌ	فَاعِلٌ

Derived Forms II - X:

The active participle has the prefix *mu-* and the sequence of vowels *a-i*.

The passive participle has the prefix *mu-* and the sequence of vowels *a-a*.

The basic structure of the forms given in the perfect tense is preserved. The sequence of vowels that follows the prefix is the same as is found in the imperfect tense of the active or passive voice, except for the active participle of Forms V and VI:

Table 49: ACTIVE AND PASSIVE PARTICIPLES (SOUND VERBS, FORMS I – X)

Form	passive participle	active participle
I	مَفْعُولٌ	فَاعِلٌ
II	مُفَعَّلٌ	مُفَعِّلٌ

III	مُفَاعَل	مُفَاعِل
IV	مُفْعَل	مُفْعِل
V	مُتَفَعَّل	مُتَفَعِّل
VI	مُتَفَاعَل	مُتَفَاعِل
VII	مُنْفَعَل	مُنْفَعِل
VIII	مُفْتَعَل	مُفْتَعِل
X	مُسْتَفْعَل	مُسْتَفْعِل

The quadriliteral verbs form the following participles:

I (q)		II (q)	
active	passive	active	passive
مُفَعْلِل	مُفَعْلَل	مُتَفَعْلِل	مُتَفَعْلَل

The feminine form takes the ending ﺔ_ .

Without auxiliary signs it is not distinguishable in Forms II to X whether the respective form is an active or a passive participle. Additional possibilities of ambiguity arise from the participles of Forms II and IV appearing in the same typeface. There are some peculiarities in the participles of the weak verbs. In the following, we only mention some patterns of the participle of Form I where the underlying pattern is not easily identifiable.

Form I	passive participle	active participle
Verbs R2 = و / ى	مَقُوم / مَبِيع / مَخُوف	قَائِم / بَائِع / خَائِف
Verbs R3 = و	مَدْعُوٌّ م مَدْعُوَّة	دَاعٍ م دَاعِيَة def. الدَّاعِي م الدَّاعِيَة
Verbs R3 = ى	مَمْشِيٌّ م مَمْشِيَّة مَلْقِيٌّ م مَلْقِيَّة	مَاشٍ / لاقٍ def. الْمَاشِي / اللاَّقِي
Forms II up to X		
Verbs R3 = و / ى	endings: -āt ﺓ_ـ م -an ـَى def. -āt اة ... أَل م -ā ـَى ... أَل	endings: -iya ـِيَة م -in - def. ـِي ... أَل م ـِيَة ... أَل

The following tables provide a full survey of all participles of the model verbs.

Table 50 : ACTIVE PARTICIPLE (ALL VERBS, FORMS **I** - **X**)

	fa'ala	R₁ و	R₁ ى	R₂ و	R₂ ى	R₂ و	R₃ و
I	فَاعِلٌ	وَاصِلٌ	يَابِسٌ	قَائِمٌ	بَائِعٌ	خَائِفٌ	دَاعٍ
II	مُفَعِّلٌ	مُوَصِّلٌ	مُيَبِّسٌ	مُقَوِّمٌ	مُبِيِّعٌ	مُخَوِّفٌ	مُدَعٍّ
III	مُفَاعِلٌ	مُوَاصِلٌ	مُيَابِسٌ	مُقَاوِمٌ	مُبَايِعٌ	مُخَاوِفٌ	مُدَاعٍ
IV	مُفْعِلٌ	مُوصِلٌ	مُوبِسٌ	مُقِيمٌ	مُبِيعٌ	مُخِيفٌ	مُدْعٍ
V	مُتَفَعِّلٌ	مُتَوَصِّلٌ	مُتَيَبِّسٌ	مُتَقَوِّمٌ	مُتَبِيِّعٌ	مُتَخَوِّفٌ	مُتَدَعٍّ
VI	مُتَفَاعِلٌ	مُتَوَاصِلٌ	مُتَيَابِسٌ	مُتَقَاوِمٌ	مُتَبَايِعٌ	مُتَخَاوِفٌ	مُتَدَاعٍ
VII	مُنْفَعِلٌ	-	-	مُنْقَامٌ	مُنْبَاعٌ	مُنْخَافٌ	مُنْدَعٍ
VIII	مُفْتَعِلٌ	مُتَّصِلٌ	مُتَّبِسٌ	مُقْتَامٌ	مُبْتَاعٌ	مُخْتَافٌ	مُدَّعٍ
X	مُسْتَفْعِلٌ	مُسْتَوْصِلٌ	مُسْتَيْبِسٌ	مُسْتَقِيمٌ	مُسْتَبِيعٌ	مُسْتَخِيفٌ	مُسْتَدْعٍ

	R₃ ى	R₃ ى	R₂=R₃	R₁ ء	R₂ ء	R₃ ء
I	مَاشٍ	لَاقٍ	مَارٌّ	آخِذٌ	سَائِلٌ	قَارِئٌ
II	مُمَشٍّ	مُلَقٍّ	مُمَرِّرٌ	مُؤَخِّذٌ	مُسَئِّلٌ	مُقَرِّئٌ
III	مُمَاشٍ	مُلَاقٍ	مُمَارٌّ	مُؤَاخِذٌ	مُسَائِلٌ	مُقَارِئٌ
IV	مُمْشٍ	مُلْقٍ	مُمِرٌّ	مُؤْخِذٌ	مُسْئِلٌ	مُقْرِئٌ
V	مُتَمَشٍّ	مُتَلَقٍّ	مُتَمَرِّرٌ	مُتَأَخِّذٌ	مُتَسَئِّلٌ	مُتَقَرِّئٌ
VI	مُتَمَاشٍ	مُتَلَاقٍ	مُتَمَارٌّ	مُتَأَاخِذٌ	مُتَسَائِلٌ	مُتَقَارِئٌ
VII	مُنْمَشٍ	مُنْلَقٍ	مُنْمَرٌّ	-	مُنْسَئِلٌ	مُنْقَرِئٌ
VIII	مُمْتَشٍ	مُلْتَقٍ	مُمْتَرٌّ	مُتَّخِذٌ	مُسْتَئِلٌ	مُقْتَرِئٌ
X	مُسْتَمْشٍ	مُسْتَلْقٍ	مُسْتَمِرٌّ	مُسْتَأْخِذٌ	مُسْتَسْئِلٌ	مُسْتَقْرِئٌ

Table 51 : PASSIVE PARTICIPLE (ALL VERBS, FORMS I - X)

R₃ و (f.)	R₃ و	R₂ و	R₂ ى	R₂ و	R₁ ى	R₁ و	fa'ala	
مَدْعُوَّةٌ	مَدْعُوٌّ	مَخُوفٌ	مَبِيعٌ	مَقُومٌ	مَيْبُوسٌ	مَوْصُولٌ	مَفْعُولٌ	I
مُدَعَاةٌ	مُدَّعًى	مُخَوَّفٌ	مُبِيعٌ	مُقَوَّمٌ	مُيَبَّسٌ	مُوَصَّلٌ	مُفَعَّلٌ	II
مُدَاعَاةٌ	مُدَاعًى	مُخَاوَفٌ	مُبَايَعٌ	مُقَاوَمٌ	مُيَابَسٌ	مُوَاصَلٌ	مُفَاعَلٌ	III
مُدَعَاةٌ	مُدَّعًى	مُخَافٌ	مُبَاعٌ	مُقَامٌ	مُوبَسٌ	مُوصَلٌ	مُفْعَلٌ	IV
مُتَدَعَّاةٌ	مُتَدَعًّى	مُتَخَوَّفٌ	مُتَبِيعٌ	مُتَقَوَّمٌ	مُتَيَبَّسٌ	مُتَوَصَّلٌ	مُتَفَعَّلٌ	V
مُتَدَاعَاةٌ	مُتَدَاعًى	مُتَخَاوَفٌ	مُتَبَايَعٌ	مُتَقَاوَمٌ	مُتَيَابَسٌ	مُتَوَاصَلٌ	مُتَفَاعَلٌ	VI
مُنْدَعَاةٌ	مُنْدَعًى	مُنْخَافٌ	مُنْبَاعٌ	مُنْقَامٌ	-	-	مُنْفَعَلٌ	VII
مُدَّعَاةٌ	مُدَّعًى	مُخْتَافٌ	مُبْتَاعٌ	مُقْتَامٌ	مُتَّبَسٌ	مُتَّصَلٌ	مُفْتَعَلٌ	VIII
مُسْتَدْعَاةٌ	مُسْتَدْعًى	مُسْتَخَافٌ	مُسْتَبَاعٌ	مُسْتَقَامٌ	مُسْتَيْبَسٌ	مُسْتَوْصَلٌ	مُسْتَفْعَلٌ	X

R₃ ء	R₂ ء	R₁ ء	R₂=R₃	R₃ ى	R₃ ى	
مَقْرُوءٌ	مَسْؤُولٌ	مَأْخُوذٌ	مَمْرُورٌ	مَلْقِيٌّ	مَمْشِيٌّ	I
مُقْرَأٌ	مُسَأَّلٌ	مُؤَخَّذٌ	مُمَرَّرٌ	مُلَقًّى	مُمَشًّى	II
مُقَارَأٌ	مُسَاءَلٌ	مُؤَاخَذٌ	مُمَارٌّ	مُلَاقًى	مُمَاشًى	III
مُقْرَأٌ	مُسْأَلٌ	مُؤْخَذٌ	مُمَرٌّ	مُلْقًى	مُمْشًى	IV
مُتَقَرَّأٌ	مُتَسَأَّلٌ	مُتَأَخَّذٌ	مُتَمَرَّرٌ	مُتَلَقًّى	مُتَمَشًّى	V
مُتَقَارَأٌ	مُتَسَاءَلٌ	مُتَآخَذٌ	مُتَمَارٌّ	مُتَلَاقًى	مُتَمَاشًى	VI
مُنْقَرَأٌ	مُنْسَأَلٌ	-	مُنْمَرٌّ	مُنْلَقًى	مُنْمَشًى	VII
مُقْتَرَأٌ	مُسْتَأَلٌ	مُتَّخَذٌ	مُمْتَرٌّ	مُلْتَقًى	مُمْتَشًى	VIII
مُسْتَقْرَأٌ	مُسْتَسْأَلٌ	مُسْتَأْخَذٌ	مُسْتَمَرٌّ	مُسْتَلْقًى	مُسْتَمْشًى	X

PLURAL OF THE PARTICIPLES

There are some regularities in the forming of the plural of the participles:

Form I: active participle / persons (often descriptions of occupations)		
m.		فَاعِلٌ ج فَاعِلُونَ
f.		فَاعِلَةٌ ج فَاعِلاتٌ
m.		فَاعِلٌ ج فُعَّالٌ
m.		فَاعِلٌ ج فَعَلَةٌ
seller		بَائِعٌ ج بَائِعُونَ
driver, chauffeur		سَائِقٌ ج سَائِقُونَ
exhibitor		عَارِضٌ ج عَارِضُونَ
student (f.)		طَالِبَةٌ ج طَالِبَاتٌ
female worker		عَامِلَةٌ ج عَامِلاتٌ
merchant		تَاجِرٌ ج تُجَّارٌ
passenger		رَاكِبٌ ج رُكَّابٌ
tourist		سَائِحٌ ج سُيَّاحٌ
student		طَالِبٌ ج طُـلّابٌ
worker		عَامِلٌ ج عُمَّالٌ
seller		بَائِعٌ ج بَاعَةٌ > (بَيَعَة)
student		طَالِبٌ ج طَلَبَةٌ

Form I: active participle / non-persons		
m.		فَاعِلٌ ج فَاعِلاتٌ
f.		فَاعِلَةٌ ج فَاعِلاتٌ
m.		فَاعِلٌ ج فَوَاعِلُ
f.		فَاعِلَةٌ ج فَوَاعِلُ

duty, task	وَاجِبٌ ج وَاجِبَاتٌ
university	جَامِعَةٌ ج جَامِعَاتٌ
family	عَائِلَةٌ ج عَائِلاتٌ
side	جَانِبٌ ج جَوَانِبُ
stamp	طَابِعٌ ج طَوَابِعُ
circle	دَائِرَةٌ ج دَوَائِرُ
capital city	عَاصِمَةٌ ج عَوَاصِمُ
fruit(s)	فَاكِهَةٌ ج فَوَاكِهُ
list	قَائِمَةٌ ج قَوَائِمُ

Form I: passive participle / persons	
m.	مَفْعُولٌ ج مَفْعُولُونَ
f.	مَفْعُولَةٌ ج مَفْعُولاتٌ
responsible person, official (m.)	مَسْؤُولٌ ج مَسْؤُولُونَ
responsible person, official (f.)	مَسْؤُولَةٌ ج مَسْؤُولاتٌ

Form I: passive participle / non-persons	
m.	مَفْعُولٌ ج مَفْعُولاتٌ / مَفْعُولٌ ج مَفَاعِيلُ
drink	مَشْرُوبٌ ج مَشْرُوبَاتٌ
project, plan	مَشْرُوعٌ ج مَشْرُوعَاتٌ ومَشَارِيعُ

Derived Forms:

The active or passive participles which denote persons have the sound masculine or feminine plural.

teacher	مُعَلِّمٌ ج مُعَلِّمُونَ	II
official/officer/civil servant	مُوَظَّفٌ ج مُوَظَّفُونَ	II
companion, attendant	مُرَافِقٌ ج مُرَافِقُونَ	III
viewer/spectator/onlooker	مُتَفَرِّجٌ ج مُتَفَرِّجُونَ	V

woman teacher	مُعَلِّمَة ج مُعَلِّمَاتٌ	II
nurse	مُمَرِّضَة ج مُمَرِّضَاتٌ	II
stewardess	مُضِيفَةٌ ج مُضِيفَاتٌ	IV

The active or passive participles which denote non-persons have the sound feminine plural, regardless of whether they are used in the masculine or feminine form in the singular.

alarm clock	مُنَبِّهٌ ج مُنَبِّهَاتٌ	II
representative team	مُنْتَخَبٌ ج مُنْتَخَبَاتٌ	VIII

Some participles of Form IV have a broken plural as well, e.g. *"problem"* مُشْكِلٌ

and مُشْكِلَة with the plural مَشَاكِلُ in addition to مُشْكِلَاتٌ or مُدِيرٌ *"director"* with

the plural مُدَرَاءُ in addition to مُدِيرُونَ.

THE USE OF THE PARTICIPLES

The participle combines the meaning of the verb with the formal properties of the noun:

noun = subject, object and predicate complement and
adjective = attributive adjunct and predicate complement.

Most participles are lexicalized as adjectives or nouns, i.e. they are pure nouns without any verbal characteristics. Some participles belong to both categories, adjectives and nouns.

adjective: بَارِدٌ cold (active part., Form I)

مَقْبُولٌ acceptable (passive part., Form I)

noun: طَابِعٌ stamp (active part., Form I)

مُوَظَّفٌ official/officer (passive part., Form II)

adjective and noun عَامِلٌ active; worker, factor (active part., Form I)

مَشْرُوعٌ legitimate; project (passive part., Form I)

Participles which are used as nouns do not lose their ability of being used as participles in the strict sense of the meaning, which has been derived from the verb. طَالِبٌ *"student"* can also mean *"claimer/claimant; someone who claims (something)"*.

This extract is given to anybody who claims (it) (< to any claimer)".	هذا الْمُسْتَخْرَج يُعْطَى لِكلِّ طَالِبٍ.

Active and passive participles are frequently used in the Arabic language for expressing so-called **shortened relative clauses** by taking a subject or an object while being employed as attributive adjuncts related to nouns. Adjectives are occasionally found in such constructions as well.

Rule:

If the antecedent is definite, the participle (or the adjective) also takes the article; if it is indefinite, the participle (or the adjective) does not take an article either. If the subject of the shortened relative clause is not identical with the antecedent, the following rule of agreement applies: The participle (or adjective) agrees with the antecedent in case and state and with the subject of the relative clause in gender and number.

The direct object, when following the active participle, either takes on the accusative (i.e. the verbal government is preserved) or is introduced by the preposition لِ . If the verb governs an object by means of a preposition, this prepositional goverment is also preserved with the participle.

Passive participles of verbs with a prepositional government accordingly do not express the gender by the participle, but by the preposition + affixed pronoun:

the desired goods	أَلْبَضَائِعُ الْمَرْغُوبُ فِيهَا

This construction is analogous to the passive construction of verbs with a prepositional government.

Active participle (the subject being the same):

the event, ending or having ended at 10 o'clock *= the event which ends or ended at 10 o'clock*	أَلْحَفْلَةُ الْمُنْتَهِيَةُ فِي السَّاعَةِ الْعَاشِرَةِ

The basis of the shortened form is a relative clause, which is either

أَلْحَفْلَةُ الَّتِي تَنْتَهِي فِي السَّاعَةِ الْعَاشِرَةِ or الْحَفْلَةُ الَّتِي انْتَهَتْ فِي السَّاعَةِ الْعَاشِرَةِ.

As the participles per se do not express a tense in the Arabic language, it must be decided from the context which temporal reference is given in particular cases.

Active participle (the subject not being the same):

lit.: the delegation the visit of which is coming to an end or has come to an end	أَلْوَفْدُ الْمُنْتَهِيَةُ زِيَارَتُهُ
Underlying relative clause:	أَلْوَفْدُ الَّذِي انْتَهَتْ زِيَارَتُهُ or أَلْوَفْدُ الَّذِي تَنْتَهِي زِيَارَتُهُ

Passive participle (the subject being the same):

the books existing with me = the books which are or were existing with me	أَلْكُتُبُ الْمَوْجُودَةُ عِنْدِي
Underlying relative clause:	أَلْكُتُبُ الَّتِي كَانَتْ تُوجَدُ عِنْدِي or أَلْكُتُبُ الَّتِي تُوجَدُ عِنْدِي
the desired goods = *the goods which are desired*	أَلْبَضَائِعُ الْمَرْغُوبُ فِيهَا
Underlying relative clause:	أَلْبَضَائِعُ الَّتِي يُرْغَبُ فِيهَا

Passive participle (the subject not being the same):

the man whose books are sold or *have been sold*	اَلرَّجُلُ الْمَبِيعَةُ كُتُبُهُ
Underlying relative clause:	اَلرَّجُلُ الَّذي بِيعَتْ كُتُبُهُ or الرَّجُلُ الّذي تُبَاعُ كُتُبُهُ

Participles as Nominal Predicate

The active and the passive participle may be a nominal predicate in the principal clause. It is often difficult to differentiate whether the participle or whether the corresponding verb should be used. Often both are interchangeable.

a)	*He is walking in the street.*	هُوَ مَاشٍ في الشَّارِعِ.
	The verbal sentence with the same meaning is:	= (هو) يَمْشِي في الشَّارِعِ.
b)	*She travels to London for a month.*	هِيَ مُسَافِرَة إلى لندن لِمُدَّة شَهرٍ.
	The verbal sentence with the same meaning is:	= (هي) تُسَافِرُ إلى لندن لِمُدَّة شَهرٍ.
c)	*This letter was written a week ago.*	هَذِه الرِّسَالَةُ مَكْتُوبَةً قَبْلَ أُسْبُوعٍ.
	The verbal sentence with the same meaning is:	= هَذِه الرِّسَالَةُ كُتِبَتْ قَبْلَ أُسْبُوعٍ.

With respect to the verbs which indicate an event (☞ examples a-c), the participle and the verb are interchangeable and are consequently to be regarded as stylistic variants.

As to the verbs which indicate a state, the participle or an adjective derived from the same verb is given preference, accordingly:

The merchandise is (was) good.	جَادَت الْبِضَاعَةُ instead of كَانَت الْبِضَاعَةُ جَيِّدَةً.

With regard to the verbs which indicate both an event and a state, e.g. قَامَ "*to stand up*" and "*to stand*", جَلَسَ "*to sit down*" and "*to sit*", رَقَدَ "*to lie down to rest/to go to bed, to abate/to subside*" and "*to lie*", the verb indicates the event, the participle indicates the state; consequently:

He is standing. / He stands up.	هُوَ قَائِمٌ. / (هو) يَقُومُ.
He was standing. / He stood up.	كَانَ قَائِماً. / (هو) قَامَ.
He is sleeping (just now). / He is falling asleep.	هُوَ نَائِمٌ. / هُوَ يَنَامُ.

The adjective and the participle (nearly exclusively the passive participle) also serve the purpose of rendering impersonal expressions such as in the construction مِنَ الـــ ... "*it is ...*" at the beginning of the sentence.

participle:

it is usual/customary/it is (a) common practice	مِنَ الْمَأْلُوف
it is allowed, legal, lawful	مِنَ الْمُبَاح
it is impossible, inconceivable	مِنَ الْمُحَال
it is probable/likely, it is assumed	مِنَ الْمُحْتَمَل
it is forbidden	مِنَ الْمُحَرَّم
it is better	مِنَ الْمُسْتَحْسَن
it is impossible	مِنَ الْمُسْتَحِيل
it is doubtful	مِنَ الْمَشْكُوك فيه
it is (well-)known	مِنَ الْمَعْرُوف
it is known	مِنَ الْمَعْلُوم
it is understandable	مِنَ الْمَفْهُوم (أَنْ / أَنَّ)
it is decided	مِنَ الْمُقَرَّر
it is possible	مِنَ الْمُمْكِن
it is suitable	مِنَ الْمُنَاسِب
it is to be expected	مِنَ الْمُنْتَظَر
it is important	مِنَ الْمُهِمّ (أَنْ / أَنَّ)
it is agreed	مِنَ الْمُتَفَّق عَلَيْه (أَنْ / أَنَّ)
it is a pity	مِنَ الْمُؤْسِف (أَنْ / أَنَّ)
it is self-evident	مِنَ الْبَدِيهِي (أَنْ / أَنَّ)

adjective:

it is better	مِنَ الأَحْسَن
it is allowed	مِنَ الْجَائِز
it is worth mentioning that …	مِنَ الْجَدِيرِ بِالذِّكْر

it is difficult	مِنَ الصَّعْبِ
it is necessary	مِنَ الضَّرُورِيّ
it is natural	مِنَ الطَّبِيعِيّ (أَنْ / أَنَّ)
it is strange, odd	مِنَ الْغَرِيبِ (أَنْ / أَنَّ)
it is easy	مِنَ الْيَسِيرِ

There are also expressions with nouns:

it is clever	مِنَ الذَّكَاءِ
it is not fair	مِنَ الظُّلْمِ
it is fair	مِنَ الْعَدْلِ
it is stupid	مِنَ الْغَبَاءِ

Such constructions are mostly followed by أَنْ and negated with لَيْسَ.

NOUNS OF INTENSITY (اسْمُ الْمُبَالَغَة)

There are patterns which denote the intensity of the action of the active participle.

They are called أَسْمَاءُ الْمُبَالَغَة and have the following patterns:

Table 52: PATTERNS OF THE NOUNS OF INTENSITY

effective, efficacious	فَعَّالٌ	فَعَّالٌ
sharp sighted	مِنْظَارٌ	مِفْعَالٌ
very thankful	شَكُورٌ	فَعُولٌ
informed, learned	عَلِيمٌ	فَعِيلٌ
cautious	حَذِرٌ	فَعِلٌ
heavy drinker	سِكِّيرٌ	فِعِّيلٌ
very big	كُبَّارٌ	فُعَّالٌ
very eloquent	مِنْطِيقٌ	مِفْعِيلٌ
faultfinder	لُمَزَةٌ	فُعَلَةٌ

unbeliever, freethinker	زِنْدِيقٌ	فِعْلِيلٌ

Originally, they expressed intensive and routine actions, but they are hardly productive any more nowadays. The last two patterns are not frequent.

Nouns of the structure فَعَّالٌ, which are derived from both verbs and nouns, are also used to denote occupations:

seaman	بَحَّارٌ (< بَحْر)
gatekeeper	بَوَّابٌ (< بَاب)
porter/carrier	حَمَّالٌ (< حَمَلَ)
money changer	صَرَّافٌ (< صَرَفَ)

All these words have the sound masculine plural.

The feminine form فَعَّالة denotes appliances and vehicles (☞ Nouns of Instruments and Vehicles):

refrigerator	بَرَّادَةٌ
excavator	حَفَّارَةٌ
bicycle	دَرَّاجَةٌ
earphone, (telephone) receiver	سَمَّاعَةٌ
car	سَيَّارَةٌ
(can) opener	فَتَّاحَةٌ
lighter	قَدَّاحَةٌ
dumper	قَلاَّبَةٌ
glasses	نَظَّارَةٌ
lighter	وَلاَّعَةٌ

All these words have the sound feminine plural.

NOUNS OF PLACE AND TIME (أَسْمَاءُ الْمَكَانَ وَالزَّمَانِ)

The nouns of place and time have the pattern structure مَفْعَلٌ if the imperfect vowel is *Fatḥa* or *Ḍamma* and with all verbs ending in ا , و or ي . If the imperfect vowel is *Kasra* the subsequent pattern is مَفْعِلٌ . The patterns مَفْعَلَةٌ and مَفْعِلَةٌ are less widespread.

مَفْعَل(ة)

aim, goal	مَرْمَّى	station	مَحَطَّة
print shop	مَطْبَعة	exit	مَخْرَج
seat	مَقْعَد	entrance	مَدْخَل
office	مَكْتَب	chimney	مَدْخَنة
clothes	مَلْبَس	school	مَدْرَسة
shelter	مَلْجَأ	way out	مَذْهَب
playground	مَلْعَب	grassland	مَرْعًى

مَفْعِل

strait, stricture	مَضيق	council	مَجْلِس
date, promise	مَوْعِد	bank	مَصْرِف

There are also some nouns of the same type which take the pattern of the passive participle of the derived forms of the verb.

future	مُسْتَقْبَل	laboratory	مُخْتَبَر
store	مُسْتَوْدَع	open staircase	مُدَرَّج
clinic	مُسْتَوْصَف	pillar	مُرْتَكَز
turn	مُنْعَطَف	extract	مُسْتَخْرَج
		hospital	مُسْتَشْفى

NOUNS OF INSTRUMENTS, VEHICLES AND VESSELS (أَسْمَاءُ الآلَةِ وَالوِعَاءِ)

Nouns denoting instruments have the following patterns:

مِفْعَلٌ

scalpel, lancet	مِشْرَط	*file, rasp*	مِبْرد
spindle	مِغْزل	*scalpel*	مِبْضع
steering wheel	مِقْود	*borer*	مِثْقب
sickle	مِنْجل	*cannon*	مِدْفع

مِفْعَالٌ

key	مِفْتاح	*plow*	مِحْراث
scissors	مِقْراض	*bolt*	مِزْلاج
saw	مِنْشار	*probe (med.)*	مِسْبار
air pump	مِنْفاخ	*nail*	مِسْمار

مِفْعَلَةٌ

washer	مِغْسلة	*shovel*	مِجْرفة
knocker	مِقْرعة	*lathe*	مِخْرطة
kohl stick	مِكْحلة	*refinery*	مِصْفاة
broom	مِكْنسة	*hammer*	مِطْرقة

فَعَّالَةٌ

plane	طَيَّارة	*seeding machine*	بذَّارة
squeezer	عصَّارة	*refrigerator*	برَّادة
washer	غسَّالة	*mowing machine*	حصَّادة
submarine	غوَّاصة	*excavator*	حفَّارة
opener	فتَّاحة	*mixer*	خلاَّطة

spring, fountain	فَوَّارة	bicycle	دَرَّاجة
lighter	قَدَّاحة	sprayer	رَشَّاشة
(nut)cracker	كَسَّارة	ear phone	سَمَّاعة
spectacles	نَظَّارة	car	سَيَّارة
vibrator	هَزَّازة	mill	طَحَّانة

فَعَالٌ

ribbon	رِباط	needle	خِياط
swaddle, diaper	قِماط	gate, gateway	رِتاج

فَاعِلَةٌ

crusher	ساحِقة	calculator	حاسِبة
locomotive	قاطِرة	puller, drawer	ساحِبة

فَاعُولٌ

soap	صابُون	calculator	حاسُوب
bell	ناقُوس	cleaver	ساطُور

There are some other patterns denoting instruments:

dagger	خَنْجَرٌ	chisel	إِزْمِيلٌ
whirlpool, eddy	دُوَّامَةٌ	corkscrew, borer	بَرِّيمَةٌ
ax, hatchet	فَأْسٌ	stator / knife	ثَبِّيتٌ / سِكِّينٌ
adze	قَدُّومٌ	hook / cramp	خُطَّافٌ / كُلَّابٌ

In Modern Standard Arabic the active participle is far more widespread to denote instruments than the patterns mentioned before:

cooler	مُبَرِّد	steamer	بَاخِرة
telex	مُبَرْقَة	seeding machine	بَاذِرة
tester	مُخْتَبِر	protector	حَاجِب

ammunition passer	مُدَخِّر	mowing machine	حَاصِدَة
destroyer	مُدَمِّرَة	incubator	حَاضِنَة
sender	مُرْسِل	injector	حَاقِن
filter	مُرَشِّح	controller	حَاكِم
synchronizer	مُزَامِن	carrier	حَامِل
projector	مُسْقِط	elevator, crane	رَافِع
radiator	مُشِعّ	crane, lifter	رَافِعَة
accelerator	مُعَجِّل	puller, drawer	سَاحِبَة
disinfector	مُعَقِّم	crusher	سَاحِقَة
reactor	مُفَاعِل	loader	شَاحِن
enlarger	مُكَبِّر	lorry	شَاحِنَة
intensifier	مُكَثِّف	insulator	عَازِل
sensor	مُلَامِس	reflector	عَاكِس
activator	مُنَشِّط	locomotive	قَاطِرَة
balancer	مُوَازِن	ice crusher	كَاسِحَة جَلِيد
distributor	مُوَزِّع	detector	كَاشِف
generator	مُوَلِّد	indicator	مُؤَشِّر
telephone	هَاتِف	evaporator	مُبَخِّر

The pattern مِفْعَلَة (rarely مِفْعَال) is used to denote vessels and containers:

incubator	مِعْقَام	inkwell	مِحْبَرَة
washbowl	مِغْسَلَة	capsule	مِحْفَظَة
frying pan	مِقْلىً	oiler	مِزْيَتَة
measure for grain	مِكْيَال	grease box	مِشْحَمَة

COLLECTIVE NOUNS (اِسْمُ الْجَمْعِ)

There are many nouns in the Arabic language which have a collective meaning when taking the form of the masculine singular. Collective nouns are also known in the English language. Think of collective formations with the suffixes *-ment* or *-y* (*government, assembly*), compound words formed with *-ware* (*glassware*), and also simple words with a collective content (*cattle, hair*).

GENERIC COLLECTIVE NOUNS (اِسْمُ الجِنْسِ الْجَمْعِيُّ)

The generic collective nouns denote a certain genus, mostly animals or plants. They are characterized by the fact that their corresponding specimens are formed by means of *Tā' marbūṭa* ة. The form which denotes the unit is called *Nomen unitatis* (اِسْمُ الْوَحْدَةِ) . The sound feminine plural is used in order to indicate a certain quantity of specimens.

ducks	بَطّ	*apples*	تُفَّاحٌ
a duck	بَطَّة	*an apple*	تُفَّاحَةٌ
five ducks	خَمْسُ بَطَّاتٍ	*three apples*	ثَلاثُ تُفَّاحَاتٍ

The following nouns follow the same rules:

fish	سَمَكٌ	*camels*	إِبْلٌ
trees	شَجَرٌ	*cattle*	بَقَرٌ
bananas	مَوْزٌ	*eggs*	بَيْضٌ
bees	نَحْلٌ	*dates*	تَمْرٌ
palms	نَخْلٌ	*figs*	تِينٌ
ants	نَمْلٌ	*horses*	خَيْلٌ
paper	وَرَقٌ	*chickens*	دَجَاجٌ

However, some such generic collective nouns have a broken plural.

grapes	عِنَبٌ ج أَعْنَابٌ	*paper*	وَرَقٌ ج أَوْرَاقٌ	*fish*	سَمَكٌ ج أَسْمَاكٌ

Many names of animals and plants, however, have no generic collective nouns, and consequently, no *Nomen unitatis* is derived from them either.

COLLECTIVES PROPER (اِسْمُ الْجَمْعِ)

Collectives proper are designations of groups without *Nomen unitatis*. They have broken plurals.

multitude, public; pl.: masses	جُمْهُورٌ ج جَمَاهِيرُ
people, nation; pl.: peoples, nationalities	قَوْمٌ ج أَقْوَامٌ
sheep, small cattle	غَنَمٌ ج أَغْنَامٌ

NAMES OF NATIONALITIES (أَسْمَاءُ الْأُمَمِ والشُّعُوبِ)

the Russians	أَلرُّوسُ	*the Arabs*	أَلْعَرَبُ
the Greeks	أَلْيُونَانُ	*the Germans*	أَلْأَلْمَانُ
the Americans	أَلْأَمْرِيكَانُ	*the English*	أَلْإِنْكْلِيزُ
the Serbians	أَلصِّرْبُ	*the Jewish*	أَلْيَهُودُ

These words are actually not plural in Arabic, but they are treated as such:

the English merchants	أَلتُّجَّارُ الْإِنْكْلِيزُ

Most names of nationalities are formed, however, by means of the *Nisba*:
أَلْفَرَنْسِيُّونَ "*the French*", أَلْجَزَائِرِيُّونَ "*the Algerians*" etc.

There is no rule specifying which nationalities have one form and which nationalities have the other. In any case, the individual representatives of these nationalities are denoted by the *Nisba*:
عَرَبِيٌّ "*an Arab*", أَلْمَانِيٌّ "*a German*", فِرْنْسِيٌّ "*a Frenchman*".

The corresponding adjectives are also formed by the *Nisba* :
عَرَبِيٌّ "*Arab/Arabic/Arabian*", رُوسِيٌّ "*Russian*", يُونَانِيٌّ "*Greek*".

PROPER NAMES (اِسْمُ الْعَلَمِ)

Arabic has three types of proper nouns:

a) name	b) title, epitheton	c) surname, agnomen
مُحَمَّدٌ، أَحْمَدُ، مِصْرُ	الصِّدِّيقُ، الرَّشِيدُ، الْفَارُوقُ	أَبُو سَالِمٍ، أَبُو بَكْرٍ، أُمُّ عَلِيٍّ

DIMINUTIVES (أَلتَّصْغِيرُ)

The diminutive can be formed from any suitable noun. The respective pattern is formed as follows: the first consonant of the noun is vocalized by *Damma*, and the second one by *Fatha* and a following يْ (يَاءُ التَّصْغِيرِ), for expressing diminution and sometimes degradation (أَلتَّحْقِيرُ).

1. Triliteral nouns: فُعَيْل (ة)

slave	عُبَيْدٌ	عَبْدٌ ⇦
bag	شُنَيْطَةٌ	شَنْطَةٌ ⇦

2. Quadriliteral nouns: فُعَيْعِل (ة)

scorpion	عُقَيْرِبٌ	عَقْرَبٌ ⇦
dirhem	دُرَيْهِمٌ	دِرْهَمٌ ⇦

3. Nouns having the structure فَاعِلٌ : فُوَيْعِل (ة)

companion	صُوَيْحِبٌ	صَاحِبٌ ⇦
student	طُوَيْلِبَةٌ	طَالِبَةٌ ⇦

4. Nouns having the structures فَعِيلٌ , فَعُولٌ and فَعِيلٌ : فُعَيِّلٌ

book	كُتَيِّبٌ	كِتَابٌ ⇦
old man/woman	عُجَيِّزٌ	عَجُوزٌ ⇦
beautiful, handsome	جُمَيِّلٌ	جَمِيلٌ ⇦

5. Nouns with a long vowel in front of the last radical: فُعَيْعِيل

box	صُنَيْدِيقٌ	صُنْدُوقٌ ⇦
key	مُفَيْتِيحٌ	مِفْتَاحٌ ⇦

6. Nouns having the structures مَفْعَل (ة) and مُفَاعَل (ة) : مُفَيْعِل (ة)

library	مُكَيْتِبَةٌ	مَكْتَبَةٌ ⇦
lecture	مُحَيْضِرَةٌ	مُحَاضَرَةٌ ⇦

The diminutives of أَبٌ، أَخٌ، ابنٌ and أُبَيٌّ، أُخَيٌّ، بُنَيٌّ are أَبُيٌّ.

ADJECTIVES (أَلصِّفَة / أَلنَّعْتُ)

Adjectives in Arabic are called أَلصِّفَة or أَلنَّعْتُ (الْمُشَبَّهَةُ). Another type of the adjective is the relative adjective (☞ *Nisba*).

Each adjective has a masculine and a feminine singular form as well as a masculine sound or broken and a feminine plural form. Determining which form has to be used depends on the word which the adjective belongs to. (☞ Number)

These adjectives are derived from the triliteral root. The most important patterns are the following:

black	أَسْوَدُ م سَوْدَاءُ	أَفْعَلُ م فَعْلَاءُ
salty	مَالِحٌ	فَاعِلٌ
cowardly	جَبَانٌ	فَعَالٌ
courageous	شُجَاعٌ	فُعَالٌ
not a kinsman	جُنُبٌ	فُعُلٌ
pretty	حَسَنٌ	فَعَلٌ
bitter	مُرٌّ	فُعْلٌ
loose, slack	رِخْوٌ	فِعْلٌ
giant	ضَخْمٌ	فَعْلٌ
active	نَشِطٌ	فَعِلٌ
lazy	كَسْلَانٌ م كَسْلَى	فَعْلَانُ م فَعْلَى
lazy	كَسُولٌ	فَعُولٌ
big	كَبِيرٌ	فَعِيلٌ
dead	مَيِّتٌ	فَيْعِلٌ

The function can be predicative or attributive:

predicative

The house is big.	أَلْبَيْتُ كَبِيرٌ.
The room is new.	أَلْغُرْفَةُ جَدِيدَةٌ.

attributive

the big house	أَلْبَيْتُ الكَبِيرُ
the new room	أَلْغُرْفَةُ الجَديدَةُ
a big house	بَيْتٌ كَبِيرٌ
a new room	غُرْفَةٌ جَديدَةٌ

There is agreement in number and gender between the noun and the adjective in their singular forms:

in number

The house is big.	singular	أَلْبَيْتُ كَبِيرٌ.
the big house	singular	أَلْبَيْتُ الْكَبِيرُ

in gender

The house is big.	m.	أَلْبَيْتُ كَبِيرٌ.
the big house	m.	أَلْبَيْتُ الْكَبِيرُ
The room is new.	f.	أَلْغُرْفَةُ جَديدَةٌ.
the new room	f.	أَلْغُرْفَةُ الْجَديدَةُ

If the adjective has an attributive function, there is also **agreement in state** (i.e. definite or no article)

the big house	definite	أَلْبَيْتُ الْكَبِيرُ
the new room	definite	أَلْغُرْفَةُ الجَديدَةُ
a big house	indefinite	بَيْتٌ كَبِيرٌ
a new room	indefinite	غُرْفَةٌ جَديدَةٌ

and **in case** (☞ Declension).

If the noun and the adjective are in the plural, the agreement between them depends on whether the noun denotes a person or not.
If it denotes a person, agreement in number and gender applies; if the adjective is used in an attributive function, there is also agreement in state and case.

predicative:

The teachers are diligent.	أَلْمُعَلِّمُونَ مُجْتَهِدُونَ.
The teachers (f.) are diligent.	أَلْمُعَلِّمَاتُ مُجْتَهِدَاتٌ.

The men are tall.	أَلرِّجَالُ طِوَالٌ.

attributive:

the diligent teachers	أَلْمُعَلِّمُونَ الْمُجْتَهِدُونَ
the diligent teachers (f.)	أَلْمُعَلِّمَاتُ الْمُجْتَهِدَاتُ
the tall men	أَلرِّجَالُ الطِّوَالُ
tall men	رِجَالٌ طِوَالٌ

If the noun denotes a non-person, the adjective takes the feminine singular form both when fulfilling an attributive and when fulfilling a predicative function.

Strictly speaking, there is only agreement when the adjective is used as an attribute, i.e. agreement in state and case.

Nevertheless, we also refer to it as agreement in gender and number, because the plural of words denoting non-persons is treated as a feminine singular.

predicative:

The tables are big.	أَلطَّاوِلَاتُ كَبِيرَةٌ.
The pens are new.	أَلْأَقْلَامُ جَدِيدَةٌ.

attributive:

the big tables	أَلطَّاوِلَاتُ الْكَبِيرَةُ
the new pens	أَلْأَقْلَامُ الْجَدِيدَةُ

If the adjective is used as a predicate, the subject can be replaced by the respective personal pronoun.

هُنَّ مُجْتَهِدَاتٌ.	أَلْمُعَلِّمَاتُ مُجْتَهِدَاتٌ.	هُوَ كَبِيرٌ.	أَلْبَيْتُ كَبِيرٌ.
هِيَ* كَبِيرَةٌ.	أَلطَّاوِلَاتُ كَبِيرَةٌ.	هِيَ كَبِيرَةٌ.	أَلْغُرْفَةُ كَبِيرَةٌ.
هِيَ* جَدِيدَةٌ.	أَلْأَقْلَامُ جَدِيدَةٌ.	هُمْ مُجْتَهِدُونَ.	أَلْمُعَلِّمُونَ مُجْتَهِدُونَ.

*In the last two examples above, هِيَ must be used because أَقْلَامٌ and طَاوِلَاتٌ are regarded as feminine singulars because they denote non-persons.

RELATIVE ADJECTIVES (أَلنِّسْبَةُ)

The soc. *Nisba* ending is ـِيٌّ, *f.* ـِيَّةٌ (in transcription -*ī*, *f.* -*īya*, with *Nunation* -*īyun* or -*īyatun*). It is added to nouns and various verbal nouns (مَصْدَرٌ), but rarely to numbers, prepositions and pronouns, and forms (relative) adjectives and nouns. The *Nisba* ending is the most productive word forming suffix in Arabic, and it is comparable to the English suffixes -*al*, -*en* a.o. which form adjectives and to the suffixes -*ian*, -*ese* which form nouns.

The endings ة and ـِيَ are omitted when the *Nisba* is added.

Lebanon ⇨	*Lebanese; a Lebanese*	لُبْنَانُ ⇦ لُبْنَانِيٌّ
Syria ⇨	*Syrian; a Syrian*	سُورِيَا ⇦ سُورِيٌّ
policy ⇨	*political; politician*	سِيَاسَةٌ ⇦ سِيَاسِيٌّ
gold ⇨	*gold(en)*	ذَهَبٌ ⇦ ذَهَبِيٌّ

Details about certain changes of sounds which occur when the *Nisba* is added, especially to words which terminate in rather rare endings, can be seen from a more detailed grammar (e.g. the "Grammar of the Arabic Language" by W. Wright).

A noun followed by an adjective with the *Nisba* is often equivalent in English to constructions of the type noun + noun:

school-book, textbook	كِتَابٌ + مَدْرَسَةٌ ⇦ كِتَابٌ مَدْرَسِيٌّ

The rules of agreement for the nominal sentence (subject - adjectival predicate) and for the attributive construction (noun - adjectival attributive adjunct) also apply to the relative adjective. Nouns and relative adjectives terminating in a *Nisba* which denote persons, mostly have the sound plural:

لُبْنَانِيٌّ / لُبْنَانِيُّونَ، لُبْنَانِيَّةٌ / لُبْنَانِيَّاتٌ : طُلَّابٌ لُبْنَانِيُّونَ، طَالِبَاتٌ لُبْنَانِيَّاتٌ

Some *Nisba*-nouns or relative adjectives have a (collective) endingless plural:

عَرَبِيٌّ / Arab students طُلَّابٌ عَرَبٌ . *Arab* (adj.), *Arab(s)* عَرَبٌ / عَرَبِيٌّ

Some of them terminate in the plural ending ة or have a broken plural, e.g. صَيْدَلِيٌّ pl. صَيَادِلَةٌ "*pharmacist*", تُرْكِيٌّ pl. أَتْرَاكٌ "*Turkish; Turk*", عَبْقَرِيٌّ pl. عَبَاقِرَةٌ "*genius*".

The adjectival suffix وِيٌّ and its long form ـَاوِيٌّ are sometimes used to form an extended *Nisba*. They are attached to nouns based on weak 3rd radical or defective nouns:

female	أُنْثَى ⇦ أُنْثَوِيٌّ	*Meccan*	مَكَّةُ ⇦ مَكَّاوِيٌّ	*bloody*	دَمٌ ⇦ دَمَوِيٌّ

If attached to relative adjectives which usually have the regular Nisba, the meaning changes and becomes (in most cases) negative:

economistic	اِقْتِصَادَوِيٌّ	economic	اِقْتِصَادِيٌّ
traditionalistic	تَقْلِيدَوِيٌّ	traditional	تَقْلِيدِيٌّ
scholastic	مَدْرَسَوِيٌّ	school-	مَدْرَسِيٌّ

THE FEMININE *NISBA* (ألنِّسْبَةُ الْمُؤَنَّثَةُ / الْمَصْدَرُ الصِّنَاعِيُّ)

The feminine *Nisba* (ـِيَّة) is the basic structure for abstract nouns. They are equivalent to English nouns with the suffixes *-ance*, *-ence*, *-ness*, *-ty*, *-cy* etc. Also, nouns ending with "*-ism*" are rendered by means of the feminine *Nisba* in the Arabic language.

expressionism	تَعْبِيرِيَّةٌ	socialism	اِشْتِرَاكِيَّةٌ
democracy	دِيمُقْرَاطِيَّةٌ	possibility	إِمْكَانِيَّةٌ
capitalism	رَأْسْمَالِيَّةٌ	productivity	إِنْتَاجِيَّةٌ
slavery	عُبُودِيَّةٌ	impressionism	اِنْطِبَاعِيَّةٌ
nationalism, patriotism	قَوْمِيَّةٌ	significance, importance	أَهَمِّيَّةٌ

This feminine *Nisba* also serves the forming of collective nouns:

interior, internal affairs	دَاخِلِيَّةٌ	navy	بَحْرِيَّةٌ
direction/administration/ management, province	مُدِيرِيَّةٌ	republic	جُمْهُورِيَّةٌ
finances	مَالِيَّةٌ	foreign affairs	خَارِجِيَّةٌ

and of some other nouns (also concrete nouns).

Some formations are ellipses:

"the Arabic language"	ألْعَرَبِيَّةُ ⇐ ألْلُّغَةُ الْعَرَبِيَّةُ	"cooperative (society)"	تَعَاوُنِيَّةٌ ⇐ جَمْعِيَّةٌ تَعَاوُنِيَّةٌ

The plural is formed by means of ـَات . However, most words of this structure are Singularia tantum. Moreover, there are *Nisba Pluralia tantum* endings with ـِيَّات . While they are plurals in form, they mostly have a collective meaning: اِقْتِصَادِيَّاتٌ "*social affairs*", اِجْتِمَاعِيَّاتٌ "*glassware*", زُجَاجِيَّاتٌ, "*ceramics*", خَزَفِيَّاتٌ "*economics*", أَدَبِيَّاتٌ "*chemicals*", كِيمْيَاوِيَّاتٌ "*humanities*", إِنْسَانِيَّاتٌ "*literature*".

ADJECTIVES OF COLOUR AND DEFECT

Adjectives which denote colours, certain physical characteristics and defects take
the patterns أَفْعَلُ / فَعْلَاءُ. The indefinite singular is diptote.

	sg.m.	sg.f.	pl.m.
white	أَبْيَضُ	بَيْضَاءُ	بِيضٌ
red	أَحْمَرُ	حَمْرَاءُ	حُمْرٌ
green	أَخْضَرُ	خَضْرَاءُ	خُضْرٌ
blue	أَزْرَقُ	زَرْقَاءُ	زُرْقٌ
brown	أَسْمَرُ	سَمْرَاءُ	سُمْرٌ
yellow	أَصْفَرُ	صَفْرَاءُ	صُفْرٌ
blonde	أَشْقَرُ	شَقْرَاءُ	شُقْرٌ
dumb/mute	أَخْرَسُ	خَرْسَاءُ	خُرْسٌ
deaf	أَطْرَشُ	طَرْشَاءُ	طُرْشٌ
blind	أَعْمَى	عَمْيَاءُ	عُمِي/ عُمْيَانٌ
stupid	أَحْمَقُ	حَمْقَاءُ	حُمْقٌ

The feminine plural ends in *-āt*: بَيْضَاوَاتٌ، حَمْرَاوَاتٌ etc. - The plural is only used
with persons. Some examples: أَلْبِيضُ "*the whites*", أَلسُّودُ "*the blacks*", أَلْهُنُودُ الْحُمْرُ
"*the American Indians*", فَتَيَاتٌ شَقْرَاوَاتٌ "*blonde girls*".

The usual rules of concord which apply to the attributive construction or to the
nominal sentence containing an adjectival predicate apply to their construction:

the Mediterranean	أَلْبَحْرُ الْأَبْيَضُ الْمُتَوَسِّطُ
Casablanca (دار *is f.*)	أَلدَّارُ الْبَيْضَاءُ
the black market (سوق *is f.*)	أَلسُّوقُ السَّوْدَاءُ
The car is blue.	أَلسَّيَّارَةُ زَرْقَاءُ.
Its colour is blue. / It is blue.	لَوْنُها أَزْرَقُ.

ADVERBS AND ADVERBIAL CONSTRUCTIONS (أَلظَّرْفُ)

The definite or indefinite accusative is the case the adverb takes in the Arabic language. Besides, there are adverbial phrases (for formal reasons they are also called prepositional phrases), which consist of a preposition + noun in the genitive. Many nouns are used as prepositions when taking the form of the (adverbial) accusative (☞ Accusative):

after	بَعْدَ
on the basis of, according to, etc.	بناء على
under/below/beneath/underneath	تَحْتَ
in accordance with, according to	طِبْقاً لِ/ طِبْقَ/ وَفْقاً لِ / وَفْقَ
above/over	فَوْقَ
before/prior to	قَبْلَ

Some of them are additionally used as adverbs and take the ending *u* as such:

up/upstairs/on top/above	فَوْقُ
to the top/upward(s)	إلى فَوْقُ
then/thereupon/ afterwards, further(more)/moreover	بَعْدُ
afterwards, later, etc.	فِيمَا بَعْدُ

Adverbial relations are expressed by the accusative or by prepositional phrases. Adverbs serve the purpose of:
a) modifying a verb, an adjective, a participle or an adverb
b) making the circumstances clear under which the fact or action expressed by the predicate comes about.
The following adverbs belong to a):

the **qualitative adverbs** as a modification of a verb:

well	جَيِّداً / حَسَناً
strongly, violently/vehemently	شَديداً

the **quantitative adverbs** as a modification of a verb, an adjective, a participle or an adverb:

approximately	تَقْرِيباً
very/much	جِدًّا
little/seldom	قَلِيلاً
much	كَثِيراً
(he) alone/(he) by himself	وَحْدَهُ

The following adverbs belong to b):
adverbs **of time:**

now	أَلآنَ
today	أَلْيَوْمَ
yesterday	أَمْسِ
formerly/previously	سَابِقاً (في السَّابِقِ)
in the morning	صَبَاحاً (في الصَّبَاحِ)
tomorrow	غَداً
at once	فَوْراً
in the evening	مَسَاءً (في المَساءِ)

of place:

up/on top/above/upstairs	فَوْقَ
here	هُنَا
there	هُناكَ

of manner:

secretly	سِرًّا
officially, openly, publicly	عَلَناً

THE USE

Position in the sentence

The qualitative and quantitative adverbs invariably follow the words they modify:

He has done that well.	فَعَلَ ذَلِكَ جَيِّداً.
He has eaten much.	أَكَلَ كَثِيراً.

The adverbs are often at the end of the sentence. However, they are not restricted to this position:

The Syrian team arrived on Saturday, the Egyptian team on Sunday.	وَصَلَ الْفَرِيقُ السُّورِيُّ يَوْمَ السَّبْتِ وَفِي يَوْمِ الأَحَدِ وَصَلَ الْفَرِيقُ الْمِصْرِيُّ.

Adverbs as predicates

The adverbs and adverbial phrases cannot only be modifiers of other words or specify a predicate, but may also be the predicate of a nominal sentence and as such an inseparable part of it.

Here is a teacher.	هُنَا مُعَلِّمٌ.
The teacher is here.	أَلْمُعَلِّمُ هُنَا.

Other adverbial constructions

Instead of the qualitative adverb, constructions are often used in which it is replaced by a verbal noun or is put to a noun as its attributive adjunct.

Preposition بـ + (verbal) noun:

I walked fast.	مَشَيْتُ سَرِيعاً. (instead of)	مَشَيْتُ بِسُرْعَةٍ.
I walked slowly.	مَشَيْتُ بَطِيئاً. (instead of)	مَشَيْتُ بِبُطْءٍ.
I liked to do that.	فَعَلْتُ ذَلِكَ مَسْرُوراً. (instead of)	فَعَلْتُ ذَلِكَ بِسُرُورٍ.

Preposition بـ + شَكْل or صُورَة "*form/shape, manner/mode, way*" + adjective:

He has done that extremely well. (lit.: in an excellent manner).	فَعَلَ ذَلِكَ مُمْتَازاً. (instead of)	فَعَلَ ذَلِكَ بِشَكْلٍ مُمْتَازٍ.
He has done that well. (lit.: in a good manner)		فَعَلَ ذَلِكَ بِصُورَةٍ جَيِّدَةٍ.

in general, generally	بِصُورَةٍ عَامَّةٍ
especially, particularly	بِصُورَةٍ خَاصَّةٍ

Cognate accusative: A verb is modified by a following indefinite noun (mostly an infinitive) in the accusative, which is combined with an attributive adjective.

He read the letter slowly. (lit.: He read the letter a slow reading).	قَرَأَ الرِّسَالَةَ قِرَاءَةً بَطِيئَةً.

This cognate accusative, possibly the starting point of the adverb modifying a verb purely and simply, has become rare in modern Arabic. Determining which of the adverbial constructions must be used, depends, to a large extent, on the structure and semantics of the nouns to be employed.(☞ Accusative)

INTERROGATIVE ADVERBS

The interrogative adverbs are the following:

How	How did he leave the city?	كَيْفَ خَرَجَ مِنَ الْمَدِينَةِ؟	كَيْفَ
	He left the city secretly.	خَرَجَ مِنَ الْمَدِينَةِ سِرًّا.	
Where	Where do we meet?	أَيْنَ نَلْتَقِي؟	أَيْنَ
	We'll meet there.	نَلْتَقِي هُنَاكَ.	
When	When will he arrive?	مَتَى سَيَصِلُ؟	مَتَى
	He will arrive tomorrow.	سَيَصِلُ غَدًا.	
Why	Why did he die?	لِمَاذَا مَاتَ؟	لِمَاذَا / لِمَا
	He starved to death.	مَاتَ جَوْعاً.	لِمَ (short)

PRONOUNS (ألضَّمَائِرُ)

PERSONAL PRONOUNS / SUBJECT PRONOUNS

The independent personal or subject pronouns (ألضَّمِيرُ الْمُنْفَصِلُ) are:

		sg.	pl.	
3rd p. m.	*he*	هُوَ	*they (m.)*	هُمْ*
3rd p. f.	*she*	هِيَ	*they (f.)*	هُنَّ
2nd p. m.	*you (m.)*	أَنْتَ	*you (m.)*	أَنْتُمْ*
2nd p. f.	*you (f.)*	أَنْتِ	*you (f.)*	أَنْتُنَّ
1st p. m. / f.	*I*	أَنَا	*we*	نَحْنُ
		dual		
2nd p. m./ f.		*both of you*	أَنْتُمَا	
3rd p. m./f.		*both of them*	هُمَا	

*The auxiliary vowel for هُمْ and أَنْتُمْ is *Damma -u*. This vowel must be inserted when the pronoun is followed by a noun with the article.

The Arabic terms are as follows: 1st p. (مُتَكَلِّمٌ), 2nd p. (مُخَاطَبٌ), 3rd p. (غَائِبٌ).

These pronouns are usually omitted when no emphasis is required and the person in question is obvious from the context. If the pronoun is used, it is called ضَمِيرٌ بَارِزٌ (*distinct pronoun*) and if not, ضَمِيرٌ مُسْتَتِرٌ (*hidden/implied pronoun*).

The 2nd and the 3rd persons masculine plural pronouns (هُمْ and أَنْتُمْ) are used to denote masculine persons and also mixed groups of male and female persons. The 2nd and the 3rd persons feminine plural pronouns (هُنَّ and أَنْتُنَّ) are only used to denote female persons. The 1st person plural pronoun (نَحْنُ) is used also for the dual.

AFFIXED PRONOUNS (ألضَّمِيرُ الْمُتَّصِلُ) (Direct Object pronoun suffixes)

The following suffixes are used as pronouns:

		sg.	pl.	
3rd p. m.	*him /it*	هُ	*them (m.)*	هُمْ
3rd p. f.	*her / it / them*	هَا	*them (f.)*	هُنَّ
2nd p. m.	*you (m.)*	كَ	*you (m.)*	كُمْ
2nd p. f.	*you (f.)*	كِ	*you (f.)*	كُنَّ
1st p. m. / f.	*me*	ي	*us*	نَا

	dual	
2ⁿᵈ p. m./ f.	both of you	كُمَا
3ʳᵈ p. m./f.	both of them	هُمَا

The auxiliary vowel after هُمْ and كُمْ is -*u*.

The 2ⁿᵈ and the 3ʳᵈ persons masculine plural pronouns (هُمْ and كُمْ) are used to denote male persons and also mixed groups of male and female persons. The 2ⁿᵈ and the 3ʳᵈ persons feminine plural pronouns (هَنَّ and كُنَّ) are only used to denote female persons. The 1ˢᵗ person plural pronoun (نَا) is also used for the dual.

The affixed pronouns can be added to
- nouns,
- prepositions,
- various particles and conjunctions and
- verbs.

When combined with nouns, the affixed pronouns are equivalent to the possessive pronouns in English. The noun is to the affixed pronoun what the 1ˢᵗ term of a definite genitive construction is to its 2ⁿᵈ term. The noun is the governing word and is in the construct state, i.e. it does not take an article or the nunation.

pl.		sg.	
their (m.) house	بَيْتُهُمْ	*his house*	بَيْتُهُ
their (f.) house	بَيْتُهُنَّ	*her house*	بَيْتُهَا
your (m.) house	بَيْتُكُمْ	*your (m.) house*	بَيْتُكَ
your (f.) house	بَيْتُكُنَّ	*your (f.) house*	بَيْتُكِ
our house	بَيْتُنَا	*my house*	بَيْتِي

An adjective added as an attributive adjunct must take the article:

your new house	بَيْتُكُمُ الْجَدِيدُ

Peculiarities of pronunciation and spelling:
The affixed pronoun of the 1ˢᵗ p.sg. assimilates every short vowel that immediately precedes it.

my book / in my book	كِتَابِي / فِي كِتَابِي
Have you seen my book?	هَلْ رَأَيْتَ كِتَابِي؟

If the vowel *-i* or *-ī* (also *-ay*), usually found as an ending of the genitive case, precedes the affixed pronoun, the *-u* of the suffixes of the 3rd person changes into *-i*:

هِنَّ ⇦ هُنَّ   هِمْ ⇦ هُمْ   هِ ⇦ هُ

in his house	فِي بَيْتِهِ
in their (pl. m.) house/ in their (pl. f.) house	فِي بَيْتِهِمْ / فِي بَيْتِهِنَّ

The *-u* or *-i* following the suffix ه is pronounced as a long vowel: *baytuhū / fī baytihī*.

The final ة changes into ت if affixed pronouns are added.

A bag/ my bag/ your bag etc.	شَنْطَةٌ / شَنْطَتِي / شَنْطَتُكَ

The sound masculine plural drops not only the ن of the suffix ـون when used as the 1st term of an *Iḍāfa*, but also if affixed pronouns are added.

Your teachers are with their teachers.	مُعَلِّمُوكَ عِنْدَ مُعَلِّمِيهِمْ.
I have seen your teachers.	رَأَيْتُ مُعَلِّمِيكُمْ.

The affixed pronoun of the 1st p. sg. changes into يَ after the long vowels *ā*, *ī* and *ay*.

my teachers	مُعَلِّمُوِيَ
with my teachers	(مُعَلِّمِي [نَ] + يَ) مَعَ مُعَلِّمِيَّ

When combined with prepositions, the affixed pronouns are equivalent to the objective of the personal pronouns in English with the personal pronoun functioning as a prepositional complement.

with him	مَعَهُ
of / from among them	مِنْهُمْ
with us	عِنْدَنَا

The English word "*to have*" is rendered by means of the prepositions مَعَ، لِ، عِنْدَ + affixed pronoun. The preposition عِنْدَ "*at/with*" is the one most frequently used:

Do you have many books?	هَلْ عِنْدَكَ كُتُبٌ كَثِيرَةٌ؟

The preposition ﻝ *"for"*, which mainly serves to emphasize ownership, and the preposition مَعَ *"with"*, which is used to express that somebody has something with him at the moment, are employed for this purpose as well.

Peculiarities of pronunciation and spelling:

ﻝ takes on the form ﻟَ , when it precedes suffixes: لَكَ ، لَهَا ، لَهُ etc., except for the suffix of the 1st p. sg.: لِي .

The ﻥ in مِنْ is doubled if the suffix of the 1st p. sg. is added: مِنِّي .

إِلَى, عَلَى und لَدَى take on the forms - ـَيْ إِلَـ , ـَيْ عَلَـ and ـَيْ لَدَ, when followed by suffixes:

	pl.			sg.	
لَدَيْهِمْ	عَلَيْهِمْ	إِلَيْهِمْ	لَدَيْهِ	عَلَيْهِ	إِلَيْهِ
لَدَيْهِنَّ	عَلَيْهِنَّ	إِلَيْهِنَّ	لَدَيْهَا	عَلَيْهَا	إِلَيْهَا
لَدَيْكُمْ	عَلَيْكُمْ	إِلَيْكُمْ	لَدَيْكَ	عَلَيْكَ	إِلَيْكَ
لَدَيْكُنَّ	عَلَيْكُنَّ	إِلَيْكُنَّ	لَدَيْكِ	عَلَيْكِ	إِلَيْكِ
لَدَيْنَا	عَلَيْنَا	إِلَيْنَا	لَدَيَّ	عَلَيَّ	إِلَيَّ

If added to a verb, the affixed pronouns fulfil the function of a direct object.

I have bought the book. / I have bought it.	اِشْتَرَيْتُ الكِتَابَ. / اِشْتَرَيْتُهُ.
You have written the letters. / You have written them.	كَتَبْتُمُ الرَّسَائِلَ. / كَتَبْتُمُوهَا.
Take the pencil. / Take it.	خُذِ الْقَلَمَ. / خُذْهُ.
Have they drunk the juice?/Yes, they have drunk it.	هَلْ شَرِبُوا الْعَصِيرَ؟/ نَعَمْ شَرِبُوهُ.
Did you attend the event?/Yes, I attended it.	هَلْ حَضَرْتَ الْحَفْلَةَ؟/ نَعَمْ حَضَرْتُهَا.

Peculiarities of pronunciation and spelling:

The 3rd p. pl. m. of the perfect form drops the *Alif* if an affixed pronoun is added:

شَرِبُوهُ

Wāw is inserted in front of the affixed pronoun in the 2nd p. pl. m.:

كَتَبْتُمُوهَا

INDEPENDENT DIRECT OBJECT PRONOUNS (أَلضَّمِيرُ الْمُنْفَصِلُ لِلنَّصْبِ)

These pronouns are formed by adding the affixed pronouns to إِيَّا:

		sg.	pl.	
3rd p. m.	*him /it*	إِيَّاهُ	*them (m.)*	إِيَّاهُمْ
3rd p. f.	*her / it / them*	إِيَّاهَا	*them (f.)*	إِيَّاهَنَّ
2nd p. m.	*you (m.)*	إِيَّاكَ	*you (m.)*	إِيَّاكُمْ
2nd p. f.	*you (f.)*	إِيَّاكِ	*you (f.)*	إِيَّاكُنَّ
1st p. m. / f.	*me*	إِيَّايَ	*us*	إِيَّانَا

		dual	
2nd p. m./ f.		*both of you*	إِيَّاكُمَا
3rd p. m./f.		*both of them*	إِيَّاهُمَا

These pronouns are rather rare in modern Arabic and more or less restricted in use to the 3rd p. sg. (☞ Accusative)

He gave me the book. / He gave it to me.	أَعْطَانِي الْكِتَابَ. / أَعْطَانِي إِيَّاهُ

DEMONSTRATIVE PRONOUNS (أَسْمَاءُ الإِشَارَةِ)

· The demonstrative pronouns that indicate what is near with respect to place or time:

	pl.	dual		sg.
this, these	هَؤُلاءِ أُلاءِ	هَذَانِ، هَذَيْنِ (ذَانِ، ذَيْنِ / ذَانَكَ، ذَيْنَكَ)	هَذَا (ذَا، ذَاكَ)	m.
		هَاتَانِ، هَاتَيْنِ (تَانِ، تَيْنِ / تَانَكَ، تَيْنَكَ)	هَذِه (ذِي، هَذِي، تِيكَ)	f.

The demonstrative pronoun that indicates what is farther or more distant with respect to place or time is:

	pl.		sg.
that, those	أُولَئِكَ (أُولائِكُمْ)	ذَلِكَ (ذلِكُمْ/ ذلِكُما / ذلِكُنَّ)	m.
		تِلْكَ (تِلْكُمْ)	f.

The first syllable in هَذَا، هَذِه، هَؤُلَاء and ذَلِكَ , and the second in أُولَئِكَ, contain the long vowel *ā*, which is not expressed by *Alif*, as is otherwise usual. However, the initial *u* in أُولَئِكَ is short. The forms in brackets are extremely rare.

The demonstrative pronoun is placed in front of the noun which is defined by the article:

this man / that man	هَذَا الرَّجُلُ / ذَلِكَ الرَّجُلُ
this girl / that girl	هَذِه الْفَتَاةُ / تِلْكَ الْفَتَاةُ
these houses / those houses	هَذِه الْبُيُوتُ / تِلْكَ الْبُيُوتُ
these men / those men	هَؤُلَاء الرِّجَالُ / أُولَئِكَ الرِّجَالُ
these girls / those girls	هَؤُلَاء الْفَتَيَاتُ / أُولَئِكَ الفَتَيَاتُ

The demonstrative pronoun follows the noun which is defined by an affixed pronoun:

this friend of mine	صَدِيقِي هَذَا
these books of his	كُتُبُهُ هَذِه
these friends of ours	أَصْدِقَاؤُنَا هَؤُلَاء

If the demonstrative pronoun refers to the 1st term of an *Iḍāfa*, it follows the genitive construction as well:

this book of the teacher	كِتَابُ الْمُعَلِّم هَذَا
those friends of my teacher	أَصْدِقَاءُ مُعَلِّمِي أُولَئِكَ

If it refers to the 2nd term of the *Iḍāfa*, it precedes it, i.e. its position is between the 1st and the 2nd term:

the book of this / that student	كِتَابُ هَذَا / ذَلِكَ الطَّالِب

However, it follows the 2nd term of the genitive construction if the latter is a noun which is defined by an affixed pronoun:

the book of this friend of mine	كِتَابُ صَدِيقِي هَذَا

Consequently, it is possible that a construction of this kind may be ambiguous, as the demonstrative pronoun may refer to the 1st term (*this book of my friend*) as well as to the 2nd term of the *Iḍāfa* (if both terms of the latter have the same gender).

The demonstrative pronouns do not only fulfil a deictic function, but they are also used as nouns. They can fulfil the function of the subject in a nominal sentence, and of the subject or the object in a verbal sentence:

This is a teacher.	هَذَا مُعَلِّمٌ.
These have drunk the juice.	شَرِبَ هَؤُلَاءِ الْعَصِيرَ.
Muḥammad has done that.	فَعَلَ ذَلِكَ مُحَمَّدٌ.

Agreement in gender and number between subject and predicate has to be observed here in the nominal sentence; if the predicate is defined by the article, the independent pronoun should be inserted:

feminine predicate	masculine predicate
هَذِه مُعَلِّمَةٌ./ هَذِه كَبِيرَةٌ.	هَذَا مُعَلِّمٌ./ هَذَا كَبِيرٌ.
هَذِه هِيَ الْمُعَلِّمَةُ./ هَذِه هِيَ الْكُتُبُ.	هَذَا هُوَ الْمُعَلِّمُ.
هَؤُلَاءِ هُنَّ الْمُعَلِّمَاتُ.	هَؤُلَاءِ هُمُ الْمُعَلِّمُونَ.

With respect to a near or a more distant place, Arabic also uses the following demonstrative pronouns:

there (more distant)	here (near)
هُنَاكَ، هُنَالِكَ / ثَمَّ، ثَمَّةَ	هُنَا، ها هُنَا
We walked from here to there.	مَشَيْنَا مِنْ هُنَا إِلَى هُنَاكَ.
Is there something that will make us laugh today?	هَلْ ثَمَّةَ مَا يُضْحِكُنَا الْيَوْمَ؟
Is there anybody whom we make responsible for the lies ?	هَلْ ثَمَّةَ مَنْ نُحَاسِبُهُ عَلَى الْأَكَاذِيبِ؟

RELATIVE PRONOUNS

The relative pronouns (أَلْأَسْمَاءُ الْمَوْصُولَةُ) are:

after a masc. noun in the singular	أَلَّذِي
after a fem. noun in sg. and after plurals which denote non-persons	أَلَّتِي
after a masc. noun in the plural which denotes persons	أَلَّذِينَ
after a fem. noun in the plural which denotes persons	أَللَّاتِي، أَللَّوَاتِي
after a masc. dual	أَللَّذَانِ

after a fem. dual	أَللَّتَانِ
related to persons	مَنْ
related to non-persons	مَا

Whereas the four first-mentioned forms are neutral as to case, the two dual forms are inflected. After a noun in the genitive or accusative, they are أَللَّتَيْنِ / أَللَّذَيْنِ.
Note the different spelling:

with one ل:	with two ل :
اَلَّذِينَ / اَلَّتِي / اَلَّذِي	اَللَّتَانِ / اَللَّذَانِ / اَللَّوَاتِي / اَللَّاتِي

The article اَل is the first component of the relative pronoun, therefore the initial *Hamza* is *Hamzat waṣl*. (☞ Attributive Relative Clause and Nominal Relative Clause)

INTERROGATIVE PRONOUNS AND PARTICLES

Which	*In which city?*	فِي أَيَّةِ مَدِينَةٍ؟	أَيُّ / أَيَّةُ
Where	*Where is the museum?*	أَيْنَ الْمَتْحَفُ؟	أَيْنَ
			كَمْ *
How	*How are you?*	كَيْفَ الْحَالُ؟	كَيْفَ
Why	*Why don't we ask him?*	لِمَا لا نَسْأَلُهُ؟	لِمَا/لِمَ
Why	*Why did he come late?*	لِمَاذَا تَأَخَّرَ؟	لِمَاذَا
What	*What is his profession?*	مَا عَمَلُهُ.	مَا
About what	*We asked him about what is new.*	سَأَلْنَاهُ عَمَّا هُوَ جَدِيدٌ.	عَمَّا
From what	*We don't know from what the bag was made.*	لا نَعْرِفُ مِمَّا صُنِعَتِ الشَّنْطَةُ.	مِمَّا/مِمَّ
What	*What did he say?*	مَاذَا قَالَ؟	مَاذَا
When, at what time	*When do we start?*	مَتَى نَنْطَلِقُ؟	مَتَى
Who	*Who is the enemy?*	مَنْ هُوَ الْعَدُوُّ؟	مَنْ
About whom	*He asked about whom was there.*	سَأَلَ عَمَّنْ كَانَ هُنَاكَ.	عَمَّنْ
From whom	*We don't know from whom he came.*	لا نَعْرِفُ مِمَّنْ جَاءَ.	مِمَّنْ

Whose	*Whose is this house?*	لِمَنْ هَذَا الْبَيْتُ؟	لِمَنْ	لِمَنْ
Interrog. particle	*Who is present, Muhammad or Ahmad?*	أَ مُحَمَّدٌ حَاضِرٌ أَمْ أَحْمَدُ؟	أَ
	Is the lesson new?	هَلِ الدَّرْسُ جَدِيدٌ؟	هَلْ

*كَمْ is used to ask about the quantity of people or things. The construction is as follows:

a) كَمْ + indefinite noun in the accusative singular:

how many books?	كَمْ كِتَابًا؟
how many men?	كَمْ رَجُلًا؟
how many times = how often?	كَمْ مَرَّةً؟

b) كَمْ + مِنْ + definite noun in the genitive plural:

how many books, how many of the books?	كَمْ مِنَ الْكُتُبِ؟
how many men, how many of the men?	كَمْ مِنَ الرِّجَالِ؟

c) Uncountable nouns or single concepts (usually designated in the singular) are treated as follows:

how much time, how long?	كَمْ مِنَ الْوَقْتِ؟
how much meat?	كَمْ مِنَ اللَّحْمِ؟
how much money?	كَمْ مِنَ النُّقُودِ؟

d) The predicate follows the post-positive indefinite noun:

How many books have you bought?	كَمْ كِتَابًا اشْتَرَيْتَ؟
How many books do you have?	كَمْ كِتَابًا عِنْدَكَ؟

d) The same word order applies to interrogative sentences which are introduced by كَمْ + مِنْ + definite noun. However, the predicate is set directly after كَمْ in some cases:

How many books do you have?	كَمْ لَكَ / عِنْدَكَ مِنَ الْكُتُبِ؟

e) كَمْ can be combined with various prepositions. The following noun is either in the accusative according to the given rule, or in the genitive, in subordination to the preposition:

for how much, by how much?	بِكَمْ؟
For how many pounds did you buy that?	بِكَمْ لِيرَة / لِيرَةٍ اشْتَرَيْتَ ذَلِكَ؟
with how much/many?	مَعَ كَمْ؟
With how many students did you study there?	مَعَ كَمْ طَالِباً / طَالِب دَرَسْتَ هُنَاكَ؟
for how long?	مُنْذُ كَمْ
For how many years have you been studying there?	مُنْذُ كَمْ سَنَة / سَنَةٍ تَدْرُسُ هُنَاكَ؟

f) كَمْ also occurs as a (predicative) term of a nominal sentence. Here, the noun – the subject of the sentence – which follows كَمْ is not in the accusative, but in the nominative:

How (much) is your age? = How old are you?	كَمْ عُمْرُكَ؟
How (much) is its price? = How much does it cost?	كَمْ سِعْرُهُ؟
How (much) is its height? = How high is it?	كَمْ ارْتِفَاعُهُ؟
How (much) is the hour? = What time is it?	كَمِ السَّاعَةُ؟

g) An inversion of the word order is also usual in the last example: أَلسَّاعَةُ كَمْ؟

It is possible that هُوَ or هِيَ comes between كم and the subject, especially if the latter is a noun which is defined by the article:

How much is the rent?	كَمْ هِيَ الْأُجْرَةُ؟
How (much) is the distance between ... and ...? = How far is it from ... to ...?	كَمْ هِيَ الْمَسَافَةُ بَيْنَ ... و...؟

ما can be used in the same meaning instead of the predicative كم:

What is the price?	مَا هُوَ السِّعْرُ؟

PREPOSITIONS (حُرُوف الْجَرِّ)

The following table shows the most common Arabic particles and nouns which fulfil the function of prepositions. All prepositions govern the genitive case.

Table 53: **PREPOSITIONS**

	إِلَى
To, toward, up to, till, until, for, with	
He went to the house.	ذَهَبَ إِلَى الْبَيْتِ.
The lecture continued until 10 o'clock.	دَامَ الدَّرْسُ إِلَى السَّاعَةِ الْعَاشِرَةِ.
What is the best gift for the people?	مَا هِيَ أَجْمَلُ هَدِيَةٍ إِلَى النَّاسِ؟
Whom does he like best?	مَنْ هُوَ أَحَبُّ النَّاسِ إِلَيْهِ؟
A Rial with a Rial makes two Rials.	أَلرِّيَالُ إِلَى الرِّيَالِ رِيَالَانِ.
	أَمَامَ
In front of, in the presence of	
He stood in front of the house.	وَقَفَ أَمَامَ الْبَيْتِ.
He delivered his speech in the presence of the president.	أَلْقَى كَلِمَتَهُ أَمَامَ الرَّئِيسِ.
He had no other alternative but to resign.	لَمْ يَكُنْ أَمَامَهُ إِلاَّ أَنْ يَسْتَقِيلَ.
	بِ
In, at, on, with, through, by, by means of	
He works at night and sleeps during daytime.	هُوَ يَعْمَلُ بِاللَّيْلِ وَيَنَامُ بِالنَّهَارِ.
She is a lecturer at the university.	هِيَ مُدَرِّسَةٌ بِالْجَامِعَةِ.
He works with his hand.	يَشْتَغِلُ بِالْيَدِ.
I bought it for five pounds.	إِشْتَرَيْتُهُ بِخَمْسَةِ جُنَيْهَاتٍ.
They solved the problem by negotiations.	حَلُّوا الْمُشْكِلَةَ بِالْمُحَادَثَاتِ.
	بِسَبَبِ
Because of, on account of, due to, by	
He came late because of the strike.	تَأَخَّرَ بِسَبَبِ الاِضْرَابِ.
He didn't sleep because of the examinations.	لَمْ يَنَمْ بِسَبَبِ الاِمْتِحَانَاتِ.

After, in addition to, beside, aside from	بَعْدَ
He succeeded after the end of the conference.	نَجَحَ بَعْدَ انْتِهَاءِ الْمُؤْتَمَرِ.
After that he met the president.	وَبَعْدَ ذَلِكَ الْتَقَى بِالرَّئِيسِ.
By *(introducing oaths)*	تَ
By God!	تَاللهِ
Under, below, beneath, underneath, on, in	تَحْتَ
The book is underneath the bag.	الْكِتَابُ تَحْتَ الشَّنْطَةِ.
The army has been under arms for two years.	الْجَيْشُ تَحْتَ السِّلَاحِ مُنْذُ عَامَيْنِ.
The project is in an experimental stage.	الْمَشْرُوعُ تَحْتَ التَّجْرِبَةِ.
They killed him before our eyes.	قَتَلُوهُ تَحْتَ أَعْيُنِنَا.
What is in print is at his disposal.	مَا هُوَ تَحْتَ الطَّبْعِ تَحْتَ تَصَرُّفِهِ.
Beside, next to, near at, by	جَنْبَ
We saw him next to the station.	رَأَيْنَاهُ جَنْبَ الْمَحَطَّةِ.
They stood side by side.	وَقَفُوا جَنْباً إِلَى جَنْبٍ.
Until, till, up to, as far as	حَتَّى
He remained sitting until the morning.	بَقِيَ جَالِساً حَتَّى الصَّبَاحِ.
He walked from the house up to the university.	مَشَى مِنَ الْبَيْتِ حَتَّى الْجَامِعَةِ.
Around, about	حَوْلَ
The world turned around him.	دَارَ الْعَالَمُ حَوْلَهُ.
He submitted the question about his position.	طَرَحَ السُّؤَالَ حَوْلَ مَوْقِفِهِ.
They discussed his apartment.	نَاقَشُوا حَوْلَ شُقَّتِهِ.
Around, about, roughly, nearly	حَوَالَى
About twenty students came.	جَاءَ حَوَالَى عِشْرِينَ طَالِباً.

Outside, outer, outward	خَارِجَ
We met him outside the city.	إِلْتَقَيْنَا بِهِ خَارِجَ الْمَدِينَةِ.
He went outside the usual ways.	ذَهَبَ خَارِجَ الطُّرُقِ الْمَأْلُوفَةِ.
During, between, through	خِلَالَ
Across, through, right through the middle of, out of, from within, by, on the basis of	مِنْ خِلال
During, in the course of, within, in a given period of	فِي خِلَلِ/خِلال
He arrived during the first week.	وَصَلَ خِلَالَ الْأُسْبُوعِ الْأَوَّلِ.
He succeeded through his wide knowledge.	نَجَحَ مِنْ خِلال مَعْرِفَتِهِ الْوَاسِعَةِ.
He will be elected within two years.	سَيُنْتَخَبُ فِي خِلال عَامَيْنِ.
Behind, after, in the rear of	خَلْفَ
He stood behind the president.	وَقَفَ خَلْفَ الرَّئِيسِ.
He came from behind the house.	جَاءَ مِنْ خَلْفِ الْبَيْتِ.
He was sitting in the rear.	كَانَ يَجْلِسُ فِي الْخَلْفِ.
Inside, within, in	دَاخِلَ
He disappeared in the city.	إِخْتَفَى دَاخِلَ الْمَدِينَةِ.
They discussed the plan inside the council.	نَاقَشُوا الْخُطَّةَ دَاخِلَ الْمَجْلِسِ.
Below, beneath, under, short of, without	دُونَ / بِدُونِ / مِنْ دُونِ
It came to less than ten.	جَاءَ دُونَ الْعَشَرَةِ.
He is an expert in ultra/short waves.	هُوَ خَبِيرٌ فِي الْمَوْجَاتِ دُونَ الْقَصِيرَةِ.
They were late without a reason.	تَأَخَّرُوا دُونَ/بِدُونِ/مِنْ دُونِ سَبَبٍ.
This prevented the writing of the plan.	هَذَا حَالَ دُونَ كِتَابَةِ الْخُطَّةِ.
Perhaps, may/might be (with foll. indef. gen.)	رُبَّ
A clever enemy might be better than a stupid friend.	رُبَّ عَدُوٍّ عَاقِلٍ أَفْضَلُ مِنْ صَدِيقٍ جَاهِلٍ.

Silence may be more informative than words.	رُبَّ صَمْتٍ أَبْلَغُ مِنْ كَلامٍ.
Against	ضِدَّ
They voted against the government.	صَوَّتُوا ضِدَّ الْحُكُومَة.
during, throughout	طُولَ / طِيلَةَ / طَوَالَ
He didn't work during this period.	لَمْ يَعْمَلْ طُولَ/طِيلَةَ هَذِهِ الْفَتْرَة.
The project was built alongside the river.	بُنِيَ الْمَشْرُوعُ عَلَى طُولِ النَّهْرِ.
Across, over, beyond, on the other side of	عَبْرَ
He went over the bridge to the city.	ذَهَبَ عَبْرَ الْجِسْرِ إِلَى الْمَدِينَة.
He was not forgotten over the centuries.	إِنَّهُ لَمْ يُنْسَ عَبْرَ الْقُرُون.
Immediately after, subsequent to	عَقِبَ
He came immediately after the battle.	جَاءَ عَقِبَ انْتِهَاءِ الْمَعْرَكَة.
On, upon, on top of, above, over, at, by, in, to, toward, against, on the condition that, provided that, for	عَلَى
We met on board ship.	إِلْتَقَيْنَا عَلَى مَتْنِ السَّفِينَة.
We agreed on the details.	إِتَّفَقْنَا عَلَى التَّفَاصِيل.
He must write the letter.	عَلَيْهِ أَنْ يَكْتُبَ الرِّسَالَة.
Provided that it is allowed to travel.	عَلَى أَنَّهُ يَجُوزُ السَّفَر.
It is a date before the examinations.	وَهُوَ تَارِيخٌ سَابِقٌ عَلَى الامْتِحَان.
He solved the problem in the best manner.	حَلَّ الْمُشْكِلَةَ عَلَى أَفْضَلِ وَجْهٍ.
He worked for unification of the country.	عَمِلَ عَلَى تَوْحِيدِ الْبَلَد.
He agreed in the desire for peace.	وَافَقَ حِرْصاً عَلَى السَّلام.
There is no insurance for houses.	لا يُوجَدُ تَأْمِينٌ عَلَى الْبُيُوت.
He will at least get a book.	سَيَحْصُلُ عَلَى كِتَاب عَلَى الأَقَلِّ.
He invested the capital in a very wide range.	إِسْتَثْمَرَ مَالَهُ عَلَى أَوْسَعِ نِطَاقٍ.

	عَنْ
Off, away from, out of, about, on, for, in defence of, above, via, by	

He kept away from the university.	إِبْتَعَدَ عَنِ الْجَامِعَةِ.
It was solved through negotiations.	تَمَّ حَلُّهُ عَنْ طَرِيقِ الْمُحَادَثَاتِ.
He came day after day.	جَاءَ يَوْمًا عَنْ يَوْمٍ.
He disliked the new project.	رَغِبَ عَنِ الْمَشْرُوعِ الْجَدِيدِ.
He told us about what he saw there.	حَكَى لَنَا عَمَّا شَاهَدَ هُنَاكَ.

	عِنْدَ
At, near, by, with, on, upon	

We met at the university.	إِلْتَقَيْنَا عِنْدَ الْجَامِعَةِ.
He came from the house.	جَاءَ مِنْ عِنْدِ الْبَيْتِ.
They came together at sunset.	إِجْتَمَعُوا عِنْدَ غُرُوبِ الشَّمْسِ.
I have a new car.	عِنْدِي سَيَّارَةٌ جَدِيدَةٌ.
At that moment he submitted his resignation.	وَعِنْدَ ذَلِكَ قَدَّمَ الاسْتِقَالَةَ.

	غَيْرَ
Except, save, but	

| *He likes all the people except the teachers.* | يَحِبُّ كُلَّ النَّاسِ غَيْرَ الْمُعَلِّمِينَ. |

	فَوْرَ
Immediately after	

| *He was appointed immediately after the end of the conference.* | عُيِّنَ فَوْرَ انْتِهَاءِ الْمُؤْتَمَرِ. |
| *I met him immediately after his arrival.* | قَابَلْتُهُ فَوْرَ وُصُولِهِ. |

	فَوْقَ
Above, over, on, on top of, beyond, more than	

He met him on the top of the mountain.	قَابَلَهُ فَوْقَ الْجَبَلِ.
He developed beyond all expectations.	تَطَوَّرَ فَوْقَ كُلِّ التَّوَقُّعَاتِ.
He is successful beyond all bounds.	إِنَّهُ نَاجِحٌ فَوْقَ كُلِّ الْحُدُودِ.
And in addition to this he wrote two novels.	وَفَوْقَ ذَلِكَ كَتَبَ رِوَايَتَيْنِ.
He welcomed more than a thousand visitors.	إِسْتَقْبَلَ أَلْفَ زَائِرٍ وَمَا فَوْقَهُ.

In(side), at, on, by, during, among, with, about, concerning, for	**فِي**
I brought him inside the university.	أَدْخَلْتُهُ فِي الْجَامِعَةِ.
He doesn't know laziness in his life.	لَا يَعْرِفُ الْكَسَلَ فِي حَيَاتِه.
He left his house in/with his new suit.	خَرَجَ مِنْ بَيْتِه فِي بَدْلَتِهِ الْجَدِيدَةِ.
Before, prior to	**قَبْلَ**
He arrived before the delegation (arrived).	وَصَلَ قَبْلَ وُصُولِ الْوَفْدِ.
This didn't happen before.	هَذَا لَمْ يَحْدُثْ مِنْ قَبْلُ.
In front of	**قُدَّامَ**
We meet in front of the station.	نَلْتَقِي قُدَّامَ الْمَحَطَّةِ.
As, like, all but, as good as, in ... capacity of, as from,	**كَ**
He works as an expert.	يَعْمَلُ كَخَبِيرٍ.
It seems that he doesn't know the truth.	يَبْدُو وَكَأَنَّهُ لَا يَعْرِفُ الْحَقِيقَةَ.
This is impossible for a student like this.	هَذَا مُسْتَحِيلٌ لِطَالِبٍ كَهَذَا.
He as a teacher cannot fail.	هُوَ كَمُعَلِّمٍ لَا يُمْكِنُ أَنْ يَفْشَلَ.
For, on behalf of, in favour of, to, because of, due to, for the purpose of	**لِ**
This is good for normal days.	هَذَا جَيِّدٌ لِلْأَيَّامِ الْعَادِيَّةِ.
He worked for them.	عَمِلَ لَهُمْ.
He failed because of different reasons.	فَشِلَ لِأَسْبَابٍ مُخْتَلِفَةٍ.
He escaped to avoid the problems.	هَرَبَ لِلْحَيْلُولَةِ دُونَ حُدُوثِ الْمَشَاكِلِ.
At, by (place and time), in the presence of, in front of, before, with	**لَدَى**
He is our ambassador at the council.	هُوَ سَفِيرُنَا لَدَى الْمَجْلِسِ.
He has all the books.	لَدَيْه كُلُّ الْكُتُبِ.
He will pay the bill in case of need.	سَيُسَدِّدُ الْحِسَابَ لَدَى الْحَاجَةِ.

Similar to, like, as much as	مِثْلَ
He lived like the kings.	عَاشَ مِثْلَ الْمُلُوكِ.
His life is like a novel.	حَيَاتُهُ مِثْلَ رِوَايَةٍ.

With, together with, in spite of, for	مَعَ
He travelled with him to Egypt.	سَافَرَ مَعَهُ إِلَى مِصْرَ.
He is not for the new government.	هُوَ لَيْسَ مَعَ الْحُكُومَةِ.
In spite of this, he continued the dialogue.	مَعَ ذَلِكَ وَاصَلَ الْحِوَارَ.

From, away from, of (in partitive expressions), out of, beginning, since, through, belonging to, among, consist of, at, on, toward, with respect to, by, than (comparison)	مِنْ
He has a house (made) from wood.	عِنْدَهُ بَيْتٌ مِنْ خَشَبٍ.
He was diligent from the beginning.	إِجْتَهَدَ مِنَ الْبِدَايَةِ.
He is bigger than me.	هُوَ أَكْبَرُ مِنِّي.
We know his position towards them.	نَعْرِفُ مَوْقِفَهُ مِنْهُمْ.
He entered through the window.	دَخَلَ مِنَ النَّافِذَةِ.
He was afraid of what could be there.	خَافَ مِمَّا (مِنْ+مَا) قَدْ يَكُونُ هُنَاكَ.

Since, for, ago	مُنْذُ / مُذْ
I have know him for a month.	أَعْرِفُهُ مُنْذُ شَهْرٍ.
He has been in Cairo for two weeks.	هُوَ فِي الْقَاهِرَةِ مُنْذُ أُسْبُوعَيْنِ.

By (introducing oaths) (☞ ACCUSATIVE AFTER وَ)	وَ
By God!	وَاللهِ

Behind, in the rear of, at the back of, after, beyond, past, over and above, beside, in addition to	وَرَاءَ
He stood behind the chair.	وَقَفَ وَرَاءَ الْكُرْسِيِّ.
He is living overseas.	يَعِيشُ مَا وَرَاءَ الْبَحْرِ.
She left four sons behind.	تَرَكَتْ وَرَاءَهَا أَرْبَعَةَ أَوْلَادٍ.

PARTICLES (أَلْحُرُوفُ)

Particles with Jussive

The following particles are followed by a verb in the Jussive (☞ Verbs):

Conditional "if" (☞ *Conditional Sentences*)	*If you continue, I will help you.*	إِنْ تَسْتَمِرُّوا أُسَاعِدْكُمْ.	إِنْ
Negative imperative "Do not ...!"	*Do not forget the book!*	لا تَنْسَ الْكِتَابَ!	لا النَّاهِيَّة
فَلـ / وَلِـ / لِـ + 1st or 3rd p. = "let, so let him/her/ it/us ..."	*Let us go.* *So let him go.*	لِنَذْهَبْ. وَ/ فَلْيَذْهَبْ.	لامُ الأَمْر
Negation of the perfect tense (☞ *Negation*)	*He didn't sleep.*	لَمْ يَنَمْ.	لَمْ

Particles with Subjunctive (☞ Verbs):

☞ *Objective Clauses*	*He asked him not to write.*	طَلَبَ مِنْهُ أَلاَّ يَكْتُبَ.	أَنْ / أَلاَّ
☞ *Infinitives; Verbs/Subjunctive*	*He works to earn money.*	يَعْمَلُ حَتَّى يَحْصُلَ عَلَى فُلُوسٍ.	حَتَّى
☞ *Verbs/ Subjunctive*	*He works to earn money.*	يَعْمَلُ كَيْ يَحْصُلَ عَلَى فُلُوسٍ.	كَيْ(لا)
☞ *Infinitives ; Verbs/Subjunctive*	*He works to earn money.*	يَعْمَلُ لِيَحْصُلَ عَلَى فُلُوسٍ.	لِ
☞ *Verbs/ Subjunctive*	*He works to earn money.*	يَعْمَلُ لِكَيْ يَحْصُلَ عَلَى فُلُوسٍ.	لِكَيْ(لا)
☞ *Negation*	*He will never sleep.*	لَنْ يَنَامَ أَبَدًا.	لَنْ

Particles Introducing Oaths

By God, do not sleep in the lecture.	بِاللهِ، لا تَنَمْ في الدَّرْسِ.	بِ
By God!	تَاللهِ	تَ
By God, Ahmad is right.	وَاللهِ، إِنَّ أَحْمَدَ لَعَلَى حَقٍّ.	وَ
By God, he doesn't know the details.	وَاللهِ، لا يَعْرِفُ التَّفَاصِيلَ.	
By God, life is good.	وَاللهِ، الْحَيَاةُ جَمِيلَةٌ.	

Particles for Answers

Yes, indeed! Certainly! By all means!	*Did he arrive? Cetainly!*	هَلْ وَصَلَ؟ أَجَلْ	أَجَلْ
Yes, by God! Yes, indeed!	*Yes, by God!*	إِي وَاللهِ	إِي

Yes. Yes, indeed! Certainly!	Ahmad did not come. Yes, indeed!	لَمْ يَحْضُرْ أَحْمَدُ. بَلَى	بَلَى
No! not	Did you see your friend? No, I didn't.	أَ رَأَيْتَ صَديقَكَ؟ لا.	لا
Yes, certainly	Is he popular? Yes, he is.	هَلْ هُوَ مَحْبُوبٌ؟ نَعَم.	نَعَم

Particles Provoking Attention

Verily, truly, oh yes	Oh yes, the boys are here.	أَلا، الشُّبّان هُنَا!	أَلا
Verily, truly, oh yes	Oh, look, he is the director.	أَمَا، هُوَ الْمُدِيرُ!	أَمَا
Ha! Look! There!	Look, there he is.	هَا هُوَ!	هَا
O, oh	Good Lord!	يَا سَلام!	يَا

Particles Introducing Conditions (☞ Conditional Sentences)

Particles Followed by the Accusative (☞ Accusative)

Particles of Exception (☞ Exceptive Sentences)

Particles Introducing Exclamations (☞ Accusative/Exclamations)

Particles of Negation (☞ Negation)

The Particle فَ

فَ is a coordinating and sometimes a subordinating particle. It is mainly used to separate two or more (verbal) actions from each other and can render a temporal, consecutive (☞ Clauses of Time) or causative (☞ Clauses of Reason) or adversative meaning (☞ Adversative Sentences). It is often used in conditional and concessive sentences to separate the two parts of such sentences.

The delegations and the president arrived.	وَصَلَت الْوُفُودُ فَوَصَلَ الرَّئِيسُ. وَصَلَت الْوُفُودُ فَالرَّئِيسُ*.
I welcomed him and thanked him and returned back home.	اسْتَقْبَلْتُهُ فَشَكَرْتُهُ فَرَجَعْتُ إِلَى الْبَيْتِ.
I entered the university and found him sleeping in his office.	دَخَلْتُ الْجَامِعَةَ فَوَجَدْتُهُ نَائِمًا في مَكْتَبِه.

* If both actions are rendered by the same verb, there is no need to repeat the verb.

فَ is obligatory after أَمَّا، بِالنِّسْبَة لِ، فِيمَا يَتَعَلَّقُ بِ، فِيمَا يَخْتَصُّ بِ which are used to emphasize a certain topic:

| As for the president, he is in London. | أَمَّا الرَّئِيسُ فَهُوَ في لندن. |
| As for the internal situation, it is stable. | أَمَّا بِالنِّسْبَة لِلْوَضْعِ الدَّاخِلي فَهُوَ ثَابِتٌ. |

As for the university, it passes a new period.	وَفِيمَا يَتَعَلَّقُ بِالْجَامِعَةِ فَهِيَ تَمُرُّ بِمَرْحَلَةٍ جَدِيدَةٍ.
As for the program, it was submitted.	فِيمَا يَخْتَصُّ بِالْبَرْنَامَجِ فَقَدْ تَمَّ تَقْدِيمُهُ.

ف can also have a final meaning, i.e. it is used to introduce a certain purpose:

I take this opportunity in order to say ...	أَغْتَنِمُ هَذِهِ الْفُرْصَةَ فَأَقُولُ ...

ف is often used to introduce conclusions:

subsequently	... فَ بِالتَّالِي	*therefore*	... فَ مِنْ ثَمَّ
eventually	... فَ أَخِيرًا	*therefore*	... فَ لِذَلِكَ
consequently	... فَ إِذَنْ	*for this reason*	... فَ مِنْ هُنَا

or to complete or continue a sentence:

Moreover, he is the head of the department.	وَبِالْإِضَافَةِ إِلَى ذَلِكَ فَهُوَ رَئِيسُ الْقِسْمِ.
Furthermore, this bank is extremely small.	وَفَضْلاً عَنْ ذَلِكَ فَهَذَا الْمَصْرِفُ صَغِيرٌ لِلْغَايَةِ.

It is also used in collocations:

faster and faster	أَسْرَعَ فَأَسْرَعَ
bit by bit, one after the other	شَيْئًا فَشَيْئًا
year after year	عَامًا فَعَامًا
day after day	يَوْمًا فَيَوْمًا

The Particle قَدْ

قَدْ is a particle which precedes the verb. It is often combined with ف. If قَدْ or its variant لَقَدْ precede the perfect tense (كَانَ قَدْ فَعَلَ، قَدْ فَعَلَ), the definite execution of the action in the past or the execution of the action with certainty in the future (يَكُونُ قَدْ فَعَلَ) is emphasized.

If قَدْ precedes the imperfect tense (قَدْ يَفْعَلُ), it indicates a possibility that the verbal action is taking place or will take place. (☞ Conditional Sentences; Perhaps, Maybe, Possibly)

GENDER (أَلْجِنْس) AND NUMBER (أَلْعَدَدُ)

Gender

There are two genders in Arabic: masculine (مُذَكَّرٌ) and feminine (مُؤَنَّثٌ). Words ending with -a (ة = *Tā´ marbūṭa*) are almost always feminine, whereas words which do not end with *Tā´ marbūṭa* are mostly masculine. *Tā´ marbūṭa* is normally not pronounced as *t*, but as a short *a* when the word occurs isolated or at the end of a clause or a sentence. (☞ Genitive).

A number of words denoting feminines do not end with *Tā´ marbūṭa*:

a. words for persons or animals which are feminine by nature:

spinster, old maid	عَانِسٌ	mother	أُمٌّ
mare	فَرَسٌ	sister	أُخْتٌ
she-goat	مَاعِزٌ	daughter	بِنْتٌ

b. the names of most countries and of all cities

masculine		feminine	
Jordan	أَلْأُرْدُنُّ	Bahrain	أَلْبَحْرَيْنُ
Sudan	أَلسُّودَانُ	Tunisia	تُونِسُ
Iraq	أَلْعِرَاقُ	Algeria	أَلْجَزَائِرُ
Lebanon	لُبْنَانُ	Oman	عُمَانُ
Morocco	أَلْمَغْرِبُ	Palestine	فِلَسْطِينُ
Yemen	(sometimes f.) أَلْيَمَنُ	Qatar	قَطَرُ
		Al-Kuwait	أَلْكُوَيْتُ
		Egypt	مِصْرُ

c. designations of many parts of the body which exist in pairs:

eye	عَيْنٌ	ear	أُذْنٌ
leg	فَخْذٌ	leg	رِجْلٌ
foot	قَدَمٌ	forearm	سَاعِدٌ
hand	يَدٌ	thigh, leg, shank	سَاقٌ

The following are masculine:

cheek	خَدٌّ	armpit	إِبْطٌ
temple (anat.)	صُدْغٌ	eyebrow	حَاجِبٌ

d. Some words are always used as feminines:

stick, rod	عَصًا	earth, ground	أَرْضٌ
ax	فَأْسٌ	well, spring	بِئْرٌ
liver	كَبِدٌ	war	حَرْبٌ
soul	نَفْسٌ	house	دَارٌ
fire	نَارٌ	heaven	سَمَاءٌ
oath	يَمِينٌ	sun	شَمْسٌ

e. Some words which are attributed to feminines:

divorced	طَالِقٌ	pregnant	حَامِلٌ
menstruating	طَامِثٌ	menstruating	حَائِضٌ
woman, who because of her age, has ceased to bear children	قَاعِدٌ	foster mother	مُرْضِعٌ

f. Arabic also uses *Alif maqṣūra* (أَلِفُ التَّأْنِيثِ الْمَقْصُورَةِ) to denote feminines:

vision, dream	رُؤْيَا	good news	بُشْرَى
smaller, smallest	صُغْرَى	pregnant	حُبْلَى
better, best	فُضْلَى	fever	حُمَّى
higher, highest	قُصْوَى	hermaphrodite	خُنْثَى
bigger, biggest	كُبْرَى	nearer, nearest; world	دُنْيَا
middle	وُسْطَى	anniversary	ذِكْرَى

g. The so called prolonged *Alif* (أَلِفُ التَّأْنِيثِ الْمَمْدُودَةِ) is also used to denote the feminine gender:

black	سَوْدَاءُ	*white*	بَيْضَاءُ
yellow	صَفْرَاءُ	*red*	حَمْرَاءُ

h. Some words are used as either masculine or feminine:

way	سَبِيلٌ	*finger*	إِصْبَعٌ
knife	سِكِّينٌ	*thousand*	أَلْفٌ
tooth	سِنٌّ	*door*	بَابٌ
market	سُوقٌ	*land, village*	بَلَدٌ
an idol, a false god	طَاغُوتٌ	*situation*	حَالٌ
way	طَرِيقٌ	*store, tavern*	حَانُوتٌ
scorpion	عَقْرَبٌ	*shop*	دُكَّانٌ
neck, nape	عُنُقٌ	*arm*	ذِرَاعٌ
spider	عَنْكَبُوتٌ	*beard*	ذَقْنٌ
glass	كَأْسٌ	*head*	رَأْسٌ
shoulder	كَتْفٌ	*soul*	رُوحٌ
palm of the hand	كَفٌّ	*wind*	رِيحٌ
shoe	نَعْلٌ	*lane*	زُقَاقٌ

NUMBER (أَلْعَدَدُ)

Arabic has three numbers as far as nouns, pronouns and verbs are concerned: singular (أَلْمُفْرَدُ), plural (أَلْجَمْعُ) and dual (أَلْمُثَنَّى) (☞ Dual).

The Arabic noun and the adjective (which is also a noun) have two types of plurals: the external and the internal, i.e.

a) the sound plural (أَلْجَمْعُ السَّالِمُ) and

b) the broken plural (جَمْعُ التَّكْسِيرِ / أَلْجَمْعُ الْمُكَسَّرُ).

Sound Plural

The external or sound plural is formed by suffixes being added. The internal or broken plural is formed by altering the structure of the vowels of the singular form and/or by adding prefixes, infixes or suffixes to the singular form.

The sound plural has two forms: The suffix ‍ون — (-ūna) for the masculine (جَمْع مُذَكَّر سَالِمٌ) and the suffix ات – (-āt) for the feminine plural (جَمْع مُؤَنَّث سَالِمٌ) are added to the masculine singular.

		pl.		sg.
m.	diligent teachers	مُعَلِّمُونَ مُجْتَهِدُونَ	a diligent teacher	مُعَلِّمٌ مُجْتَهِدٌ
f.	diligent teachers (f.)	مُعَلِّمَاتٌ مُجْتَهِدَاتٌ	a diligent teacher (f.)	مُعَلِّمَةٌ مُجْتَهِدَةٌ

Each adjective has a masculine and a feminine singular form:

m.	big	كَبِيرٌ	long	طَوِيلٌ	many	كَثِيرٌ	diligent	مُجْتَهِدٌ
f.		كَبِيرَةٌ		طَوِيلَةٌ		كَثِيرَةٌ		مُجْتَهِدَةٌ

as well as a masculine sound or broken and a feminine plural form:

m.	كِبَارٌ	طِوَالٌ	كَثِيرُونَ	مُجْتَهِدُونَ
f.	كَبِيرَاتٌ	طَوِيلَاتٌ	كَثِيرَاتٌ	مُجْتَهِدَاتٌ

Broken Plural

The majority of nouns have the broken plural. There are hardly any rules according to which the appropriate plural form can be derived with certainty from the singular form. Regularities in the forms of the plural only occur in some groups of verbal nouns which have the sound feminine plural.

There are numerous patterns for the broken plural. The ones which occur most frequently are the following:

birds	فُعُولٌ: طُيُورٌ
pencils	أَفْعَالٌ: أَقْلَامٌ
men	فِعَالٌ: رِجَالٌ

Other patterns of the broken plural are the following:

free, independent	فُعَّلٌ: بُهَّلٌ	big, great	أَفَاعِلُ: أَكَابِرُ
greens	فُعْلٌ: خُضْرٌ	legs	أَفْعُلٌ: أَرْجُلٌ

rooms	فُعَل: غُرَفٌ	relatives	أَفْعِلَاءُ: أَقْرِبَاءُ
pieces	فُعَل: قِطَعٌ	wings	أَفْعِلَة: أَجْنِحَةٌ
books	فُعُل: كُتُبٌ	Africans	أَفَاعِلَة: أَفَارِقَةٌ
directors	فُعَلَاءُ: مُدَرَاءُ	experiments, tests	تَفَاعِل: تَجَارِبُ
countries	فُعْلَانٌ: بُلْدَانٌ	squadrons	فَعَائِل: كَتَائِبُ
students	فُعَلَة: طَلَبَةٌ	formal legal opinions	فَعَال: فَتَاوٍ
monkeys	فِعَلَة: قِرَدَةٌ	stones	فَعَالَة: حِجَارَةٌ
judges	فُعَلَة: قُضَاةٌ	companions	فَعَالَة: صَحَابَةٌ
wounded	فَعْلَى: جَرْحَى	dirhems	فَعَالِل: دَرَاهِمُ
unclehood (pl. of عَمّ)	فُعُولَة: عُمُومَةٌ	doctors	فَعَالِلَة: دَكَاتِرَةٌ
slaves	فَعِيل: عَبِيدٌ	desert	فَعَالَى: صَحَارَى
coffers, safes	فَوَاعِلُ: خَزَائِنُ	masses	فَعَالِيل: جَمَاهِيرُ
storehouses	مَفَاعِلُ: مَخَازِنُ	writers	فُعَّال: كُتَّابٌ

DUAL (أَلْمُثَنَّى)

The Arabic language has a third number in addition to the singular and the plural: the dual. It is used when two things or persons are denoted. The dual is formed by means of suffixes. The characteristic morpheme of the suffix is the long vowel *ā*, which is expanded by *n* in some cases.

Dual of the Noun

Suffix: ــَانِ in the nominative, ــَيْنِ in the genitive and accusative

	dual		sg.	
n.	أَلْمُعَلِّمَانِ	مُعَلِّمَانِ	أَلْمُعَلِّمُ	مُعَلِّمٌ
g.	أَلْمُعَلِّمَيْنِ	مُعَلِّمَيْنِ	أَلْمُعَلِّمِ	مُعَلِّمٍ
a.	أَلْمُعَلِّمَيْنِ	مُعَلِّمَيْنِ	أَلْمُعَلِّمَ	مُعَلِّماً

The genitive and the accusative of the dual cannot be distinguished from the same cases of the sound masculine in unpointed typeface.

	dual		sg.	
n.	أَلْمُعَلِّمَتَان	مُعَلِّمَتَان	أَلْمُعَلِّمَة	مُعَلِّمَة
g.	أَلْمُعَلِّمَتَيْن	مُعَلِّمَتَيْن	أَلْمُعَلِّمَة	مُعَلِّمَة
a.	أَلْمُعَلِّمَتَيْن	مُعَلِّمَتَيْن	أَلْمُعَلِّمَة	مُعَلِّمَة

The ending ن is dropped if the dual is in the construct state, e.g. if it functions as the 1st term óf an *Idāfa* or if an affixed pronoun has been added. The same applies to the sound plural.

the two companions of the delegation	مُرَافِقَا الْوَفْد
with the two companions of the delegation	مَعَ مُرَافِقَي الْوَفْد
her two escorts/ with her two escorts	مُرَافِقَاهَا / مَعَ مُرَافِقَيْهَا

The affixed pronoun of the 1st p.sg., if added to a dual form, is يَ :

my two friends	صَدَيقَايَ

There is agreement in case, state, gender and number between a noun in the dual and an adjectival attributive adjunct:

indef.	(أَل)مُعَلِّمَتَان (ال)جَدِيدَتَان	(أَل)مُعَلِّمَان (ال)جَدِيدَان
g.	عِنْدَ الْمُعَلِّمَتَيْن الْجَدِيدَتَيْن	عِنْدَ الْمُعَلِّمَيْن الْجَدِيدَيْن
a.	رَأَيْتُ الْمُعَلِّمَتَيْن الْجَدِيدَتَيْن	رَأَيْتُ الْمُعَلِّمَيْن الْجَدِيدَيْن

Two attributive adjuncts in the singular can also be employed instead of one attributive adjunct in the dual. In this case, each of them belongs to only one of the two concepts embodied in the dual form of the noun respectively:

the two teachers, the old one and the new one = the old and the new teacher	أَلْمُعَلِّمَان الْقَدِيمُ وَالْجَدِيدُ
the Syrian and the Iraqi government	أَلْحُكُومَتَان السُّورِيَّةُ وَالْعِرَاقِيَّةُ

Dual of the Pronoun
Both the independent and the affixed pronouns have dual forms in the 3rd and 2nd p. The suffix is -ā.

affixed pronouns		independent pronouns	
them both; both their	- هُمَا	*both of them*	هُمَا
both of you/you both; both your	- كُمَا	*both of you*	أَنْتُمَا

The duals of "*father*", "*brother*", "*father-in-law*" are as follows (☞ p. 125):

	dual		sg.		
	a./g.	n.	a.	g.	n.
father	أَبَوَيْنِ	أَبَوَان	أَبًا	أَبٍ	أَبٌ
brother	أَخَوَيْنِ	أَخَوَان	أَخًا	أَخٍ	أَخٌ
father-in-law	حَمَوَيْنِ	حَمَوَان	حَمًا	حَمٍ	حَمٌ

The following forms must be used when combining the dual with "*my*", "*your*"...:

	g./a.		n.			
	my two...	*your two...*	*my two*	*your two...*	*two...*	*my ...*
teacher	مُعَلِّمَيَّ	مُعَلِّمَيْكَ	مُعَلِّمَايَ	مُعَلِّمَاكَ	مُعَلِّمَان	مُعَلِّمِي
bags	شَنْطَتَيَّ	شَنْطَتَيْكَ	شَنْطَتَايَ	شَنْطَتَاكَ	شَنْطَتَان	شَنْطَتِي
brother	أَخَيَّ	أَخَيْكَ	أَخَايَ	أَخَوَاكَ	أَخَوَان	أَخِي
sister	أُخْتَيَّ	أُخْتَيْكَ	أُخْتَايَ	أُخْتَاكَ	أُخْتَان	أُخْتِي
building	بِنَاءَيَّ	بِنَاءَيْكَ	بِنَاءَايَ	بِنَاءَاكَ	بِنَاءَان	بِنَائِي

The Use of كِلا (m.) and كِلْتا (f.)

Arabic uses كِلا and كِلْتا to emphasize "*both*" which is already expressed by a noun in the dual. They are not declined when preceding a noun in the dual:

Both students are diligent.	n.	كِلا الطَّالِبَيْنِ مُجْتَهِدَانِ.
with both students	g.	مَعَ كِلا الطَّالِبَيْنِ
I saw both students.	a.	رَأَيْتُ كِلا الطَّالِبَيْنِ
Both students are diligent (f.).	n.	كِلْتا الطَّالِبَتَيْنِ مُجْتَهِدَتَانِ.
with both students (f).	g.	مَعَ كِلْتا الطَّالِبَتَيْنِ
I saw both students (f.).	a.	رَأَيْتُ كِلْتا الطَّالِبَتَيْنِ

كِلا and كِلْتا are declined when connected to a dual possessive suffix:

I was welcomed by both the students.	n.	اِسْتَقْبَلَنِي الطَّالِبَانِ كِلَاهُمَا.
He met both the students.	g.	اِجْتَمَعَ بِالطَّالِبَيْنِ كِلَيْهِمَا.
He saw both the students.	a.	رَأَيْتُ الطَّالِبَيْنِ كِلَيْهِمَا.
I was welcomed by both the students (f).	n.	اِسْتَقْبَلَتْنِي الطَّالِبَتَانِ كِلْتَاهُمَا.
He met both the students(f).	g.	اِجْتَمَعَ بِالطَّالِبَتَيْنِ كِلْتَيْهِمَا.
He saw both the students (f).	a.	رَأَيْتُ الطَّالِبَتَيْنِ كِلْتَيْهِمَا.

If كِلَا or كِلْتَا are the subject, the following verb or adjective is usually singular:

They both left yesterday.	كِلَاهُمَا غَادَرَ أَمْسِ.
They both (f.) left yesterday.	كِلْتَاهُمَا غَادَرَتْ أَمْسِ.
They are both new.	كِلَاهُمَا جَدِيدٌ.
They are both (f.) new.	كِلْتَاهُمَا جَدِيدَةٌ.

The Dual of the Demonstrative Pronouns

The demonstratives هَذَا / هذه have the same dual suffix that the noun has:

	f.	m.
n.	هَاتَانِ	هَذَانِ
g. / a.	هَاتَيْنِ	هَذَيْنِ

In the feminine dual form of the demonstrative the long vowel *ā* in the first syllable is also expressed in the typeface.

The Verbal Dual Forms (☞ the verbs for details)

Perfect tense: The suffix *-ā* is added to the 3ʳᵈ p.sg. m. and f. and to the 2ⁿᵈ p.pl.m.
Imperfect tense: The suffix *-āni* is added to the 3ʳᵈ p.sg.m. and f. and to the 2ⁿᵈ p.sg.m.:

	imperfect tense	perfect tense	
3ʳᵈ p.m.	يَفْعَلَانِ	فَعَلَا	(هُمَا)
3ʳᵈ p.f.	تَفْعَلَانِ	فَعَلَتَا	(هُمَا)
2ⁿᵈ p.	تَفْعَلَانِ	فَعَلْتُمَا	(أَنْتُمَا)

The ending ن is dropped in the subjunctive and in the jussive.

Imperative: The dual suffix *ā* is added to the masculine imperative of the singular:
. اُكْتُبَا ، اِفْعَلَا

There is no verbal dual form in any modern Arabic dialect, but some dialects have the nominal dual. Adjectives, however, are not attested in the dual in any known colloquial.

DECLENSION (أَلتَّصْرِيفُ) AND NUNATION (أَلتَّنْوِينُ)

An Arabic noun may be declinable (مُعْرَبٌ) or indeclinable (مَبْنِيٌّ). The majority of nouns have three cases which are characterized in Arabic by means of the three short vowels: -*u* = nominative (أَلرَّفْعُ), -*i* = genitive (أَلْجَرُّ / أَلْخَفْضُ), -*a* = accusative (أَلنَّصْبُ). *Damma, Kasra* and *Fatha* represent them in vocalized texts.

n.	the new teacher	أَلْمُعَلِّمُ الجَدِيدُ	al-muʿallimu l-ǧadīdu
g.	of the new teacher	أَلْمُعَلِّمِ الجَدِيد	al-muʿallimi l-ǧadīdi
a.	the new teacher	أَلْمُعَلِّمَ الجَدِيدَ	al-muʿallima l-ǧadīda
n.	the new teacher (f.)	أَلْمُعَلِّمَةُ الجَدِيدَةُ	al-muʿallimatu l-ǧadīdatu
g.	of the new teacher (f.)	أَلْمُعَلِّمَةِ الجَدِيدَة	al-muʿallimati l-ǧadīdati
a.	the new teacher (f.)	أَلْمُعَلِّمَةَ الجَدِيدَة	al-muʿallimata l-ǧadīdata

An -*n* (*Nūn*) is pronounced after the case endings -*u, -i, -a* as a characteristic sign of indefiniteness. This process is called *Nunation*. Consequently, the endings -*un*, -*in*, -*an* are formed. *Nunation* is expressed in vocalized texts by the doubling of the respective sign that represents the vowel: ٌ = -*un*, ٍ = -*in*, ً = -*an*.

Indefinite nouns in the accusative case which do not end with ة *(Tā' marbūṭa)* terminate in *Alif*, which, however, does not express a sound quality.

n.	a new teacher	مُعَلِّمٌ جَدِيدٌ	muʿallimun ǧadīdun
g.	of a new teacher	مُعَلِّم جَدِيد	muʿallimin ǧadīdin
a.	a new teacher	مُعَلِّمًا جَدِيدًا	muʿalliman ǧadīdan
n.	a new teacher (f.)	مُعَلِّمَةٌ جَدِيدَةٌ	muʿallimatun ǧadīdatun
g.	of a new teacher (f.)	مُعَلِّمَة جَدِيدَة	muʿallimatin ǧadīdatin
a.	a new teacher (f.)	مُعَلِّمَةً جَدِيدَة	muʿallimatan ǧadīdatan

Certain Arabic words have only two case endings because of their word structure, some even only one (☞ Diptotes, Indeclinable Nouns).

The declensional endings of the sound plural of masc. words are: ـُونَ -ūna = nominative and ـِينَ -īna = genitive and accusative, of feminine words: ـَاتٌ - ātu(n) = nominative and ـَاتِ -āti(n) = genitive and accusative.

	definite	indefinite	
n.	أَلْمُعَلِّمُونَ	مُعَلِّمُونَ	(al-)mu'allimūna
g.	أَلْمُعَلِّمِينَ	مُعَلِّمِينَ	(al-)mu'allimīna
a.	أَلْمُعَلِّمِينَ	مُعَلِّمِينَ	(al-)mu'allimīna
n.		مُعَلِّمَاتٌ	mu'allimātun
g.		مُعَلِّمَاتٍ	mu'allimātin
a.		مُعَلِّمَاتٍ	mu'allimātin
n.	أَلْمُعَلِّمَاتُ		(al-)mu'allimātu
g.	أَلْمُعَلِّمَاتِ		(al-)mu'allimāti
a.	أَلْمُعَلِّمَاتِ		(al-)mu'allimāti

The broken plural has the same declensional endings as the singular.

	pl.		sg.	
indefinite				
n.	أَقْلَامٌ	aqlāmun	قَلَمٌ	qalamun
g.	أَقْلَامٍ	aqlāmin	قَلَمٍ	qalamin
a.	أَقْلَامًا	aqlāman	قَلَمًا	qalaman
definite				
n.	أَلْأَقْلَامُ	al-aqlāmu	أَلْقَلَمُ	al-qalamu
g.	أَلْأَقْلَامِ	al-aqlāmi	أَلْقَلَمِ	al-qalami
a.	أَلْأَقْلَامَ	al-aqlāma	أَلْقَلَمَ	al-qalama

The functions of the cases:

nominative = case of the subject,

genitive = case required by prepositions and case of the attributive adjunct,

accusative = case of the direct object and of adverbs.

There is no universal rule whether the endings are pronounced or not. Only some endings are pronounced in colloquial language, whereas they can be fully heard in recitations.

DIPTOTES (أَلْأَسْمَاءُ غَيْرُ الْمُنْصَرِفَة / أَلْأَسْمَاءُ الْمَمْنُوعَةُ مِنَ الصَّرْف)

Indefinite nouns with nunation and three cases are called triptotes. Indefinite nouns without nunation and only two cases are called diptotes. Diptotes are usually indicated by a final *Ḍamma*. Accordingly, the characteristic of diptotes is that the final *Nūn* is missing and that the genitive and accusative endings are the same if the diptotes are not defined by the article or otherwise. Diptotes which are defined by the article or otherwise consequently change into triptotes.

	diptotes/triptotes (definite)	diptotes (indefinite)	triptotes
n.	أَلْخَزَائِنُ الْبَيْضَاءُ	خَزَائِنُ بَيْضَاءُ	رَجُلٌ كَبِيرٌ
g.	أَلْخَزَائِنِ الْبَيْضَاءِ	خَزَائِنَ بَيْضَاءَ	رَجُلٍ كَبِيرٍ
a.	أَلْخَزَائِنَ الْبَيْضَاءَ	خَزَائِنَ بَيْضَاءَ	رَجُلاً كَبِيراً

The following nouns are usually diptotes:

a) proper names

proper names with the ending ان :	عَدْنَانُ، عُثْمَانُ، رَمَضَانُ
feminine proper names regardless of having a feminine ending:	زَيْنَبُ، سُعَادُ، فَاطِمَةُ، عَائِشَةُ
masculine proper names with a feminine ending:	طَلْحَةُ، حَمْزَةُ
proper names of foreign origin when consisting of more than three letters:	إِبْرَاهِيمُ، يَعْقُوبُ
combined proper names forming one word:	حَضْرَمَوْتُ، بَعْلَبَكُ، بُورسَعِيدُ
proper names of the pattern فُعَل:	عُمَرُ، مُضَرُ، زُحَلُ، قُزَحُ
proper names with the following structures:	يَزِيدُ، أَحْمَدُ، أَشْرَفُ، تَغْلَبُ

b) adjectives having the following patterns:

أَفْعَلُ / فَعْلانُ / فُعَلُ / فُعَالُ / مَفْعَلُ

c) broken plurals with the following patterns (☞ Number):

> مَفَاعِلُ /فَوَاعِلُ / مَفَاعِيلُ / فَعَالِيلُ / فُعَلاءُ / أَفْعِلاءُ / فَعَائِلُ / أَفَاعِلُ / فَعَالِلُ

d) nouns with the ending ءا: (صَحْرَاءُ)

INDECLINABLE NOUNS (أَلْمَبْنِيُّ مِنَ الأَسْمَاء)

Arabic has numerous indeclinable nouns which never change their endings regardless of their position in a sentence.

There are two types of indeclinable nouns:

a) Nouns indeclinable by origin:

personal and affixed pronouns	... ،كَ ،هَا ،ُه ،... ،أَنْتَ ،هِيَ ،هُوَ

But if the vowel *-i* or *-ī* (also *-ay*), usually found as an ending of the genitive case, precedes the affixed pronoun, the *-u* of the suffixes of the 3rd person changes into *-i*:

> هِنَّ ⇦ هُنَّ   هِمْ ⇦ هُمْ   ِه ⇦ ُه

demonstrative pronouns (except the dual of هَذَا and هَذِه)
relative pronouns (except the dual of أَلَّذِي and أَلَّتِي)

particles for conditions	مَنْ، مَا، حَيْثُمَا، أَيْنَمَا، مَتَى، إِذَا
interrogative pronouns	مَنْ، مَا، كَيْفَ، مَتَى، أَيْنَ، كَمْ
some adverbial particles	حَيْثُ، إِذْ، أَمْسِ

b) Nouns indeclinable by their position or construction

numbers from 11 – 19 (except 12)	مَعَ سِتَّةَ عَشَرَ طَالِباً
لا + following noun in the accusative	لا شَكَّ، لا رَيْبَ فِي، لا مَفَرَّ مِنْ، لا بُدَّ مِنْ
some nouns denoting time and directions	بَعْدُ، قَبْلُ، فَوْقُ، تَحْتُ، وَرَاءُ، خَلْفُ، أَمَامَ، قُدَّامَ، يَمِينَ، شَمَالَ
the particle غَيْرُ after لا / لَيْسَ	عِنْدَهُ خَمْسَةُ بُيُوتٍ لا غَيْرُ

THE "FIVE NOUNS" (أَلأَسْمَاءُ الْخَمْسَةُ) AND OTHER IRREGULAR NOUNS

Some nouns have anomalous plurals and special patterns when being in the construct state or when followed by a suffix starting with a consonant. The following table gives the respective patterns of the so-called *"Five Nouns"* and some frequent nouns with special patterns for singular, dual and plural:

g./a.	n.	g./a.	n.	a.	g.	n.	
pl.		dual					s.
أَبَاءٍ /أَبَاءَ	أَبَاءٌ	أَبَوَيْنِ	أَبَوَانِ	أَبَا*	أَبِي*	أَبُو*	أَبٌ
إخْوَةً/إخْوَةٍ	إخْوَانٌ/إخْوَةٌ	أخَوَيْنِ	أخَوَانِ	أخَا*	أخِي*	أخُو*	أخٌ
أحْمَاءٍ/أحْمَاءَ	أحْمَاءٌ	حَمَوَيْنِ	حَمَوَانِ	حَمَا*	حَمِي*	حَمُو*	حَمٌ
أفْوَاهٍ/أفْوَاهاً	أفْوَاهٌ	فَمَيْنِ	فَمَانِ	فَا*	فِي*	فُو*	فَمٌ
☞ Genitive with ذُو and ذَاتُ							ذُو / ذَاتُ
أخَوَاتٍ	أخَوَاتٌ	أخْتَيْنِ	أخْتَانِ	أخْتاً	أخْتِ	أخْتُ	أخْتٌ
أمَّهَاتٍ	أمَّهَاتٌ	أمَّيْنِ	أمَّانِ	أمّاً	أمِّ	أمُّ	أمٌّ
النَّاسَ/النَّاسِ	أنَاسٌ/النَّاسُ	إنْسَانَيْنِ	إنْسَانَانِ	إنْسَاناً	إنْسَانِ	إنْسَانٌ	إنْسَانٌ
بَيْنَ/بَنِي* أبْنَاءٍ/ أبْنَاءَ	بَنُونَ / بنو* أبْنَاءٌ	ابْنَيْنِ	ابْنَانِ	ابْناً	ابْنِ	ابْنٌ	ابْنٌ**
رِجَالٍ/رِجَالاً	رِجَالٌ	رَجُلَيْنِ	رَجُلاَنِ	امْرَءاً	امْرِئٍ	امْرُؤٌ	امْرَءٌ/امْرُؤٌ
نِسَاءٍ/نِسَاءَ	نِسَاءٌ	امْرَأتَيْنِ	امْرَأتَانِ	امْرَأةً	امْرَأةٍ	امْرَأةٌ	امْرَأةٌ
شِفَاهٍ/ شِفَاهاً	شِفَاهٌ	شَفَتَيْنِ	شَفَتَانِ	شَفَةً	شَفَةٍ	شَفَةٌ	شَفَةٌ
مِيَاهٍ/مِيَاهاً	مِيَاهٌ / أمْوَاهٌ	مَاءَيْنِ	مَاءانِ	مَاءً	مَاءٍ	مَاءٌ	مَاءٌ
أيَادٍ / أيَادِيَا ألأيَادِي / ألأيَادِيَ	أيَادٍ ألأيَادِي	يَدَيْنِ	يَدَانِ	يَداً	يَدٍ	يَدٌ	يَدٌ

* These special patterns are only used when being in the construct state or when followed by a suffix starting with a consonant.

** Ibn is written with *Alif* (ابن) only at the beginning of a sentence or a new line or if it is the first part of a name.

SYNTAX

THE ARABIC (أَدَاةُ التَّعْرِيفِ)

The definite article *"the"* is أَلْ in Arabic. It remains unchanged for any noun, adjective, participle or numeral regardless of gender, case and number. It is connected with the following word, forming a phonetical unit with it. There is no indefinite article in Arabic.

the house	أَلْبَيْتُ	*house*	بَيْتٌ
the room	أَلْغُرْفَةُ	*room*	غُرْفَةٌ

A noun which is preceded by the article أَلْ is called a definite noun.

Although proper names are definite as such and therefore do not need the definite article, many Arab names contain the article.

لُبْنَانُ *"Lebanon"*, مُحَمَّد *"Muhammad"*, دِمَشْقُ *"Damascus"*

But: عَبْدُ الله *"Abdullāh"*, أَلْأُرْدُنُّ *"Jordan"*, أَلْقَاهِرَةُ *"Cairo"*

If the noun begins with one of the following consonants

ت ، ث ، د ، ذ ، ر ، ز ، س ، ش ، ص ، ض ، ط ، ظ ، ل ، ن

the ل of the article is assimilated, and therefore not pronounced, and the respective above-mentioned consonant is doubled, i.e. it takes the *Šadda*:

assimilated			not assimilated		
the friend	aṣ-ṣadīqu	أَلصَّدِيقُ	*the house*	al-baytu	أَلْبَيْتُ
the man	ar-raǧulu	أَلرَّجُلُ	*the room*	al-ġurfatu	أَلْغُرْفَةُ
the sun	aš-šamsu	أَلشَّمْسُ	*the moon*	al-qamaru	أَلْقَمَرُ

The letters the ل of the article is assimilated to are called حُرُوفٌ شَمْسِيَّةٌ *"sun letters"*, the others are called حُرُوفٌ قَمَرِيَّةٌ *"moon letters"*.

The *Hamza* of the article أ is only pronounced as a glottal stop when the respective word preceded by the article introduces a sentence or an independent part of a sentence. Otherwise *Hamza* is replaced by *Waṣla* ٱ which denotes that the ا is no longer pronounced as a glottal stop.

A pronounced *Hamza* is called *Hamzat al-qaṭ'*. *Hamza* that is not pronounced is called *Hamzat al-waṣl* or simply *Waṣla*.

He is the teacher.	هُوَ ٱلْمُعَلِّمُ	the teacher	أَلْمُعَلِّمُ
pronounced:	huwal-muʿallimu		al-muʿallimu
with the friend	مَعَ ٱلصَّدِيقِ	the friend	أَلصَّدِيقُ
pronounced:	maʿaṣ-ṣadīqi		aṣ-ṣadīqu
Where is the sun?	أَيْنَ ٱلشَّمْسُ؟	the sun	أَلشَّمْسُ
pronounced:	aynaš-šamsu		aš-šamsu

All final vowels followed by the article اَل of the next word are pronounced as short vowels in order to allow smooth linkage between the words:

fī + al-bayt ⇨ fil-bayti (in the house)	فِي + أَلْبَيْت ⇦ فِي ٱلْبَيْتِ
ʿalā + aṭ-ṭāwila ⇨ ʿalaṭ-ṭāwilati (on the table)	عَلَى + أَلطَّاوِلة ⇦ عَلَى ٱلطَّاوِلَة

The final *Sukūn* of a word usually turns into *Kasra* acting as an auxiliary vowel if it is followed by the article اَل of the next word:

Take the book!	خُذْ ⇦ خُذِ ٱلْكِتَابَ
She wrote the letter.	كَتَبَتِ ٱلرِّسَالَةَ.

However, the preposition مِنْ takes *Fatḥa* as an auxiliary vowel:

from /out of the house	مِنَ ٱلْبَيْتِ

Some pronouns and verbal suffixes which contain the vowel *u* take *Ḍamma* as their auxiliary vowel.

The preposition لِ is directly linked to the following noun and the *Alif* is therefore omitted:

Pronounced: lir-raǧuli	لِ + أَلرَّجُلُ = لِلرَّجُلِ

If the definite article is preceded by وَ "*and*", this وَ is always directly linked (i.e. without space) to the article followed by ٱ (*Waṣla*):

the director, the teachers and the students	أَلْمُدِيرُ وَٱلْمُعَلِّمُونَ وَٱلطُّلَّابُ

CONSTRUCT (أَلْإِضَافَةُ) AND GENITIVE (أَلْجَرُّ/ الْخَفْضُ)

A noun can be defined more closely by a subsequent noun in the genitive. The relation of both nouns to each other is that of a governing noun to an attributive adjunct in the function of the 1st term (أَلْمُضَافُ) and the 2nd term (أَلْمُضَافُ إِلَيْهِ) of an *Iḍāfa* (الْإِضَافَة), i.e. genitive construction.

The first (governing) noun is in the so-called **construct state**; i.e. it does not take the article or nunation. The last noun is always in the genitive case and may be definite or indefinite according to the intended meaning of the whole expression.

the house of a man	بَيْتُ رَجُلٍ
the house of the man	بَيْتُ الرَّجُلِ

If the word in the construct state terminates in ة, the *Tā' marbūṭa* changes

into *-tu* in the nominative	شَنْطَةُ الْمُعَلِّمَةِ	***Pronounce:** šanṭatu-l-muʻallimati*
into *-ti* in the genitive	شَنْطَةِ الْمُعَلِّمَةِ	***Pronounce:** šanṭati-l-muʻallimati*
into *-ta* in the accusative	شَنْطَةَ الْمُعَلِّمَةِ	***Pronounce:** šanṭata-l-muʻallimati*

The genitive construction does not only characterize possession, like in the example بَيْتُ رَجُلٍ, it also characterizes membership or close association:

the member of an Arab delegation	عُضْوُ وَفْدٍ عَرَبِيٍّ

As well as a characteristic feature or a quality:

the symbol of credibility	رَمْزُ مِصْدَاقِيَّةٍ

Inquiring about ownership is also expressed in the form of a genitive construction.

"Whose house is this?"	بَيْتُ مَنْ هَذَا؟

Word combinations like "*a house of the man*", "*a member of the Arab delegation*" etc. are expressed by means of the preposition مِنْ (sometimes لِ).

a house of the man lit.: *a house from the houses of the man*	بَيْتٌ مِنْ بُيُوتِ الرَّجُلِ
a member of the Arab delegation lit.: a member out of the members of the Arab delegation	عُضْوٌ مِنْ أَعْضَاءِ الْوَفْدِ الْعَرَبِيِّ

All terms except the last in a genitive construction consisting of several terms (genitive chain) are in the construct state.

the doors of the buildings of the management of the faculties of the university	أَبْوَابُ مَبَانِي إِدَارَةِ كُلِّيَّاتِ الْجَامِعَةِ

Not more than one noun should constitute the 1st term of a genitive construction - in good style. Whereas we say in English e.g. *"the head and the members of the delegation"*, i.e. two nouns followed by a genitive, we only take one noun as the governing noun in Arabic, place the other one behind the genitive construction and connect it with the 2nd term of the latter by the appropriate affixed pronoun:

lit.: the head of the delegation and its members	رَئِيسُ الْوَفْدِ وَأَعْضَاؤُهُ

However, we find that the 1st term consists of more than one noun forming a more or less inseparable unit in some set expressions:

the General Secretary of the party	أَمِينُ عَامُّ الْحِزْبِ
the General Secretary of the union	أَمِينُ سِرُّ الاتِّحَادِ
the general manager of the company	مُدِيرُ عَامُّ الشَّرِكَةِ
the public prosecutor	مُدَّعِي عَامُّ الْجُمْهُورِيَّةِ
Mufti of the kingdom	مُفْتِي عَامُّ الْمَمْلَكَةِ

The following rules regarding definiteness apply to the genitive construction:

a) If the 2nd term of the *Iḍāfa* is definite, the 1st term, which is in the construct state, is also regarded as definite. Consequently, an adjectival attributive adjunct ascribed to the 1st term has to be construed with the article.

However, as the terms of the genitive construction must not be separated (with one exception: ☞ Demonstrative Pronouns), the attributive adjunct must either follow the whole genitive construction:

the new house of the man	بَيْتُ الرَّجُلِ الْجَدِيدُ
the house of the new man	بَيْتُ الرَّجُلِ الْجَدِيدُ

or else it follows the 1st term, so that ambiguity can be avoided, and the 2nd term of the genitive construction which has been dissolved by now is added by means of لِ . This type of construction is rather frequent in modern Arabic:

the new house of the man	أَلْبَيْتُ الْجَدِيدُ لِلرَّجُلِ

b) If the 2nd term of the *Iḍāfa* is indefinite, the 1st term in the construct state is regarded as indefinite:

an investment bank	بَنْكُ اسْتِثْمَارٍ

An adjectival attributive adjunct ascribed to the 1st term of an *Iḍāfa*, i.e. to بَنْكُ follows an indefinite:

a new investment bank	بَنْكُ اسْتِثْمَارٍ جَدِيدٌ

The sound masculine plural and the dual lose the final ن when being the 1ˢᵗ term of an *Iḍāfa*.

the teachers of the student	مُعَلِّمُو الطَّالِبِ
with the teachers of the student	مَعَ مُعَلِّمِي الطَّالِبِ
the two teachers of the student	مُعَلِّمَا الطَّالِبِ
with the two teachers of the student	مَعَ مُعَلِّمَيِ الطَّالِبِ

There are some examples in which the 1ˢᵗ term is an adjective or participle (☞ Improper Annexation and *Elative*):

high-ranking officers	كِبَارُ الضُّبَّاطِ
with sincere respect	مَعَ خَالِصِ التَّقْدِيرِ

If the 1ˢᵗ term is an infinitive followed by an affixed pronoun the following noun is not always in the genitive, but in the case governed by the respective verb:

the study of the Arabic language	دِرَاسَةُ اللُّغَةِ الْعَرَبِيَّةِ
their studying of the Arabic language	دِرَاسَتُهُمُ اللُّغَةَ الْعَرَبِيَّةَ
the welcoming of the guests	أَلتَّرْحِيبُ بِالضُّيُوفِ / تَرْحِيبُ الضُّيُوفِ
his welcoming of the guests	تَرْحِيبُهُ بِالضُّيُوفِ / تَرْحِيبُهُ لِلضُّيُوفِ

A demonstrative pronoun follows the noun which is defined by an affixed pronoun:

this friend of mine	صَدِيقِي هَذَا

If the demonstrative pronoun refers to the 1ˢᵗ term of an *Iḍāfa* it follows the genitive construction as well:

this book of the teacher	كِتَابُ الْمُعَلِّمِ هَذَا

If it refers to the 2ⁿᵈ term of the *Iḍāfa*, it precedes it, i.e. its position is between the 1ˢᵗ and the 2ⁿᵈ term:

the book of this student	كِتَابُ هَذَا الطَّالِبِ

However, it follows the 2ⁿᵈ term of the genitive construction if the latter is a noun which is defined by an affixed pronoun:

the book of this friend of mine	كِتَابُ صَدِيقِي هَذَا

☞ Demonstrative Pronouns

IMPROPER ANNEXATION (أَلإِضَافَةُ غَيْرُ الْحَقِيقِيَّةِ)

Adjectives and participles employed as adjectives are often used as the 1st term of a genitive construction the 2nd term of which is a definite noun. An *Iḍāfa* constructed in this way is considered a (compound) adjective, which is almost always employed as an attributive adjunct. In accordance with the agreement in state, which exists between the noun and the attributive adjunct that belongs to it, the 1st term of this genitive construction (i.e. the adjective or the participle) also takes the article if the noun is definite.

Such constructions are called *False Iḍāfa* or improper annexation because of the peculiarity of its construction in comparison with the *Iḍāfa proper* (the 1st and the 2nd term of which are nouns).

different/various (active part., Form VIII)	مُخْتَلِفٌ
kind	نَوْعٌ ج أَنْوَاعٌ
of various kinds (False Iḍāfa)	مُخْتَلِفُ الأَنْوَاعِ
problems of various kinds	مَشَاكِلُ مُخْتَلِفَةُ الأَنْوَاعِ
the problems of various kinds	أَلْمَشَاكِلُ الْمُخْتَلِفَةُ الأَنْوَاعِ

In this context it is often not possible to render the 2nd term of the genitive construction as an adjective when translating into English, as no adjective is formed out of the noun in the English language. In such cases the genitive construction is translated by a prepositional phrase or by a single word.

low + price	مُنْخَفِضٌ + سِعْرٌ
goods of a low price	بَضَائِعُ مُنْخَفِضَةُ السِّعْرِ
tall/short /medium + stature, build	طَوِيلٌ/ قَصِيرٌ/ مُتَوَسِّطٌ + الْقَامَةِ
a man of a tall build, a tall man	رَجُلٌ طَوِيلُ الْقَامَةِ
a man short of stature	رَجُلٌ قَصِيرُ الْقَامَةِ
a man of medium height	رَجُلٌ مُتَوَسِّطُ الْقَامَةِ
the tall man	أَلرَّجُلُ الطَّوِيلُ الْقَامَةِ
two tall men	رَجُلَانِ طَوِيلَا الْقَامَةِ
the two tall men	أَلرَّجُلَانِ الطَّوِيلَا الْقَامَةِ

tall men	رِجَالٌ طِوَالُ الْقَامَة
the tall men	أَلرِّجَالُ الطِّوَالُ الْقَامَة
a strongly voiced letter	رِسَالَةٌ شَدِيدَةُ اللَّهْجَة
the strongly voiced letter	أَلرِّسَالَةُ الشَّدِيدَةُ اللَّهْجَة
a fast-flying plane	طَائِرَةٌ سَرِيعَةُ الطَّيْرَان
the fast-flying plane	أَلطَّائِرَةُ السَّرِيعَةُ الطَّيْرَان
a widely distributed journal	مَجَلَّةٌ وَاسِعَةُ الاِنْتِشَار
the widely distributed journal	أَلْمَجَلَّةُ الْوَاسِعَةُ الاِنْتِشَار

Frequently in use are the following *False Iḍāfas*:

white, red, green	أَبْيَضُ/ أَحْمَرُ/ أَخْضَرُ اللَّوْن
a slow-moving man	رَجُلٌ بَطِيءُ الْحَرَكَة
a man with a nice face	رَجُلٌ حَسَنُ الْوَجْه
a fast-moving man	رَجُلٌ سَرِيعُ الْحَرَكَة
a young man	رَجُلٌ صَغِيرُ السِّنّ
a man of weak health	رَجُلٌ ضَعِيفُ الصِّحَّة
a powerful man	رَجُلٌ طَوِيلُ الْبَاع
a longsighted man	رَجُلٌ طَوِيلُ النَّظَر
a man with a good heart	رَجُلٌ طَيِّبُ الْقَلْب
a man with an ugly face	رَجُلٌ قَبِيحُ الْوَجْه
a weak man	رَجُلٌ قَصِيرُ الْبَاع
a shortsighted man	رَجُلٌ قَصِيرُ النَّظَر
a man who speaks a lot	رَجُلٌ كَثِيرُ الْكَلَام
a man with clean hands	رَجُلٌ نَظِيفُ الْيَدَيْن

a man of wide education/culture	رَجُلٌ وَاسِعُ الثَّقَافَة
easy to handle	سَهْلُ التَّنَاوُل
easy to use	سَهْلُ الاسْتِعْمَال
easily digestible, light	سَهْلُ الْهَضْم
hard to bear	صَعْبُ الاحْتِمَال
hard to please	صَعْبُ الإِرْضَاء
obstinate, self-opinionated	صَعْبُ الْمِرَاس
difficult to understand	صَعْبُ الْفَهْم

Not all genitive constructions with an adjective or a participle as 1st term followed by a noun as 2nd term are *False Iḍāfas*. This can be deduced from their function; they do not fulfil the function of an attributive adjunct like the *False Iḍāfas* do, but they express the relationship noun - attributive adjective with the attributive adjunct preceding the noun here. The nature of this construction is explained by the possibility of transforming an adjective or a participle into a noun that is used or is in general use as an adjective, which is inherent in the Arabic language.

The number of these constructions, which do not have a specific name, is relatively small, as only a few adjectives or participles employed as adjectives are used as their 1st terms (☞ the construction of the *Elative*).

the various countries	مُخْتَلِفُ الْبُلْدَان
in the various countries	في مُخْتَلِفِ الْبُلْدَان
excellent/exquisite, outstanding (active part., Form I,)	فَائِقٌ
Yours faithfully/Yours very truly	مَعَ فَائِقِ الاحْتِرَام
clear, pure, sincere/frank/candid (active part., Form I,)	خَالِصٌ
with sincere esteem	مَعَ خَالِصِ التَّقْدِير
from times of old, from time immemorial	مُنْذُ قَدِيمِ الزَّمَان

Constructions which contain a participle or adjective that is used as a noun anyway (جَمِيع "*all, entirety*", سَائِر "*rest*", مُعْظَم "*the majority*") are not listed here. (☞ Everybody, All, Whole)

GENITIVE CONSTRUCTIONS WITH ذُو AND ذَاتٌ

Genitive constructions which denote a specific quality or affiliation are formed by means of ذُو and ذَاتٌ:

a man of culture / a cultured man	رَجُلٌ ذُو ثَقَافَة
a politician of influence = an influential politician	سِيَاسِيٌّ ذُو نُفُوذ
a problem of importance	قَضِيَّةٌ ذَاتُ أَهَمِّيَّة
a state (provided) with a parliamentary system	دَوْلَةٌ ذَاتُ نِظَامٍ بَرْلَمَانِيٌّ

When used as an attributive adjunct, ذُو and ذَاتٌ agree in case, gender and number with their respective (i.e. with their **preceding**) antecedents, and the following forms arise:

	plural		dual		singular	
	f.	m.	f.	m.	f.	m.
n.	ذَوَاتُ	ذَوُو	ذَاتَا /ذَوَاتَا	ذَوَا	ذَاتُ	ذُو
g.	ذَوَاتِ	ذَوِي	ذَاتَيْ/ذَوَاتَيْ	ذَوَيْ	ذَاتِ	ذِي
a.	ذَوَاتِ	ذَوِي	ذَاتَيْ/ذَوَاتَيْ	ذَوَيْ	ذَاتَ	ذَا

In addition, the inflectional forms أُولُو (أُولُو الأَمْرِ) for the nominative and أُولِي for the genitive or accusative exist for the masculine plural. The feminine plural أُولَاتُ is very rare.

The genitive that follows ذُو or ذَاتٌ has the same state as the antecedent:

an influential politician	سِيَاسِيٌّ ذُو نُفُوذ
the influential politician	أَلسِّيَاسِيُّ ذُو النُّفُوذِ
an influential politician (f.)	سِيَاسِيَّةٌ ذَاتُ نُفُوذ
the influential politician (f.)	أَلسِّيَاسِيَّةُ ذَاتُ النُّفُوذِ
with an influential politician	مَعَ سِيَاسِيٍّ ذِي نُفُوذ
with the influential politician	مَعَ السِّيَاسِيِّ ذِي النُّفُوذِ

I saw an influential politician.	رَأَيْتُ سِيَاسِيًّا ذَا نُفُوذ
I saw the influential politician.	رَأَيْتُ السِّيَاسِيَّ ذَا النُّفُوذ
with an influential politician (f.)	مَعَ سِيَاسِيَّة ذَاتِ نُفُوذ
with the influential politician (f.)	مَعَ السِّيَاسِيَّة ذَاتِ النُّفُوذ
I saw an influential politician (f.).	رَأَيْتُ سِيَاسِيَّة ذَاتَ نُفُوذ
I saw the influential politician (f.).	رَأَيْتُ السِّيَاسِيَّةَ ذَاتَ النُّفُوذ
influential politicians	سِيَاسِيُّونَ ذَوُو نُفُوذ
the influential politicians	ألسِّيَاسِيُّونَ ذَوُو النُّفُوذ
influential politicians (f.)	سِيَاسِيَّاتٌ ذَوَاتُ نُفُوذ
the influential politicians (f.)	ألسِّيَاسِيَّاتُ ذَوَاتُ النُّفُوذ
with / I saw the influential politicians	مَعَ / رَأَيْتُ السِّيَاسِيِّينَ ذَوِي النُّفُوذ
with / I saw the influential politicians (f.)	مَعَ / رَأَيْتُ السِّيَاسِيَّات ذَوَاتِ النُّفُوذ

These constructions do not occur very frequently outside elevated style.

There are also some cases in which ذو or ذاتٌ occur without a preceding antecedent and become independent nouns/adjectives when translated into English:

healthy	ذُو صِحَّةٍ	*pneumonia*	ذَاتُ الرِّئَة
intelligent	ذُو عَقْلٍ	*disease of the chest*	ذَاتُ الصَّدْرِ
rich, wealthy	ذُو مَالٍ	*subjectivists*	الذَّاتِيُّونَ
notables	الذَّوَاتُ	*relatives*	ذَوُو الْقُرْبَى
experts	ذَوُو الْخِبْرَة	*Alexander the Great*	ذُو الْقَرْنَيْنِ
dubious people	ذَوُو الشُّبُهَات	*important*	ذُو شَأْنٍ

COMPARISON

The *Elative* (اِسْمُ التَّفْضِيلِ)

The patterns m. أَفْعَلُ and f. فُعْلَى can be formed out of many adjectives and from some participles. These patterns are called اِسْمُ التَّفْضِيلِ or "*Elative*". *Elatives* can denote a certain degree of comparison and/or express a high degree of the respective quality.

The nouns خَيْرٌ (*good, better, best*) and شَرٌّ ("*bad, worse, worst*") have a comparative or superlative meaning although they are not *Elatives* in form.

This is the best proof.	هَذَا خَيْرُ دَلِيلٍ.
Prevention is better than cure.	أَلْوِقَايَةُ خَيْرٌ مِنَ العِلَاجِ.
A living dog is better than a dead lion.	أَلْكَلْبُ الحَيُّ خَيْرٌ مِنْ أَسَدٍ مَيِّتٍ.
Their evildoing is worse than all evil.	شَرُّهُمْ شَرٌّ مِنْ كُلِّ شَرٍّ.

The Arabic *Elative* is used for expressing:
- **an (intensified) positive,**
- **the comparative,**
- **the superlative.**

The *Elative* as (intensified) Positive

pl.		sg.	
f.	m.	f.	m.
فُعَلٌ، فُعْلَيَاتٌ	أَفَاعِلُ، أَفْعَلُونَ	فُعْلَى	أَفْعَلُ

Plural forms are rarely encountered.

In an attributive use, the *Elative* as a positive is nearly exclusively found in standard terms. There is agreement in gender with the superordinate noun.

Asia Minor	آسِيَا الصُّغْرَى
Great Britain	بِرِيطَانِيَا الْعُظْمَى
maximum (= utmost limit)	أَلْحَدُّ الْأَقْصَى
minimum (= lowest limit)	أَلْحَدُّ الْأَدْنَى
of great importance	ذُو أَهَمِّيَّةٍ كُبْرَى
the big powers	أَلدُّوَلُ الْكُبْرَى

the Far East	أَلشَّرْقُ الأَقْصَى
the Middle East	أَلشَّرْقُ الأَوْسَطُ
the Near East	أَلشَّرْقُ الأَدْنَى

The following *Elatives*

near	م دُنْيَا	أَدْنَى
far(-away)/ distant/remote	م قُصْوَى	أَقْصَى
middle, central	م وُسْطَى	أَوْسَطُ

as well as

left	م يُسْرَى	أَيْسَرُ
right	م يُمْنَى	أَيْمَنُ
lower	م سُفْلَى	أَسْفَلُ
upper/higher	م عُلْيَا	أَعْلَى

(all of them direction-related adjectives) and

(an)other	م أُخْرَى	آخَرُ

do not have a positive form or one which is rarely used or employed in a different sense. Here, they are *Elatives* in form, but do not express a degree of comparison. In a predicative use the *Elative* as a positive is rarely encountered:

God/Allah is (very) great.	أَللهُ أَكْبَرُ.
God/Allah is omniscient, knows best.	أَللهُ أَعْلَمُ.

The *Elative* as Comparative
The form which exclusively occurs is: أَفْعَلُ (also in conjunction with feminine or plural words).

In attributive use: def. or indef. noun + following أَفْعَلُ:

a smaller number/quantity	عَدَدٌ أَقَلُّ
the cheaper car	أَلسَّيَّارَةُ الأَرْخَصُ

The preposition مِنْ "*than*" may follow:

a cheaper car than the one I bought.	سَيَّارَةٌ أَرْخَصُ مِنَ السَّيَّارَةِ الَّتِي اِشْتَرَيْتُهَا

In a predicative use the *Elative* as a comparative is mostly followed by مِنْ "*than*":

He is taller than I (am).	هو أَطْوَلُ مِنِّي.
She is more active than you.	هي أَنْشَطُ مِنْكَ.
They are stronger than we (are).	هُمْ أَقْوَى مِنَّا.

The preposition مِنْ may be missing if comparison is expressed in a different way:

I am tall, he is taller.	أَنا طَوِيلٌ وهو أَطْوَلُ.

The genitival construction أَفْعَلُ + definite dual (or plural) or أَفْعَلُ + affixed pronoun in a comparative sense is rare.

the older of the two children	أَكْبَرُ الوَلَدَيْنِ
the older of the two	أَكْبَرُهُمَا

Another possibility for comparison is the use of verbs (☞ *Tamyīz*):

The problems became more important.	زَادَتِ الْمَشَاكِلُ أهمِّيَّةً.
The problems became less important.	قَلَّتِ الْمَشَاكِلُ أهمِّيَّةً.

Comparison can also be expressed by كُلَّمَا ... كُلَّمَا "*the more ... the more*". In such constructions, كُلَّمَا is always followed by a verb in the perfect tense (☞ كُلَّمَا = "*whenever*" in clauses of time).

The more I try/tried the easier are/were the solutions.	كُلَّمَا حَاوَلْتُ كُلَّمَا كَانَتِ الْحُلُولُ أَسْهَلَ.
The longer the lecture (was) the less the attention (was, will be).	كُلَّمَا طَالَتِ الْمُحَاضَرَةُ كُلَّمَا قَلَّ الاهْتِمَامُ.

The *Elative* as Superlative

The exclusive pattern is: أَفْعَلُ (also in conjunction with feminine or plural words).

If the *Elative* as a superlative occurs in a genitival use, and if an attributive construction is to be expressed, the following constructions are employed:

a) أَفْعَلُ + indefinite noun in the singular

the best student	أَحْسَنُ طَالِبٍ

b) أَفْعَلُ + definite noun in the plural

the best student (= the best of the students) or: the best students	أَحْسَنُ الطُّلاب

c) أَفْعَلُ + **affixed pronoun**

the best of them or: *the best (pl.) of them*	أَحْسَنُهُمْ

In general the context will decide whether it is a singular or a plural, e.g.

He is the best student.	هُوَ أَحْسَنُ الطُّلَّابِ
They are the best students.	هُمْ أَحْسَنُ الطُّلَّابِ
sincerest greetings	أَخْلَصُ التَّحِيَّاتِ
one of the most beautiful cities	مَدِينَةٌ مِنْ أَجْمَلِ الْمُدُنِ
the greatest industrial nation(s)	أَكْبَرُ الدُّوَلِ الصِّنَاعِيَّةِ

The Arabic *Elative* does not occur in a predicative position for the purpose of expressing an absolute superlative:

These students are best.	هُمْ أَحْسَنُ الطُّلَّابِ.
They play best.	يَلْعَبُونَ أَحْسَنَ مِنْ غَيْرِهِمْ or يَلْعَبُونَ أَحْسَنَ مَا يَكُونُ.

The most frequent among these *Elative* constructions are the following:

أَفْعَلُ مِنْ = **comparative**

He is taller than I (am).	هُوَ أَطْوَلُ مِنِّي .

أَفْعَلُ + **indefinite singular = superlative**

the best student	أَحْسَنُ طَالِبٍ

أَفْعَلُ + **definite plural = superlative**

the best student/ the best students	أَحْسَنُ الطُّلَّابِ

Some phraseological expressions with *Elatives*:

at least	عَلَى الأَقَلِّ	*above(-mentioned)*	(مَذْكُورٌ) أَعْلَاهُ
at most	عَلَى الأَكْثَرِ، على أَكْثَرِ تَقْدِيرٍ	*to a very large extent*	إِلَى أَبْعَدِ حَدٍّ
below, down	فِي الأَسْفَلِ	*to the highest degree*	إِلَى أَقْصَى حَدٍّ

COMPARISON EXPRESSED BY *TAMYĪZ*-ACCUSATIVE

Comparison of adjectives which do not form an *Elative* is the main area in which the *Tamyīz* (☞ Accusative) is applied. These adjectives are:

- the adjectives which take the pattern أَفْعَل by nature
- the participles (except the active participle, Form I) and the pattern فَعَّال
- the relative adjectives (*Nisba*)
- the adjectives which take the forms فَعْلان and فَعُول, and some other adjectives.

The comparative and the superlative are formed by means of the *Elative* أَكْثَر "more" + noun in the indefinite accusative in all these cases. أَكْثَر may sometimes be replaced with أَشَدّ.

The difficulty for the non-native speaker is to find out which noun is to be used. In case of the participles, it is almost always the corresponding infinitive which follows أَكْثَر or أَشَدّ. In the case of the *Nisba* adjectives and of the adjectives having the structure فَعَّال, it is the feminine *Nisba* which follows.

The construction becomes definite by the article being placed in front of the *Elative*.

white	أَبْيَضُ
whiter	أَكْثَرُ بَيَاضاً، أَشَدُّ بَيَاضاً
the whiter, whitest paper	أَلْوَرَقُ الأَكْثَرُ بَيَاضاً /أَلْوَرَقُ الأَشَدُّ بَيَاضاً
the whitest paper	أَكْثَرُ / أَشَدُّ الأَوْرَاقِ بَيَاضاً

Constructions like أَلْوَرَقُ الأَكْثَرُ بَيَاضاً , i.e. a definite *Elative* follows the noun, primarily express a comparative. In cases of doubt, the context will decide whether a comparative or a superlative sense is meant.

The noun used for comparison takes the form فَعَال (سَوَادٌ، بَيَاضٌ) in the case of أَبْيَضُ and أَسْوَدُ, the form فُعْلَة (حُمْرَة، زُرْقَة) etc. in the case of the remaining adjectives of colour.

diligent	مُجْتَهِدٌ
more diligent	أَكْثَرُ اجْتِهَاداً
the more, most diligent students	أَلطُّلَّابُ الأَكْثَرُ اجْتِهَاداً
the most diligent student(s)	أَكْثَرُ الطُّلَّابِ اجْتِهَاداً

productive	مُنْتِجٌ
more productive	أَكْثَرُ إِنْتَاجِيَّةً
the more, most productive equipment	ٱلْأَجْهِزَةُ ٱلْأَكْثَرُ إِنْتَاجِيَّةً
the most productive equipment	أَكْثَرُ ٱلْأَجْهِزَةِ إِنْتَاجِيَّةً
popular	شَعْبِيٌّ
more popular	أَكْثَرُ شَعْبِيَّةً
the more, most popular men	ٱلرِّجَالُ ٱلْأَكْثَرُ شَعْبِيَّةً
the most popular man, men	أَكْثَرُ ٱلرِّجَالِ شَعْبِيَّةً
tired, weary	تَعْبَانُ
more tired	أَكْثَرُ تَعَبًا، أَشَدُّ تَعَبًا
the most tired one of us	أَكْثَرُنَا تَعَبًا، أَشَدُّنَا تَعَبًا
hopelessness	يَأْسٌ
the most hopeless of them	أَشَدُّهُمْ يَأْسًا
luck	حَظٌّ
the most lucky of them	أَكْثَرُهُمْ حَظًّا
influence	سَطْوَةٌ
the most influential of them	أَوْسَعُهُمْ سَطْوَةً

In the improper annexation (*False Iḍāfa*) the *Elative* of the adjective and the *Tamyīz* of the noun are used for comparison:

widespread	وَاسِعُ ٱلرَّوَاجِ
more widespread	أَوْسَعُ رَوَاجًا
the more, most widespread books	ٱلْكُتُبُ ٱلْأَوْسَعُ رَوَاجًا
the most widespread books	أَوْسَعُ ٱلْكُتُبِ رَوَاجًا
the most widespread of them	أَوْسَعُهَا رَوَاجًا

Matters are more complicated if the 1st term of the *False Iḍāfa* does not have an *Elative*, like صُلْبُ الرَّأْي "obstinate, stubborn". If the comparative and the superlative are used at all, they must be formed with أَكْثَرُ + noun + preposition فِي:

He is more stubborn than all the others.	هُوَ أَكْثَرُ صَلَابَةً فِي الرَّأْي مِنْ كُلِّ الْآخَرِينَ.

Decreasing comparison is expressed by the Elative of قَلِيل (*few, little*) = أَقَلُّ "*less*". The construction is the same as with أَكْثَرُ/أَشَدُّ:

less diligent	أَقَلُّ اجْتِهَادًا

Another possibility for comparison is the use of verbs:

The problems became more important.	زَادَتِ الْمَشَاكِلُ أَهَمِّيَّةً.
The problems became less important.	قَلَّتِ الْمَشَاكِلُ أَهَمِّيَّةً.

Everybody, All, Whole

كُلٌّ and جَمِيعٌ are nouns, which are employed in the sense of the English indefinite pronouns "*every(one)/everybody*", "*all*", "*whole*". In these cases, they are always in the construct state. They are either followed by a definite or an indefinite noun or by an affixed pronoun.

كُلٌّ and جَمِيعٌ + noun

كُلٌّ + indefinite noun in the singular = "*every*":

every student	كُلُّ طَالِبٍ
every day	كُلُّ يَوْمٍ

كُلّ + مِنْ + **definite noun in the singular or plural** often serves to introduce enumerations like:

the rector as well as the teachers and the students	كُلٌّ مِنَ الْمُدِيرِ وَالْمُعَلِّمِينَ وَالطَّلَبَةِ
Syria as well as Iraq and Libya	كُلٌّ مِن سُورِيَا وَالْعِرَاقِ وَلِيبِيَا

and should be translated by "*both ... and .../... as well as ...*".

كُلّ + **definite noun in the singular = "*whole*":**

the whole country	كُلّ البَلَد

كُلّ + **definite noun in the plural = "*all*":**

all books	كُلّ الكُتُب

جَمِيعٌ + **definite noun in the plural = "*all*":**

all students	جَمِيعُ الطُّلاب

كُلّ **and** جَمِيعٌ + **affixed pronoun**

كُلّ (seldom جَمِيعٌ) **in the meaning of "*whole*" and "*all*"** is predominantly used as an apposition when it occurs in this construction. The affixed pronoun agrees with the preceding noun in gender and number:

the whole family	أَلعَائِلَةُ كُلّها
I have seen all the friends.	رَأَيْتُ الأَصْدِقاءَ كُلّهُمْ.

Like any apposition, كُلّ and جَمِيعٌ are in the same case in this context as the antecedent.

كُلّ and جَمِيعٌ also occur without an antecedent, when connected with the affixed pronoun:

all (of it) / all of them	كُلّهُ / كُلّهُمْ
all of us	كُلّنا

The meaning of أَلجَمِيعُ is "*all (people)*" and of جَمِيعاً = "*all of them*", "*altogether*" which is post-positive as an apposition.

كَافَّةٌ "*all*" is used less frequently; it is either in anteposition, or postpositive, taking the accusative like قَاطِبَةً "*all together, all without exception, one and all*" which is always placed after the noun:

all students	كَافَّةُ الطُّلاب/ الطَّالِبَات، أَلطُّلابُ/ أَلطَّالِبَاتُ كَافَّةً
He directed his letter to all representatives of culture and thinking	وَجَّهَ الرِّسَالَةَ إِلَى أَهْلِ الثَّقَافَة والْفِكْرِ قَاطِبَةً.

Same, Himself (نَفْسٌ)

The noun نَفْسٌ (pl. نُفُوسٌ، أَنْفُسٌ) is employed in the sense of the English words of identification "*the same, himself/herself/itself*" in addition to its original meaning "*soul*". It is always in the construct state and either followed by a definite noun or by an affixed pronoun.

نَفْسٌ + **noun**

on the same day	فِي نَفْسِ الْيَوْمِ
I bought the same book.	إِشْتَرَيْتُ نَفْسَ الْكِتَابِ.

نَفْسٌ + **affixed pronoun**

The appositional construction in which نَفْس + affixed pronoun follow the noun has the same meaning:

on the same day	فِي الْيَوْمِ نَفْسِه
I bought the same book.	اِشْتَرَيْتُ الْكِتَابَ نَفْسَهُ.

نَفْسٌ + affixed pronoun also occurs without a preceding noun. The English pronouns "*he (you, I - ...) himself/yourself/myself*" are expressed by this construction in connection with the preposition بِ:

he himself, she herself	هُوَ بِنَفْسِهِ، هِيَ بِنَفْسِهَا
you yourself	أَنْتَ بِنَفْسِكَ، أَنْتِ بِنَفْسِكِ
I myself	أَنَا بِنَفْسِي
they themselves	هُمْ بِأَنْفُسِهِمْ، هُنَّ بِأَنْفُسِهِنَّ
you yourselves	أَنْتُمْ بِأَنْفُسِكُمْ، أَنْتُنَّ بِأَنْفُسِكُنَّ
we ourselves	نَحْنُ بِأَنْفُسِنَا

The same meaning is sometimes rendered by ذَات :

(He) himself, (she) herself	هُوَ بِذَاتِهِ، هُوَ ذَاتُهُ / هِيَ بِذَاتِهَا ، هِيَ ذَاتُهَا

نَفْسٌ + affixed pronoun is also employed as a reflexive pronoun (*himself / herself /itself, yourself, myself etc.*) in Arabic:

Help yourself!	أُخْدُمْ نَفْسَكَ بِنَفْسِكَ!

Some (بَعْض ، عِدَّة) **and** *One* (أَحَدٌ / إِحْدَى)

The nouns أَحَدٌ / إِحْدَى and بَعْضٌ , عِدَّة are used in the sense of various English indefinite pronouns. بَعْضٌ means *"some"*, عِدَّة *"several"* and أَحَدٌ / إِحْدَى *"one"*. عِدَّة and أَحَدٌ / إِحْدَى are followed by a definite noun or an affixed pronoun; بَعْضٌ is followed by an indefinite noun.

بَعْض + definite noun in the plural = *"some (of)"*:

some of the teachers	بَعْضُ الْمُعَلِّمِينَ
with some friends, with some of the friends	مَعَ بَعْضِ الأَصْدِقَاءِ
with some of them	مَعَ بَعْضِهِمْ
Some travel and some others don't.	يُسَافِرُ الْبَعْضُ وَلَا يُسَافِرُ الْبَعْضُ الآخَرُ.

The reciprocal بَعْضَهُمْ (ال)بَعْض/بَعْضًا means *"each other"* and is almost always used with a prepositional object, sometimes with a direct object.

We visited each other.	زُرْنَا بَعْضَنَا الْبَعْضَ / بَعْضًا
They welcomed each other.	يُرَحِّبُونَ بِبَعْضِهِم الْبَعْضَ / بَعْضًا
They left together	غَادَرُوا مَعَ بَعْضِهِم الْبَعْضَ / بَعْضًا.
They came together.	إِجْتَمَعُوا بِبَعْضِهِم الْبَعْضَ / بَعْضًا.

عِدَّة + indefinite noun in the plural = *"several"*:

several teachers	عِدَّةُ مُعَلِّمِينَ
after several days	بَعْدَ عِدَّةِ أَيَّامٍ

أَحَدٌ , f. إِحْدَى + definite noun in the plural = *"one"*:

one of the teachers	أَحَدُ الْمُعَلِّمِينَ
one of them	أَحَدُهُمْ
one of the woman teachers	إِحْدَى الْمُعَلِّمَاتِ
in one of the rooms	فِي إِحْدَى الْغُرَفِ

Other, Another (آخَرُ / أُخْرَى / غَيْرٌ)

These nouns are used as follows:

the other student	أَلطَّالِبُ الآخَرُ
the other bag	أَلشَّنْطَةُ الأُخْرَى
Germany and other countries	أَلْمَانِيَا وَغَيْرُهَا مِنَ الْبُلْدَانِ
Iraq and other countries	الْعِرَاقُ وَغَيْرُهُ مِنَ الْبُلْدَانِ
he and others	هُوَ وَالْغَيْرُ
his and other proposals	إِقْتِرَاحُهُ وَغَيْرُ ذَلِكَ مِنَ الاقْتِرَاحَاتِ

What, Which, Any (أَيٌّ)

The interrogative pronoun أَيٌّ, f. أَيَّةٌ means "*what/which*". It is always in the construct state as the 1st term of a genitive construction.

أَيٌّ **+ indefinite noun = "*what/which*":**

in which month?	فِي أَيِّ شَهْرٍ؟
Which city?	أَيَّةُ مَدِينَةٍ؟
Which city did you visit?	أَيَّةَ مَدِينَةٍ زُرْتَ؟
Which delegations?	أَيَّةُ وُفُودٍ؟

أَيٌّ +مِنْ **+ definite noun in the plural:**

which one of the friends?	أَيٌّ مِنَ الأَصْدِقَاءِ؟
which one of them?	أَيٌّ مِنْهُمْ؟

أَيٌّ/أَيَّةٌ **+ indefinite noun in the singular = "*any*"**

with any government	مَعَ أَيَّةِ حُكُومَةٍ
in any moment	فِي أَيَّةِ لَحْظَةٍ
with anybody	مَعَ أَيِّ وَاحِدٍ

أَيٌّ must not be confused with the indeclinable particle أَيْ, which has the meaning "*i.e.*".

Nouns construed like كُلّ and جَمِيعٌ :

eventually, finally*	آخِرَ الأَمْرِ	آخِرُ
most of the banks	أَغْلَبُ الْبُنُوك	أَغْلَبُ
people like Abu Bakr	أَمْثَالُ أَبِي بَكْرٍ	أَمْثَالٌ
the first conference	أَوَّلُ مُؤْتَمَر	أَوَّلُ
the remaining students	بَاقِي الطُّلَّاب	بَاقِي
the remaining victims	بَقِيَّةُ الضَّحَايَا	بَقِيَّةٌ
at 5 o'clock sharp	فِي تَمَامِ السَّاعَةِ الْخَامِسَة	تَمَامٌ
all the problems	جُمْلَةُ الْمَشَاكِلِ	جُمْلَةٌ
one day	ذَاتَ يَوْمٍ	ذَاتَ
the rest of the students	سَائِرُ الطُّلَّاب	سَائِرٌ
with various methods	بِشَتَّى الأَسَالِيب	شَتَّى
the common people	عَامَّةُ النَّاس	عَامَّةٌ
on the same day	فِي ذَاتِ الْيَوْمِ	فِي ذَاتِ
high ranking officers	كِبَارُ الْمُوَظَّفِين	كِبَارٌ
with only one word	بِمُجَرَّدِ كَلِمَةٍ وَاحِدَةٍ	مُجَرَّدٌ
the whole production	مَجْمُوعُ الإِنْتَاج	مَجْمُوعٌ
entirely of his own record	بِمَحْضِ اخْتِيَاره	مَحْضٌ
various countries	مُخْتَلَفُ الْبُلْدَان	مُخْتَلَفٌ
most of the countries	مُعْظَمُ الْبُلْدَان	مُعْظَمٌ

*If used as an attribute آخِر is replaced by أَخِيرٌ/أَخِيرَةٌ:

the last bag	أَلشَّنْطَةُ الأَخِيرَةُ	the last thing	أَلأَمْرُ الأَخِير

APPOSITIONS

In appositions (☞ Everybody, All, Same) a noun is more closely qualified by a following noun having the same case and number. Appositions in Arabic are added to

a)   measurements and numbers

| *He wrote numerous articles.* | كَتَبَ مَقَالاتٍ عِدَّةً. |

b)   what is similar to the noun in question

| *a man like Abu Bakr* | رَجُلٌ مِثْلُ أَبِي بَكْرٍ |

c)   the material

| *a ring of silver* | خَاتِمٌ فِضَّةٌ (خَاتِمٌ مِنْ فِضَّةٍ) |

d)   the contents

| *one liter of oil* | لِتْرُ زَيْتٍ |

Appositions are also used to denote titles and professions:

Brother ...	... أَلأَخُ
Professor ...	... أَلأُسْتَاذُ
Miss ...	... أَلآنِسَةُ
Dr. ...	... أَلدُّكْتُورُ
President ...	... أَلرَّئِيسُ
Mister ...	... أَلسَّيِّدُ
Mistress ...	... أَلسَّيِّدَةُ
Señor ...	... أَلسِّينْيُورُ
the poet ...	... أَلشَّاعِرُ
Sheikh ...	... أَلشَّيْخُ
Colonel ...	... أَلعَقِيدُ
Mister ...	... أَلمِسْتَرُ
Monsieur ...	... أَلمِسْيُو
King ...	... أَلمَلَكُ

His majesty the king	... جَلَالَةُ الْمَلِكُ
Mister ...	... حَضْرَةُ السَّيِّدُ
Your Grace Dr. ...	... سَعَادَةُ الدُّكْتُورُ
His Highness ...	... سُمُوُّهُ
His Excellency the president ...	... سِيَادَةُ الرَّئِيسُ
His excellency ...	... سِيَادَتُهُ
My dear!	... عَزِيزَتِي
My dear!	... عَزِيزِي
His Highness ...	... فَخَامَةُ الرَّئِيسُ
His Excellency Sheikh ...	... فَضِيلَةُ الشَّيْخُ
His Excellency the minister ...	... مَعَالِي الْوَزِيرُ

Other frequently used appositions are:

compromise	حَلٌّ وَسَطٌ ج حُلُولٌ وَسَطٌ
raw material	مَادَّةٌ خَامٌ ج مَوَادٌّ خَامٌ
member state	دَوْلَةٌ عُضْوٌ ج دُوَلٌ أَعْضَاءٌ
railway, the railway	سِكَّةٌ حَدِيدٌ/سِكَكٌ حَدِيدٌ، السِّكَّةُ الْحَدِيدُ/السِّكَكُ الْحَدِيدُ

QUASI-, SEMI-, HALF-, NON-, QUARTER-

There are genitive constructions in which a noun as the 1st term is followed by an adjective as the 2nd term. They are no *False Idāfas*, although they fulfil the function of an attributive adjunct and are regarded as compound adjectives with respect to the content of the words. The agreement in state is expressed by the 2nd term of the genitive construction. Only genitive constructions occur, the 1st term of which is constituted by the following nouns respectively:

resemblance/similarity/ likeness, semi-	شِبْهٌ ج أَشْبَاهٌ
semi-official/officious	شِبْهُ رَسْمِيٌّ

semi-official relations	عَلاقَاتٌ شِبْهُ رَسْمِيَّة
the semi-official relations	أَلْعَلاقَاتُ شِبْهُ الرَّسْمِيَّة
non-/un-/in-/dis-	غَيْرُ
unusual	غَيْرُ اعْتِيَادِيٌّ
unclear	غَيْرُ وَاضِح
unintelligible	غَيْرُ مَعْقُول
semi-, half	نِصْفٌ ج أَنْصَافٌ
semiannual	نِصْفُ سَنَوِيٌّ
semiannual journal	مَجَلَّةٌ نِصْفُ سَنَوِيَّة
the semiannual journal	أَلْمَجَلَّةُ نِصْفُ السَّنَوِيَّة
semi-finished products	مُنْتَجَاتٌ نِصْفُ مَصْنُوعَة
quarter	رُبْعٌ
quarterly	رُبْعُ سَنَوِي

Practically, these nouns have become semi-prefixes. In careless style, it can even be observed that the article الـ is not placed in front of the 2nd term, as would be grammatically correct, but in front of the 1st term of this combination of words.

ACCUSATIVE

Accusative Object

Direct Object (أَلْمَفْعُولُ بِهِ)

He has read the book.	قَرَأَ الْكِتَابَ.

Form of the object: def. or indef. noun or pronoun.
Two objects with doubly transitive verbs:

He has given Muḥammad the book.	أَعْطَى مُحَمَّدًا الكِتَابَ.

If a personal pronoun replaces the second object, it is introduced by the particle إِيَّا .

He has given it (the book) to me.	أَعْطَانِي إِيَّاهُ.

This "accusative form" of the personal pronoun may also occur in the shortened relative clause together with the active participle of transitive verbs:

the man who sells or has sold his car	أَلرَّجُلُ الْبَائِعُ سَيَّارَتَهُ
the man who sells or has sold it	أَلرَّجُلُ الْبَائِعُ إِيَّاهَا

Cognate Accusative (أَلْمَفْعُولُ الْمُطْلَقُ)

This pattern of the accusative is also called absolute accusative.
Form of the object: indef. infinitive + attributive adjunct:

He read the letter slowly (lit.: ... a slow reading).	قَرَأَ الرِّسَالَةَ قِرَاءَةً بَطِيئَةً.

The infinitive used in such constructions is not always chosen according to the Form of the verb used in the sentence:

He washed himself completely.	اِغْتَسَلَ غُسْلًا كَامِلًا.
He supported him morally.	عَاوَنَهُ عَوْنًا مَعْنَوِيًّا.
He gave him a good beating.	ضَرَبَهُ ضَرْبًا مُبْرِحًا.
They will withdraw completely.	سَيَنْسَحِبُونَ انْسِحَابًا كَامِلًا.
He made disgusting use of the situation.	اسْتَغَلَّ الْمَوْقِفَ اسْتِغْلَالًا بَشِعًا.
He completely regained his rights.	اسْتَعَادَ حُقُوقَهُ اسْتِعَادَةً كَامِلَةً.

Even if the infinitive is not followed by an adjective, an intensified or enforced character of the action of the verb is expressed. In such cases, the expression can be translated as if the infinitive is followed by an adjective:

He gave him a good beating.	ضَرَبَهُ ضَرْباً.
They will (completely, surely, really) withdraw.	سَيَنْسَحِبُونَ انْسِحَاباً.
They imposed the solution on him by force.	فَرَضُوا عَلَيْهِ الْحَلَّ فَرْضاً.
By God, we slept really well.	وَاللهِ، نِمْنَا نَوْماً.

The infinitive can also be the first term of an Iḍāfa:

| He assumed the attitude of a spectator. | وَقَفَ مَوْقِفَ الْمُتَفَرِّجِ. |
| He put the plan into force. | وَضَعَ الْخُطَّةَ مَوْضِعَ التَّنْفِيذِ. |

Another pattern, used in the same way, is اسْمُ الْمَرَّة which denotes that the action happens only once. If derived from the triliteral root, its form is فَعْلَة. The infinitives of the derived forms get an additional (*Tā' marbūṭa*). If they already have it, the infinitive must be followed by وَاحِدَة :

He gave him one strong hit.	ضَرَبَهُ ضَرْبَةً قوية.
The plane started for its very last start.	انْطَلَقَت الطَّائِرَةُ انْطِلاقَةً أَخِيرَةً.
He mentioned the subject (only) once.	أَشَارَ إِلَى الْمَوْضُوع إِشَارَةً وَاحِدَةً.

The (فَعْلَة) اسْمُ النَّوْعِ or اسْمُ الْهَيْئَة is also used in such constructions. It describes the manner or the circumstances in which the the action of the verb takes place.

| He looked at him like the rich people look. | نَظَرَ إِلَيْهِ نِظْرَةَ الأَغْنِيَاء. |
| He beats him like a boxer. | يَضْرِبُهُ ضَرْبَةَ الْمُلاكِمينَ. |

The cognate accusative is also used with كُلٌّ , بَعْضٌ and تَمَامُ :

I liked the film very much.	أَعْجَبَنِي الْفِلْمُ كُلَّ الإِعْجَابِ.
We had some differences.	إخْتَلَفْنَا بَعْضَ الاخْتِلاف.
We understood the problem completely.	فَهِمْنَا الْمُشْكِلَةَ تَمَامَ الْفَهْمِ.

Another possibility is the use of an Elative:

| He welcomed them very cordially. | رَحَّبَ بِهِمْ أَحَرَّ التَّرْحِيبِ. |
| He paid great attention to his guests. | إهْتَمَّ بِضُيُوفِه أَكْبَرَ اهْتِمَامٍ. |

Adverbial Qualification of Time, Duration, Date (ظَرْفُ الزَّمَانِ)

some day	يَوْماً، يَوْماً مَا، يَوْماً من الأَيَّامِ، ذاتَ يَوْمٍ
every day	كُلَّ يَوْمٍ
today	أَلْيَوْمَ
on Sunday	يَوْمَ الأَحَدِ
in the morning	صَبَاحاً
for days (and days)/for days on end	أَيَّاماً طِوَالاً
(for) two years	سَنَتَيْنِ
always	دَائماً
in the year 1990	سَنَةَ ١٩٩٠

Frequently a prepositional phrase replaces the accusative:

in the year ...	سَنَةَ ...	=	في سَنَةِ ...
for two years	سَنَتَيْنِ	=	لِمُدَّةِ سَنَتَيْنِ

Adverbial Qualification of Place (ظَرْفُ المَكَانِ)

in the East	شَرْقاً
in the West	غَرْباً
(at, on) the right	يَمِيناً
(at, on) the left	يَسَاراً

Adverbial Qualification of Purpose (أَلْمَفْعُولُ لَهُ / لأَجْلِهِ)

The accusative can be used to express a certain purpose or situation:

They stood up to honour him.	وَقَفُوا احْتِرَاماً لَهُ.
I left the university to work.	تَرَكْتُ الْجَامِعَةَ رَغْبَةً في الْعَمَلِ.
I left the city being afraid of him.	غَادَرْتُ الْمَدِينَةَ خَوْفاً مِنْهُ.
I attended the lecture to express my thanks.	حَضَرْتُ الدَّرْسَ تَعْبِيراً عَن شُكْرِي.

It can sometimes be replaced by ﻟ + subjunctive/infinitive:

They stood up to honour him.	وَقَفُوا لِيَحْتَرِمُوهُ /لِاحْتِرَامِه.
to express ...	لِلتَّعْبِير عَنْ = تَعْبِيراً عَنْ

The following adverbial qualifications of purpose are frequently used:

to protest against ...	إِحْتِجَاجاً عَلَى
to realize ...	تَحْقِيقاً لِ
to support ...	تَدْعِيماً لِ
to esteem highly ...	تَقْدِيراً لِ
to honour ...	تَكْرِيماً لِ
to facilitate ...	تَمْهِيداً لِ
to carry out ...	تَنْفِيذاً لِ
to preserve ...	حِفَاظاً عَلَى
to defend ...	دِفَاعاً عن

Ḥāl-Accusative (أَلْحَالُ)

The *Ḥāl*-accusative is an indefinite accusative, which is normally derived from a participle, but sometimes from an adjective:

sitting	جَالِساً
laughing	ضَاحِكاً
coming	قَادِماً
sleeping	نَائِماً

The name "*Ḥāl*"-accusative originates from the word حَالٌ "*condition, state*".

Therefore, some textbooks and grammars describe it as the accusative in *Ḥāl* or the *Ḥāl*-clause.

The *Ḥāl*-accusative has the function of a predicative, attributive adjunct with a double semantic reference:

a) to the subject (sometimes also to the object) of the sentence:

It characterizes a certain state or mode of behaviour of the subject during the execution of the verbal action expressed by the verb. The formal reference to the subject is marked by agreement in gender and number.

My friend left laughing.	خَرَجَ صَدِيقِي ضَاحِكاً.
My friends left laughing.	خَرَجَ أَصْدِقَائِي ضَاحِكِينَ.
My friend left laughing.	خَرَجَتْ صَدِيقَتِي ضَاحِكَةً.
My friends left laughing.	خَرَجَتْ صَدِيقَاتِي ضَاحِكات.
Aḥmad stood up saying ... = *Aḥmad stood up and said ...*	قَامَ أَحْمَدُ قَائِلاً...
Do not eat the fruit (when it is still) unripe!	لا تَأْكُلِ الْفَاكِهَةَ فِجَّةً !

In the last sentence the *Ḥāl*-accusative refers to the object.

b) to the verb of the sentence:

It elucidates and completes the content of the verb. The formal reference to the subject of the sentence is given here, too, by agreement in gender and number.

Aḥmad came walking *= ... came walking, on foot.*	جَاءَ أَحْمَدُ مَاشِياً.
He did the job sitting.	أَنْجَزَ الْعَمَلَ جَالِساً.
The delegation arrived in London, coming from Cairo.	وَصَلَ الْوَفْدُ إلى لندن قَادِماً مِنَ الْقَاهِرَة.
The delegations have left London, turning to Cairo.	غَادَرَتِ الْوُفُودُ لندن مُتَوَجِّهَةً إلى الْقَاهِرَةِ.

It is obvious that the *Ḥāl*-accusative can be rendered in different ways when being translated into English. There is the possibility of rendering it with a prepositional phrase, using the participle, or by a clause linked to the main clause by means of "*and*". Arab grammarians have a comprehensive classification system of the *Ḥāl*-accusative, which includes many nouns used in the indefinite accusative as well.

The *Ḥāl*-Clause (أَلْجُمْلَةُ الْحَالِيَّةُ)

A whole clause, the so-called *Ḥāl*-clause, may replace the *Ḥāl*-accusative.

a. If it begins with a verb in the imperfect tense, it is added directly to the main clause.

My friend came in laughing.	دَخَلَ صَدِيقِي يَضْحَكُ.
Muḥammad came walking, on foot.	جَاءَ مُحَمَّدٌ يَمْشِي.

b. A nominal sentence or a verbal sentence with a subject or a pronoun in anteposition is linked to the main clause by means of وَ.

Muḥammad came in with a book in his hand.	دَخَلَ مُحَمَّدٌ وَفِي يَدِه كِتَابٌ.
My friend came in laughing, ... came in and laughed (while doing so).	دَخَلَ صَدِيقِي وَهُوَ يَضْحَكُ.
He said, looking at me/He said and while doing so he looked at me, ... and looked at me (while doing so).	قَالَ وَهُوَ يَنْظُرُ إِلَيَّ.
I said and while doing so I tried to smile, ..., ... and tried to smile while doing so.	... قُلْتُ وَأَنَا أُحَاوِلُ أَنْ أَبْتَسِمَ
He received me, saying ..., ... and said, ... with the remark that/by saying that.	... إِسْتَقْبَلَنِي وَهُوَ يَقُولُ

The *Ḥāl*-clause most frequently occurs in a construction which contains a personal pronoun in anteposition.

The negated *Ḥāl*-clause is expressed by means of "*without ...-ing*" in English:

| He listened to us without saying a word. | كَانَ يَسْتَمِعُ إِلَيْنَا وَلاَ يَقُولُ كَلِمَةً. |

c. If the *Ḥāl*-clause begins with a verb in the perfect tense, it is also linked to the main clause by means of وَ. The particle قَدْ follows وَ.

| Muḥammad came in when the friends were (already) assembled. | دَخَلَ مُحَمَّدٌ وَقَدْ كَانَ الأَصْدِقَاءُ مُجْتَمِعِينَ. |

d. The temporal relation between the main clause and the *Ḥāl*-clause:

The tense expressed by the verb of the main clause (past, present) also applies to the *Ḥāl*-clause. The perfect tense in the main clause shows that an action happened in the past; accordingly, the *Ḥāl*-clause is regarded as preterite tense.

| Muḥammad entered the room and laughed (while doing so). | دَخَلَ مُحَمَّدٌ الْغُرْفَةَ وَهُوَ يَضْحَكُ. |

Accordingly, the imperfect tense of the *Ḥāl*-clause has to be translated by a verb in the past tense, although the imperfect tense in Arabic is most common to express the present tense. If, however, the imperfect tense is used in the main clause, the *Ḥāl*-clause is also present and has to be translated accordingly:

| Muḥammad enters the room and laughs (while doing so). | يَدْخُلُ مُحَمَّدٌ الْغُرْفَةَ وَهُوَ يَضْحَكُ. |

There is simultaneousness between the *Ḥāl*-clause and the main clause. The temporal relation of the *Ḥāl*-construction becomes particularly evident when the *Ḥāl*-clause has a subject different from the subject of the main clause:

| Muḥammad came in, (just) when/while I was writing a letter. | دَخَلَ مُحَمَّدٌ وَأَنَا أَكْتُبُ رِسَالَةً. |

The *Ḥāl*-clause only expresses an anteriority as compared with the main clause or the result of an action carried out before the happening expressed by the main clause when it has been formed by means of وَقَدْ + perfect tense.

There are various possibilities of translating the *Ḥāl*-clause. Conjunctions ("*when, while, and while doing so*") can be used as an introduction of subordinate clauses besides the participle and a clause linked to the main clause by means of "*and*".

Accusative of Specification (ٱلتَّمْيِيز)

We refer to the accusative of an indefinite noun which expresses a specification (= تَمْيِيز) as *Tamyīz* (accusative of specification).

According to the rules of classical Arabic language the *Tamyīz* is used, above all, **with measurements,**

Example: ذِرَاعٌ جُوخًا "*a cubit of cloth*". However, it may be replaced in modern Arabic by the prepositional phrase مِنْ + definite noun: ذِرَاعٌ مِنَ الجُوخِ .

after the numerals 11-99 (☞ Cardinal Numbers)
and for indicating the material.

Example: خَاتَمٌ فِضَّةً "*a ring made of silver, a silver ring*".

Nowadays we find: خَاتَمٌ فِضِّيٌّ or خَاتَمٌ مِنَ الفِضَّةِ

In modern language such constructions which are equivalent to prepositional phrases with "*in*" in English are considered *Tamyīz*-accusatives.

lit.: Nobody surpasses him in knowledge and diligence.	لا يَفُوقُهُ أَحَدٌ مَعْرِفَةً واجْتِهادًا.

The main area in which the *Tamyīz* is applied is the comparison of adjectives which do not have an *Elative*. (☞ Comparison/Elative)

Predicate Complement in the Accusative (☞ "*Sisters of kāna*")

The student was diligent.	كَانَ الطَّالِبُ مُجْتَهِدًا.

The predicate complement in the accusative follows some other verbs as well. A whole clause containing the imperfect tense may also replace the nominal predicate with some of these verbs in the sense of "*to begin (to do/doing sth.)*" or "*to last, to keep doing something*": ظَلَّ يَشْرَبُ "*he continued to drink/drinking, he kept to drinking*". Some verbs of beginning (أَخَذَ، شَرَعَ، بَدَأَ a.o.) as well as the verbs of perception related to an object: بَدَأَ يَشْرَبُ "*he began to drink/drinking*", رَأَيْتُهُ يَشْرَبُ "*I saw him drinking*", have the same construction. The meaning is analog to the *Ḥāl*-clause in the imperfect tense.

Subject in the Accusative (☞ إِنَّ and أَنَّ)

The delegation arrived yesterday.	إِنَّ الْوَفْدَ وَصَلَ أَمْس.
I know that the delegation arrived yesterday.	أَعْرِفُ أَنَّ الْوَفْدَ وَصَلَ أَمْس.

The subject in the accusative also follows the compounds with لِ (لِأَنَّ، لَكِنَّ a.o.). Arabic also offers the following possibility:

We have heard that the director has arrived.	سَمِعْنا أَنَّ الْمُدِيرَ قَدْ وَصَلَ.
We have heard that the director has arrived.	سَمِعْنا أَنَّهُ قَدْ وَصَلَ الْمُدِيرُ.

The suffix هُ in the second example is referred to as ضَمِيرُ الشَّأْن in Arabic here. The suffix هُ is invariable in these cases, regardless of gender and number of the following noun. The subject الْمُدِيرُ does not follow in the accusative case any more, but in the nominative case.

Exclamations in the Accusative

Thank you.	شُكْرًا.
You're welcome. I beg your pardon/excuse me!	عَفْوًا.
Good morning!	صَبَاحَ الْخَيْرِ.

There is a specific construction for the exclamation of admiration (التَّعَجُّب): ما + masc. *Elative* in the accusative + noun in the accusative.

How beautiful this city is!	مَا أَجْمَلَ هَذِه الْمَدِينَةَ!
How difficult the tasks are!	مَا أَصْعَبَ الْوَاجِبَاتِ!

Mind the "slight" difference with respect to the vowel signs and in the meaning with respect to the interrogative sentence:

What/which ones are the most difficult tasks?	مَا أَصْعَبُ الْوَاجِبَاتِ؟

The noun takes on the nominative without an article and without nunation after the vocative particle يَا (يَا مُحَمَّدُ "*o Muḥammad*", يَا أَبُو "*o father*"). However, it takes on the accusative if a genitive or a personal pronoun follows it, i.e. if the noun takes on the construct state: يَا أَبَانَا "*oh our father*".

The particle يَا can be followed by لَ (لَامُ التَّعَجُّب) and sometimes by مِنْ to express exclamations:

Oh, how wonderful!	يَا لَلْعَجَبِ
Oh, how terrible!	يَا لَلْهَوْلِ
What a stupidity!	يَا لَلْحَمَاقَةِ

What an ignorance!	يَا لَلْغَبَاء
What a shame!	يَا لَلْعَار
What a scandal!	يَا لَلْفَضِيحَة
What a disaster!	يَا لَلْكَارِثَة
What a knowledge you have!	يَا لَكَ مِنْ مَعْرِفَةٍ

Accusative after Numerals and after كَمْ (☞ Interrogative Pronouns)

The indefinite accusative singular follows the numerals 11 to 99 and the interrogative adverb كَمْ "*how much/how many*":

how many persons?	كَمْ شَخْصًا؟
24 (male) students and 14 (female) students	٢٤ طَالِبًا و ١٤ طَالِبَةً

General Negation (☞ Negations)

Form: لَا + noun taking on the accusative without having an article and without having any nunation:

without doubt, doubtless, undoubtedly	لَا شَكَّ (فِيهِ)
There is nothing new under the sun.	لَا جَدِيدَ تَحْتَ الشَّمْسِ.

Accusative in the Exceptive (☞ Exceptive Sentences)

In the affirmative exceptive the noun takes the accusative after إِلَّا :

All but Muḥammad came./(They) all came except Muḥammad.	جَاءَ كُلُّهُمْ إِلَّا مُحَمَّدًا.

Prepositions in the Accusative (☞ Prepositions)

Many prepositions are nouns and have the form of an accusative:

in accordance with, according to	*He worked according to law.*	عَمِلَ وَفْقًا لِلْقَانُونِ. وَفْقَ، وَفْقًا لِ
on the basis of, according to	*He resigned according to law*	إِسْتَقَالَ بِنَاءً عَلَى الْقَانُونِ. بِنَاءً عَلَى

Accusative of Order

Don't hurry!	مَهْلًا!
Praise the Lord!	سُبْحَانَ اللهِ!

Accusative of Greetings and Thanks

Welcome!	مَرْحَبًا
Thank you!	شُكْرًا

Accusative of Explanation

We as Syrians know this.	نَحْنُ السُّورِيِّينَ نَعْرِفُ ذَلِكَ.

Accusative after إِيَّاكَ وَ...

Beware of the lion!	إِيَّاكَ وَالْأَسَدَ!

Accusative after و (وَاو الْمَعِيَّة)

In this construction و means "*with*" and is always followed by a noun in the accusative case:

He came back with the sunset.	رَجَعَ وَغُرُوبَ الشَّمْسِ.
This is not in harmony with their policy.	هَذَا لَا يَنْسَجِمُ وَسِيَاسَتَهُمْ.

Particles Followed by the Accusative (أَخَوَاتُ إِنَّ)

The following conjunctions which are called أَخَوَاتُ إِنَّ transfer the subject of a following nominal sentence into the accusative like إِنَّ and أَنَّ do. If preceding a verbal sentence, an affixed personal pronoun instead of a noun follows:

as if	*It looks as if the situation changes.*	يَبْدُو كَأَنَّ الْوَضْعَ يَتَغَيَّرُ.	كَأَنَّ
as if	*It seems as if he will resign.*	يَبْدُو وَكَأَنَّهُ سَوْفَ يَسْتَقِيلُ.	كَأَنَّهُ
because	*He came late because his car was damaged.*	تَأَخَّرَ لِأَنَّ سَيَّارَتَهُ تَعَطَّلَتْ.	لِأَنَّ
because	*He travels because he knows the conditions.*	سَيُسَافِرُ لِأَنَّهُ يَعْرِفُ الشُّرُوطَ.	لِأَنَّهُ
perhaps	*Perhaps we see them in the university.*	لَعَلَّنَا نَرَاهُمْ فِي الْجَامِعَة.	لَعَلَّ/لَعَلَّهُ
but	*He came but the students had (already) left.*	جَاءَ لَكِنَّ الطُّلَّابَ قَدْ غَادَرُوا.	لَكِنَّ
but	*He does not buy meat but cheese.*	لَا يَشْتَرِي لُحُومًا لَكِنَّهُ يَشْتَرِي جُبْنَة.	لَكِنَّهُ
I wish; if only	*I wish I was in London.*	لَيْتَنِي كُنْتُ فِي لندن.	لَيْتَ/لَيْتَنِي

Even if the noun does not follow one of these conjunctions immediately in a nominal sentence, it must be in the accusative case:

There are a lot of students.	إِنَّ هُنَاكَ طُلَّابًا كَثِيرِينَ.
But these details have political dimensions.	وَلَكِنَّ لِهَذِهِ التَّفَاصِيلِ أَبْعَادًا سِيَاسِيَّةً.

DOUBLY TRANSITIVE VERBS

Arabic has quite a number of doubly transitive verbs, i.e. they are followed by two direct objects in the accusative.

to inform s.o. about s.th.	أَبْلَغَ / يُبْلِغُ
to take on, assume, make use	اتَّخَذَ / يَتَّخِذُ
to inform s.o. about s.th.	أَخْبَرَ / يُخْبِرُ
to choose s.o. to be s.th.	اخْتَارَ / يَخْتَارُ
to make or let enter	أَدْخَلَ / يُدْخِلُ
to show s.o. s.th.	أَرَى / يُرِي
to regard, consider	اعْتَبَرَ / يَعْتَبِرُ
to give to s.b. s.th.	أَعْطَى / يُعْطِي
to inform s.o. about s.th.	أَعْلَمَ / يُعْلِمُ
to make s.o. understand	أَفْهَمَ / يُفْهِمُ
to dress s.o. in s.th.	أَلْبَسَ / يُلْبِسُ
to elect s.o. to an office	انْتَخَبَ / يَنْتَخِبُ
to present s.th. to s.o.	أَهْدَى / يُهْدِي
to inform s.o. about s.th.	بَلَّغَ / يُبَلِّغُ
to leave, give up, let s.o. do s.th.	تَرَكَ / يَتْرُكُ
to make s.o. do s.th.	جَعَلَ / يَجْعَلُ
to call s.o. (by or with a name)	دَعَا / يَدْعُو
to give s.o s.th.	سَلَّمَ / يُسَلِّمُ

to name s.b. (by or with a name)	سَمَّى / يُسَمِّي
to become, make out of s.o/s.th. s.th.	صَيَّرَ / يُصَيِّرُ
to grant s.o. s.th.	مَنَحَ / يَمْنَحُ
to forbid s.o. s.th	مَنَعَ / يَمْنَعُ

Examples:

He regarded the director as an outstanding teacher.	اعْتَبَرَ / عَدَّ الْمُدِيرَ مُعَلِّماً مُمْتَازاً.
I made him understand the project.	أَفْهَمْتُهُ الْمَشْرُوعَ.
He dressed his son in the trousers.	أَلْبَسَ ابْنَهُ السِّرْوَالَ.
He elected the engineer as head of the department.	انْتَخَبَ الْمُهَنْدِسَ رَئِيساً لِلْقِسْمِ.
He informed the director about the details.	بَلَّغَ الْمُدِيرَ التَّفَاصِيلَ.
He gave the student a book.	سَلَّمَ الطَّالِبَ كِتَاباً.
He gave to the student a grant.	مَنَحَ الطَّالِبَ مِنْحَةً.
The teacher forbids the pupil to smoke.	يَمْنَعُ الْمُعَلِّمُ التِّلْمِيذَ التَّدْخِينَ.

There is another group of verbs denoting doubt, probability, certainty and confirmation which are followed by the object and the predicate in the accusative. These verbs are called ظَنَّ وَأَخَوَاتُهَا (*Sisters of ẓanna*).

to make s.o. (do) s.th	جَعَلَ / يَجْعَلُ
to regard, consider, think	حَسِبَ / يَحْسَبُ
to imagine, believe, suppose	خَالَ / يَخَالُ
to know, be aware, understand	دَرَى / يَدْرِي
to behold, regard, think	رَأَى / يَرَى
to believe, regard	زَعَمَ / يَزْعَمُ
to think, assume, consider	ظَنَّ / يَظُنُّ
to regard, consider, think	عَدَّ / يَعُدُّ

| to come to know | عَلِمَ / يَعْلَمُ |
| to find | وَجَدَ / يَجِدُ |

Examples:

I considered the stranger an expert.	ظَنَنْتُ الْغَرِيبَ خَبِيراً.
He thought the director was rich.	حَسِبَ المدير غَنِيًّا.
He made a castle out of the house.	جَعَلَ الْبَيْتَ قَصْرًا.
He made a paradise out of the desert.	جَعَلَ الصَّحْرَاءَ جَنَّةً.
He regarded the lecture to be useful.	وَجَدَ الْمُحَاضَرَةَ مُفِيدَةً.
He thought the plan was successful.	رَأَى الْخُطَّةَ نَاجِحَةً.
The president is considered a courageous man.	يُعَدُّ الرَّئِيسُ رَجُلاً شُجَاعاً.

THE PASSIVE VOICE OF DOUBLY TRANSITIVE VERBS

If sentences containing two direct objects are turned into passive constructions, the
1st object turns into the subject, the 2nd object remains as such in the accusative:

Example: with أَعْطَى ه هـ ــ IV *"to give (to s.o. s.th.)"*

Active voice

| I gave Muhammad money. | أَعْطَيْتُ مُحَمَّدًا نُقُودًا. |

Passive voice

| Muhammad has been given money. | أُعْطِيَ مُحَمَّدٌ نُقُودًا. |

Example with سَمَّى ه هـ ــ II *"to name s.o. (by or with a name)"*

Active voice

| The mother has named the child Muhammad. | سَمَّتِ الأُمُّ الْوَلَدَ مُحَمَّدًا. |

Passive voice

| The child was named Muhammad. | سُمِّيَ الْوَلَدُ مُحَمَّدًا. |

Even if the subject is not mentioned, the accusative object is preserved:

| He was named Muhammad. | سُمِّيَ مُحَمَّدًا. |

NEGATION (النَّفي والنَّهي)

There are several means of negation in Arabic which can be summarized as follows :

لا + imperfect tense (لا النَّافِيَّة) = **negation of actions taking place in present and future tenses:**

He does not do that / he will not do that.	لا يَفْعَلُ ذَلِكَ.

A verb preceded by the particle سَوْفَ for the future tense can be negated in the following way: سَوْفَ لا يَفْعَلُ ذَلِكَ *"He will (definitely) not do that"*. Consequently, the abridged form سـ can not be used here, and it would be **wrong** to say: (لا سَيَفْعَلُ).

لا + jussive (لا النَّاهِيَّة) = negative imperative:

Do not do that!	لا تَفْعَلْ ذَلِكَ! لا تَفْعَلي ذَلِكَ!
Do (pl.) not do that!	لا تَفْعَلُوا ذَلِكَ! لا تَفْعَلْنَ ذَلِكَ!

لا + indefinite noun in the accusative without nunation = general negation (نَفْي الْجِنْس) *"there is no ...":*

There is no god but God, Muhammad is the Messenger of God (the Muslim creed).	لا إلَهَ إلا اللهُ مُحَمَّدٌ رَسُولُ اللهِ.

لا is largely lexicalized in this particular function:

nobody	لا أَحَدَ
there is no objection, not bad	لا بَأْسَ بِه
there is no way out = it is necessary	لا بُدَّ (مِنْ)
there is no need	لا دَاعِيَ
he is not guilty	لا ذَنْبَ لَهُ
there is no doubt	لا شَكَّ في
no wonder	لا عَجَبَ
unjustifiable	لا مُبَرِّرَ لَهُ

| unrivalled, matchless | لا مَثيلَ لَهُ |
| there is no escape from it = unavoidable | لا مَفَرَّ مِنْهُ |

لا also resumes a negation already expressed by another negative particle if no new verb is mentioned:

| *"He has not drunk the beer and not the wine."* | لَمْ يَشْرَبِ البِيرَةَ ولا النَّبيذَ |

The double negation is equivalent to *"neither - nor"* in English.

لا + nouns/adjectives = negation or denoting the opposite or antonym:

inhuman	لاإنْسانيٌّ
wireless	لاسلْكيٌّ
the no-system	أَللانظامُ
the unequal globalization	أَلْعَوْلَمَةُ اللامُتَكافِئَة
point of no return	نُقْطَةُ اللاعَوْدَة
the concepts of de-centralism	مَفاهيمُ اللامَرْكَزِيَّة
the inorganic compounds	أَلْمُرَكَّباتُ اللاعُضَوِيَّةُ
the war of absurdity about nothing	حَرْبُ اللامَعْقُول حَوْلَ اللاشَيْءِ

لَمْ + jussive = negation of actions having taken place in the past:

| *He has not done that.* | لَمْ يَفْعَلْ ذَلكَ. |
| *He has not drunk the wine.* | لَمْ يَشْرَبْ* النَّبيذَ. |

*The auxiliary vowel *i-*, instead of *Sukūn*, precedes *Hamzat waṣl.*

Sometimes لَمَّا is used instead of لَمْ, meaning *"not yet"*:

| *They have not united yet.* | لَمَّا يَتَّحِدُوا. |

In a conditional sentence it is not allowed to use لَمَّا . However, it is also used in clauses of time meaning *"when"* or *"after"*, but with a following perfect tense.

لَمْ in connection with the post-positive word بَعْدُ means *"not yet"*:

| *He has not done that yet.* | لَمْ يَفْعَلْ ذَلكَ بَعْدُ. |

لَنْ + subjunctive = (strong) negation of actions taking place in the future:

He will not (or is not to) do that.	لَنْ يَفْعَلَ ذَلِكَ.

The construction with لا سوف + **imperfect form** is possible as well for the purpose of the certainty of negation in the future tense: "*He will (definitely) not write.*"

(I am sure) he will not write.	سَوْفَ لا يكْتُبُ.

مَا + perfect tense = negation of actions having taken place in the past:

He has not done that.	مَا فَعَلَ ذَلِكَ.

مَا + perfect tense is widespread in the dialects. However, in modern literary language, لَمْ + jussive is almost exclusively used. But there are several collocations with مَا, both of verbal and of nominal construction, like e.g. مَا زَالَ (يَشْرَبُ) "*he has not ceased (drinking)*" = "*(he) still (drinks)*", مَا أَنْ ... حَتَّى "*scarcely had he ... when ...; no sooner had he ... than*" a. o.

مَا is the particle in general use for negating the perfect as well as the imperfect tense in colloquial language.

لَيْسَ is the negated copula and means "*not to be*". It is regarded as being in the present tense, although it is conjugated analogously to the perfect tense.

هو لَيْسَ ، هي لَيْسَتْ ، أَنْتَ لَسْتَ ، أَنْتِ لَسْتِ ، أَنا لَسْتُ

هُمْ لَيْسُوا ، هُنَّ لَسْنَ ، أَنْتُم لَسْتُمْ ، أَنْتُنَّ لَسْتُنَّ ، نَحْنُ لَسْنَا

He is not, you are not ... etc.

The affirmative nominal sentence, which does not have a copula, is negated by لَيْسَ . The predicate complement is in the accusative after لَيْسَ :

The house is not big.	لَيْسَ البَيْتُ كَبِيراً.
I am not a student.	لَسْتُ طَالِباً.
They are not diligent men.	لَيْسُوا رِجَالاً مُجْتَهِدِينَ.
There is no teacher in the room. *(lit.: (There) is not in the room a teacher.)*	لَيْسَ في الغُرْفَةِ مُعَلِّمٌ.

مَا (مَا النَّافِيَّة) is also used in the same way as لَيْسَ :

Your journey is not forbidden.	مَا رِحْلَتُكَ مَمْنُوعاً.

He isn't an engineer.	مَا هُوَ بِمُهَنْدِس.
He is neither a student nor a teacher.	مَا هو طَالِباً ولا مُدَرِّسٌ / ولا مُدَرِّساً.

However, مَا in such construction is not followed by the accusative if the sentence contains the exceptive إلّا :

The activity of the government is only a continuous play.	مَا عَمَلُ الْحُكُومَةِ إلّا مَسْرَحِيَّةٌ مُسْتَمِرَّةٌ.

"neither ... nor"

The Arabic equivalent for *"neither ... nor"* is always indicated by the negation. If there are several verbs, each verb is negated by means of لَمْ / لا / لَنْ :

I have neither read nor written.	لَمْ أَقْرَأْ ولَمْ أَكْتُبْ.
Neither do I read nor write.	لا أَقْرَأُ وَلاَ أَكْتُبُ.
I will neither read nor write.	لَنْ أَقْرَأَ وَلَنْ أَكْتُبَ.

If there are several nouns, the first clause is negated by لَمْ / لا / لَنْ as well, followed by ولا / أَوْ / ولَيْسَ :

I wrote neither books nor letters.	لَمْ أَكْتُبْ كُتُباً وَلاَ / أَوْ / وَلَيْسَ رِسائِلَ.
I write neither books nor letters.	لا أَكْتُبُ كُتُباً وَلاَ / أَوْ / وَلَيْسَ رِسائِلَ.
I will write neither books nor letters.	لَنْ أَكْتُبَ كُتُباً وَلاَ / أَوْ / وَلَيْسَ رِسائِلَ.

If the predicates are to be negated, مَا ... وَلاَ or لَيْسَ ... وَلاَ are used:

He is neither handsome nor large / big / tall.	لَيْسَ جَمِيلاً وَلاَ كَبِيراً. / مَا هُوَ جَمِيلاً وَلاَ كَبِيراً.

غَيْرُ + adjective/noun = negation of the following noun/adjective:

not acceptable	غَيْرُ مَقْبُول
not sufficient	غَيْرُ كَاف
unintelligible	غَيْرُ مَعْقُول

غَيْرَ + adverb in the accusative or بِصُورَةٍ غَيْرِ + adverb in the genitive = negation of adverbs:

officially / unofficially	رَسْمِيّاً / غَيْرَ رَسْمِيًّا / بِصُورَةٍ غَيْرِ رَسْمِيٍّ

عَدَم + noun in the genitive = negation of nouns ("*in-, non-*")

instability	عَدَمُ الاسْتِقْرَارِ
non-allied	عَدَمُ الانْحِيازِ
inattention	عَدَمُ الاهْتِمَامِ
non-interference	عَدَمُ التَّدَخُّلِ
intolerance	عَدَمُ التَّسَامُحِ
non-existence	عَدَمُ الوُجُودِ
non-existence	عَدَمُ وُجُودٍ

عَدِيمٌ + noun in the genitive = negation of nouns ("*-less*")

useless	عَدِيمُ الْجَدْوَى
motionless	عَدِيمُ الْحَرَكَةِ
restless	عَدِيمُ الْخُلُقِ
odourless	عَدِيمُ الرَّائِحَةِ
tasteless	عَدِيمُ الطَّعْمِ
colourless	عَدِيمُ اللَّوْنِ

No one, Never, Absolutely not, Not at all, By no means, Nothing

Such expressions are formed as follows:

He never travelled.	لَمْ يُسَافِرْ أَبَدًا.	لم + أَبَدًا
I absolutely do not know him.	لا أَعْرِفُهُ إِطْلاقًا.	لا + إِطْلاقًا
I will not visit him by no means/ not at all.	لا أَزُورُهُ بِأَي حَالٍ (مِنَ الأحْوَال).	لا + بِ(أَيِّ) حَالٍ (مِنَ الأحْوَال)
Nobody is there.	لا أَحَدَ هُنَاكَ.	لا أَحَدَ
He lives from nothing	يَعِيشُ مِنْ لا شَيْءٍ.	لا شَيْء

Without

The Arabic equivalents are as follows:

without conditions	دُونَ شُرُوطٍ	دُونَ
He came in without greeting him.	دَخَلَ دُونَ أَنْ يُرَحِّبَ بِهِ.	دُونَ أَنْ
without any precautions	بِدُونِ أَيَّةِ تَحَفُّظَاتٍ	بِدُونِ (أَنْ)
without mentioning his name	مِنْ دُونِ أَنْ ذَكَرَ اسْمَهُ.	مِنْ دُونِ (أَنْ)
without conditions	بِلاَ شُرُوطٍ	بِلاَ
without conscience	بِغَيْرِ وَعْيٍ	بِغَيْرِ
without knowing	مِنْ غَيْرِ عِلْمٍ	مِنْ غَيْرِ
without thinking	فِي غَيْرِ مَا تَرَوٍّ	فِي غَيْرِ مَا

Not only ... but also

Arabic uses different expressions to render this meaning:

not only the president but also the government	لَيْسَ الرَّئِيسُ فَقَطْ وَإِنَّمَا الْحُكُومَةُ أَيْضًا / كَذَلِكَ	لَيْسَ – فَقَطْ وَإِنَّمَا أَيْضًا /كَذَلِكَ
not only the president but also the government	لَيْسَ الرَّئِيسُ فَقَطْ بَلْ الْحُكُومَةُ أَيْضًا / كَذَلِكَ	لَيْسَ – فَقَطْ بَلْ أَيْضًا/ كَذَلِكَ
not only the president but also the government	لَيْسَ الرَّئِيسُ فَقَطْ بَلْ إِنَّمَا الْحُكُومَةُ أَيْضًا / كَذَلِكَ	لَيْسَ – فَقَطْ بَلْ إِنَّمَا أَيْضًا / كَذَلِكَ
not only he but also the students	لَيْسَ هُوَ فَقَطْ / فَحَسْبْ بَلْ الطُّلاَّبُ أَيْضًا / كَذَلِكَ	لَيْسَ – فَقَطْ / فَحَسْبْ بَلْ أَيْضًا /كَذَلِكَ
He does not only sleep at home but also in the lectures.	لا يَنَامُ فِي الْبَيْتِ فَقَطْ/فَحَسْبْ بَلْ إِنَّمَا فِي الدُّرُوسِ أَيْضًا / كَذَلِكَ.	لا – فَقَطْ / فَحَسْبْ وَإِنَّمَا أَيْضًا /كَذَلِكَ

TYPES OF SENTENCES

Arabic has two basic types of sentences:
Nominal sentences are all types of sentences starting with a noun or a pronoun.
Verbal sentences are all types of sentences starting with a verb.

NOMINAL SENTENCES (أَلْجُمْلَةُ الاِسْمِيَّةُ)

The simple nominal sentence in the Arabic language consists of two parts:

the subject (أَلْمُبْتَدَأُ) and the predicate (أَلْخَبَرُ).

It denotes a general present tense or an action taking place regularly and has no copula (i.e. derivatives of the verb *to be*).

Its subject can be a noun (اِسْمٌ), a personal pronoun (ضَمِيرٌ) or a demonstrative

pronoun (اِسْمُ إِشَارَةٍ). Its predicate can be an adjective (صِفَةٌ), a noun, an adverb

(ظَرْفٌ) or a prepositional phrase.

The following structures occur frequently:
Sentence structure 1 = The subject is a definite noun (اِسْمٌ مُعَرَّفٌ) or a pronoun
and appears at the beginning of the sentence.

a1) Noun + adjective

The house is big.	أَلْبَيْتُ كَبِيرٌ.

a2) Noun + (indef.) noun

The man is a teacher.	أَلرَّجُلُ مُعَلِّمٌ.

a3) Noun + adverb

The teacher is here.	أَلْمُعَلِّمُ هُنَا.

Noun + prepositional phrase

The teacher is in the room.	أَلْمُعَلِّمُ فِي الْغُرْفَةِ.

b1) Personal pronoun + adjective

He/(it) is big.	هُوَ كَبِيرٌ.

b2) Personal pronoun + (indef.) noun

He is a teacher.	هُوَ مُعَلِّمٌ.

Personal pronoun + (def.) noun

He is the teacher.	هُوَ الْمُعَلِّمُ.

b3)   Personal pronoun + adverb

He is here.	هُوَ هُنَا.

Personal pronoun + prepositional phrase

He is in the room.	هُوَ فِي الْغُرْفَةِ.

c1)   Demonstrative pronoun + adjective

This (one) is big.	هَذَا كَبِيرٌ.

c2)   Demonstrative pronoun + (indef.) noun

This (one) is a teacher.	هَذَا مُعَلِّمٌ.

c3)   Demonstrative pronoun + adverb

This (one) is here.	هَذَا هُنَا.

Demonstrative pronoun + prepositional phrase

This (one) is in the room.	هَذَا فِي الْغُرْفَةِ.

A demonstrative pronoun followed by a definite noun may be ambiguous:
هَذَا الْمُعَلِّمُ may be translated as: *This teacher / This is the teacher.*
However, if ambiguity is to be avoided, the personal pronoun must be inserted:

This is the teacher.	هَذَا هُوَ الْمُعَلِّمُ.
This is the teacher (f.).	هَذِه هِيَ الْمُعَلِّمَةُ.

Sentence structure 2 = The subject is an indefinite noun (مُنَكَّرٌ) and therefore appears at the end of the sentence.

Adverb + noun

Here is a teacher.	هُنَا مُعَلِّمٌ.

Prepositional phrase + noun

In the room there is a teacher. (There is a teacher in the room.)	فِي الْغُرْفَةِ مُعَلِّمٌ.

In the 'yes/no' question the word order of the declarative sentence is retained, but the sentence begins with the interrogative particle هَلْ , or rarely أ.

Is he here?	هَلْ هُوَ هُنَا؟ أ هُوَ هُنَا؟
Is this big?	هَلْ هَذَا كَبِيرٌ؟ أ هَذَا كَبِيرٌ؟

In the case of alternative questions the alternative particle أَمْ must be used:

Is this big or small?	هَلْ هَذَا كَبِيرٌ أَمْ صَغِيرٌ؟

The interrogatives مَا for "*what*" and مَنْ for "*who*" act as subjects in *wh*-questions:

What is this?	مَا هَذَا / هَذِه؟
Who is this?	مَنْ هَذَا / هَذِه؟
What is here / there?	مَا هُنَا / هُنَاكَ؟
Who is here / there?	مَنْ هُنَا / هُنَاكَ؟

The interrogative pronoun must be followed by a personal pronoun if the predicate is a noun.

Who is a/(the) teacher?	مَنْ هُوَ (ال) مُعَلِّم؟

The interrogative مَاذَا is used instead of مَا if a verb follows in the question.

Agreement in Gender

There is agreement in gender between the subject and the adjectival predicate.

	feminine subject = feminine form of the adjectival predicate			**masculine subject = masculine form of the adjectival predicate**
a1)	أَلْخِزَانَةُ كَبِيرَةٌ.		*The house is big.* *The cupboard is big.*	أَلْبَيْتُ كَبِيرٌ.
b1)	هِيَ كَبِيرَةٌ.		*He/she/it is big.*	هُوَ كَبِيرٌ.
c1)	هَذِه كَبِيرَةٌ.		*This one is big.*	هَذَا كَبِيرٌ.

Agreement in gender also exists between a pronominal subject and a nominal predicate:

He is a teacher. / She is a teacher.	هُوَ مُعَلِّمٌ. / هِيَ مُعَلِّمَةٌ.

The question whether هَذَا، هَذِه، هُوَ or هِيَ should be chosen as a predicate in a *wh*-question introduced by مَا or مَنْ is determined by the gender of the persons or objects referred to:

What is this?	مَا هَذَا؟
Who is this?	مَنْ هَذَا؟
Who is he?	مَنْ هُوَ؟

when a masculine is asked about,

What is this?	مَا هَذِه؟
Who is this?	مَنْ هَذِه؟
Who is she?	مَنْ هِيَ؟

when a feminine is asked about.

The personal pronoun which has to be inserted into the *wh*-question must be هُوَ
when the predicate of the latter is masculine, and هِيَ when its predicate is
feminine:

What is the name?/ What is his/her name?	مَا هُوَ الاسْمُ؟
What is the problem?	مَا هِيَ الْمُشْكِلَةُ؟
Who is a/(the) teacher?	مَنْ هُوَ (ال)مُعَلِّم؟
Who is a/(the) teacher?	مَنْ هِيَ (ال)مُعَلِّمَة؟

Agreement in gender must also be observed between the verb which introduces a
sentence and the following noun: The masculine form يُوجَدُ and the feminine
form تُوجَدُ may be used for indicating existence, i.e. "*there is / are*":

The teacher is in the room.	(يُوجَدُ) الْمُعَلِّمُ فِي الْغُرْفَة.
The cupboard is in the room.	(تُوجَدُ) الْخِزَانَةُ فِي الْغُرْفَة.
Here is a teacher.	(يُوجَدُ) هُنَا مُعَلِّمٌ.
Here is a cupboard.	(تُوجَدُ) هُنَا خِزَانَةٌ.

In interrogative sentences introduced by مَاذَا, the masculine form يُوجَدُ is used:

| *What is in the room?* | مَاذَا يُوجَدُ فِي الْغُرْفَة؟ |

VERBAL SENTENCES (أَلْجُمْلَةُ الْفِعْلِيَّةُ)

The Arabic verbal sentence either consists of only a **verb** (فِعْلٌ)

He drank / has drunk.	شَرِبَ.
He arrived / has arrived.	وَصَلَ.

(the subject being included in the verb; the independent pronoun may be added for the purpose of emphasis),

or of a **verb + subsequent subject** (أَلْفَاعِلُ)

The man has drunk.	شَرِبَ الرَّجُلُ.
The friend has arrived.	وَصَلَ الصَّدِيقُ.

or of a **verb (+ subject) + object**

He (the man) has drunk juice.	شَرِبَ (الرَّجُلُ) العَصِيرَ.
He (the man) has asked about that.	سَأَلَ (الرَّجُلُ) عَنْ ذَلِكَ.

These sentences can be extended by prepositional phrases and subordinate clauses.

The normal word order in the verbal sentence is verb - subject - object. This word order does not change in the verbal interrogative sentence either. The verb immediately follows the interrogative هَلْ, the interrogative pronoun or interrogative adverb.

The man drank the juice.	شَرِبَ الرَّجُلُ العَصِيرَ.
Did the man drink the juice?	هَلْ شَرِبَ الرَّجُلُ العَصِيرَ؟

The word order verb - object - subject in the declarative and interrogative sentence is used when the subject is the part of the sentence which is emphasized.

Has Muḥammad done that?	هَلْ فَعَلَ ذَلِكَ مُحَمَّدٌ؟
Yes, Muḥammad has done that.	نَعَمْ ، مُحَمَّدٌ فَعَلَ ذَلِكَ.

Here, the word order depends on the sentence accent. The part of the sentence which is emphasized is usually placed at the end, but can be placed at the beginning of the sentence as well.

The word order subject - verb - (object) is possible as well in the declarative sentence. The sentence in anteposition is mostly preceded by a conjunction or particle. (☞ Objective Clauses).

Rules of agreement:

a) If the verb precedes the subject, there is always agreement in gender, but not in number, between them. The sentence is invariably introduced by a singular form of the verb. In this regard, the 3rd p. sg. m. form precedes a masculine singular noun or a plural noun that denotes male persons, the 3rd p. sg. f. form precedes all feminine singular nouns and all other types of plural.

subject:		
m. sg.	*The man arrived.*	وَصَلَ الرَّجُلُ.
pl.	*The men arrived.*	وَصَلَ الرِّجَالُ.
f. sg.	*The girl arrived.*	وَصَلَت الْفَتَاةُ .
pl.	*The girls arrived.*	وَصَلَت الْفَتَيَاتُ .
like f. sg.	*The letters arrived.*	وَصَلَت الرَّسَائِلُ إِلَى . *(pl. of non-human beings)*

The masculine form is also used with some verbs which are construed impersonally or passively - in spite of occurring together with a feminine subject. Moreover, it can be used if the (feminine) subject does not follow the verb immediately.

b) If the verb follows the subject, there is agreement in gender as well as in number between them.

subject:		
m. sg.	*I have heard that the man arrived.*	سَمِعْتُ أَنَّ الرَّجُلَ وَصَلَ.
pl.	*I have heard that the men arrived.*	سَمِعْتُ أَنَّ الرِّجَالَ وَصَلُوا.
f. sg.	*I have heard the girl arrived.*	سَمِعْتُ أَنَّ الْفَتَاةَ وَصَلَتْ.
pl.	*I have heard that the girls arrived.*	سَمِعْتُ أَنَّ الْفَتَيَاتِ وَصَلْنَ.
like f. sg.	*I have heard that the letters arrived.*	سَمِعْتُ أَنَّ الرَّسَائِلَ وَصَلَتْ. *(pl. of non-human beings)*

TENSES AND THE USE OF كَانَ

The Arabic verb has basically two tenses:

A) The **Perfect** (أَلْمَاضِي) denoting a completed act or state which (has) happened in the past (English past and imperfect). The perfect is often preceded by the particle قَدْ or لَقَدْ denoting that the act expressed by the verb is really completed.

B) The **Imperfect** (أَلْمُضَارِعُ) denoting an act or state which happens or will happen. A future meaning can be marked by سَوْفَ or the prefix ـسَ before the verb.

Nevertheless, both basic tenses of the Arabic verb can refer nearly to any tense and time when embedded in certain sentence structures.

The verb كَانَ (imperfect tense يَكُونُ) is a temporal auxiliary verb, which localizes the action (state, event) in a certain tense.

كَانَ IN THE NOMINAL SENTENCE

كَانَ is the copula in the nominal sentence and comparable to the English auxiliary verb *"to be"*.

The nominal predicate (خَبَر كَانَ) is in the accusative after كَانَ. The perfect tense of كَانَ localizes the predicate of the nominal sentence in the past tense.

The student was diligent.	كَانَ الطَّالِبُ مُجْتَهِداً.
Muḥammad was our teacher.	كَانَ مُحَمَّدٌ مُعَلِّمَنَا.

كَانَ is negated by لَمْ + jussive, accordingly لَمْ يَكُنْ

The student was not diligent.	لَمْ يَكُنِ الطَّالِبُ مُجْتَهِداً.

The imperfect tense of كَانَ localizes the predicate of the nominal sentence in the present and future tense.

The student is diligent.	يَكُونُ الطَّالِبُ مُجْتَهِداً.

كَانَ is rare in the imperfect, i.e. يَكُونُ = *"is"*, and then merely serves to emphasize the predicate. In general, affirmative nominal sentences which are regarded as being in the present tense do not have a copula.

However, the use of كَانَ is obligatory when the conjunction أَنْ *"that"* is employed, which is required to be followed by a verb in the subjunctive:

I am afraid that Aḥmad has a new illness.	أَخَافُ أَنْ يَكُونَ أَحْمَدُ مُصَاباً بِمَرَضٍ جَدِيد.

لَا يَكُونُ is negated by لَا + imperfect tense, accordingly لَا يَكُونُ:

I am afraid that Aḥmad is not /will not be the headmaster.	أَخَافُ أَلَّا يَكُونَ أَحْمَدُ مُدِيرَ الْمَدْرَسَةِ.

كَانَ is also rare in the negated imperfect, i.e. لَا يَكُونُ = "*is not*". In general, a nominal sentence in the present tense is negated by لَيْسَ. (☞ Negation)

كَانَ IN THE VERBAL SENTENCE

كَانَ also serves to temporalize the predicate in the verbal sentence. It is used in compound forms which are comparable to certain compound tenses in English:

(1) كَانَ قَدْ فَعَلَ   *he had done* = **Pluperfect Tense** as an expression of anteriority or of a completed action in the past which took place prior to another action in the past:

He had written the letter when his friend came.	كَانَ قَدْ كَتَبَ الرِّسَالَةَ عِنْدَمَا جَاءَ صَدِيقُهُ.

(2) كَانَ يَفْعَلُ   *he was doing, he used to do* = **Continuous Perfect Tense** as an expression of a constant, repeated or customary action which took place in the past:

He used to write letters in those days.	كَانَ يَكْتُبُ رَسَائِلَ فِي تِلْكَ الْأَيَّامِ.

(3) يَكُونُ قَدْ فَعَلَ   *he will have done* = **Future Perfect Tense** as an expression of an action which is expected with certainty to happen in the future:

He will have written the letter before Sunday.	يَكُونُ قَدْ كَتَبَ الرِّسَالَةَ قَبْلَ يَوْمِ الْأَحَدِ.

(4) كَانَ سَيَفْعَلُ   *he would have done* = **Past Conditional** as an expression of an action or state which could have happened in the past:

he would have died	كَانَ سَيَمُوتُ	*he would have become*	كَانَ سَيُصْبِحُ
he would have asked	كَانَ سَيَسْأَلُ	*he would have said*	كَانَ سَيَقُولُ

However, the pattern كَانَ سَيَفْعَلُ is not classical and rather new. It is often followed by a conditional or an adversative sentence. (☞ Unreal Conditional Sentence, Adversative Sentences).

Accordingly, **seven forms** are available in contemporary Arabic to describe temporal relations: the **three simple forms** فَعَلَ (قَدْ، لَقَدْ) "*he has done*", "*he did*" **(1)**, يَفْعَلُ "*he does*", "*he will do*" **(2)** and سَيَفْعَلُ / سَوْفَ يَفْعَلُ "*he will do*" **(3)** and the **four compound forms** which have just been mentioned.

كَانَ/ يَكُونُ is understood in these as a temporal marker, whereas فَعَلَ and يَفْعَلُ have their original value which is neutral with regard to tense. فَعَلَ and يَفْعَلُ are most frequently used. كَانَ يَفْعَلُ is often found both in oral and written usage as well. كَانَ سَيَفْعَلُ and يَكُونُ قَدْ فَعَلَ، كَانَ قَدْ فَعَلَ are less common.

There are difficulties when translating into Arabic, especially regarding the differentiation between the forms فَعَلَ and كَانَ يَفْعَلُ. There are no binding rules which specify that it is obligatory to use فَعَلَ in one case and كَانَ يَفْعَلُ in the other. It occurs fairly often that both forms are used as stylistic variants, so it can be assumed that they are interchangeable. The form كان يَفْعَلُ should be employed if a routine or repeated action from the past is described; it can often be translated by *"he used to ... "*.

SISTERS OF كَانَ

Verbs with similar functions are referred to in Arabic as أَخَوَات كَانَ *"Sisters of kāna"*. The most important verbs of this type are:

to become (in the morning)	أَصْبَحَ / يُصْبِحُ
to be, to become (in the forenoon)	أَضْحَى / يُضْحِي
to be, to become (in the evening)	أَمْسَى / يُمْسِي
to become	بَاتَ / يَبِيتُ
to remain, to continue to be	بَقِيَ / يَبْقَى
to persist, still to be	دَامَ / يَدُومُ / مَا دَامَ
to become	صَارَ / يَصِيرُ
to continue to do sth., to go on doing sth.	ظَلَّ / يَظَلُّ
to do sth. no more or no longer	عَادَ / مَا عَادَ / لَا يَعُودُ / لَمْ يَعُدْ
to be almost, almost, (with negation) scarcely; no sooner ...	كَادَ / يَكَادُ
still, yet; s.o. does not stop to do s.th.	لَمْ يَزَلْ / كَانَ لَا يَزَالُ / لَا يَزَالُ / مَا زَالَ / مَا يَزَالُ
not (to be)	لَيْسَ

SISTERS OF كَادَ

There is, besides بَدَأَ / يَبْدَأُ and إِبْتَدَأَ / يَبْتَدِئُ (*to begin, to start*), a number of other verbs which as auxiliary verbs denote the beginning of an action. They are called *Sisters of* كَادَ (أَخَوَاتُ كَادَ). They are always used in the perfect tense followed by a verb in the imperfect tense if their meaning is "*to begin*" and not their original meaning. كَادَ/عَسَى/أَوْشَكَ can be followed by أَنْ and the subjunctive.

to take	أَخَذَ / يَأْخُذُ
to become	أَصْبَحَ / يُصْبِحُ
to continue	إِسْتَمَرَّ / يَسْتَمِرُّ
to bring into being	أَنْشَأَ / يُنْشِئُ
to be on the point of, to be about	أَوْشَكَ / يُوشِكُ (عَلَى)
to begin, to commence	شَرَعَ / يَشْرَعُ
may be, perhaps, possibly	عَسَى أَنْ
to be on the point of, to be about	كَادَ / يَكَادُ أَنْ
hardly, scarcely, barely, no sooner ...	لَا يَكَادُ / لَمْ يَكَدْ / مَا كَادَ (حَتَّى)

Examples:

The teacher began to lecture.	أَخَذَ الْمُعَلِّمُ يُحَاضِرُ.
The army began to move.	أَصْبَحَ الْجَيْشُ يَتَحَرَّكُ.
He began to work in the institute.	شَرَعَ يَعْمَلُ فِي الْمَعْهَدِ/أَنْ يعمل في المعهد.
Perhaps silence will be in the house.	عَسَى الْهُدُوءُ يَسُودُ الْبَيْتَ/أَنْ يَسُودَ الْبَيْتَ.
He was about to be afraid.	كَادَ يَخَافُ / أَنْ يَخَافَ.
As soon as he entered the house they offered juice.	مَا كَادَ يَدْخُلُ الْبَيْتَ حَتَّى قَدَّمُوا الْعَصِيرَ.

The verbs of letting وَدَعَ / يَدَعُ and تَرَكَ / يَتْرُكُ are used accordingly although their direct object becomes the subject of the second sentence.

He doesn't let us move.	لَا يَدَعُنَا / يَتْرُكُنَا نَتَحَرَّكُ.
He let the student in.	تَرَكَ الطَّالِبَ يَدْخُلُ.

OBJECTIVE CLAUSES

The two conjunctions أَنْ and أَنَّ "*that*" introduce a clause with the syntactic function of an object when being subordinate to a transitive verb, and the function of a subject when being subordinate to an intransitive verb or a verb which is constructed passively or impersonally. The structures of such clauses can be as follows:

a) verbal clause	أَنْ	+ verb/subjunctive	
	أَنْ	+ verb/subjunctive	+ noun (subject, n.)
b1) nominal clauses	أَنَّ	+ noun (subject, a.)	+ noun (predicate)
	أَنَّ	+ noun (subject, a.)	+ adjective (predicate)
	أَنَّ	+ noun (subject, a.)	+ adverb/prepositional phrase (predicate)
	أَنَّ	+ pronoun (subject, a.)	+ noun (predicate)
	أَنَّ	+ pronoun (subject)	+ adjective (predicate)
	أَنَّ	+ pronoun (subject)	+ adverb/prepositional phrase (predicate)
b2) verbal clauses	أَنَّ	+ noun (subject, a.)	+ verb (predicate)
with the subject in anteposition	أَنَّ	+ pronoun (subject)	+ verb (predicate)

Examples of the objective clause:

a)	*Ahmad requested that he travel to London.*	طَلَبَ أَحْمَدُ أَنْ يُسَافِرَ إِلَى لندن.
	Ahmad requested that Muhammad travel to London.	طَلَبَ أَحْمَدُ أَنْ يُسَافِرَ محمَّدٌ إِلَى لندن.
b1)	*I know that Muhammad is a minister.*	أَعْرِفُ أَنَّ محمَّداً وَزِيرٌ.
	I know that Muhammad is ill.	أَعْرِفُ أَنَّ محمَّداً مَرِيضٌ.
	I know that Muhammad is in the room.	أَعْرِفُ أَنَّ محمَّداً فِي الْغُرْفَةِ.
	I know that he is a minister.	أَعْرِفُ أَنَّهُ وَزِيرٌ.
	I know that he is ill.	أَعْرِفُ أَنَّهُ مَرِيضٌ.
	I know that he is in the room.	أَعْرِفُ أَنَّهُ فِي الْغُرْفَةِ.

| b2) | *I know that Muḥammad has travelled/travels to London.* | أَعْرِفُ **أَنَّ** مُحَمَّداً سَافَرَ / يُسَافِرُ إِلَى لندن. |
| | *I know that he travels/has travelled to London.* | أَعْرِفُ **أَنَّهُ** يُسَافِرُ / سَافَرَ إِلَى لندن. |

Examples of the nominal clause (the transitive verbs in the above-mentioned examples are simply replaced by an intransitive verb or a verb which is constructed impersonally or passively):

a)	*He can travel to Berlin.*	يُمْكِنُهُ **أَنْ** يُسَافِرَ إِلَى برلين.
b1)	*It appeared that Muḥammad is ill.*	إتَّضَحَ **أَنَّ** مُحَمَّداً مَرِيضٌ.
b2)	*It appeared that Muḥammad travelled to Berlin yesterday.*	إتَّضَحَ **أَنَّ** مُحَمَّداً سَافَرَ أمس إلى برلين.

Accordingly the two basic structures are:

أَنْ + **subjunctive**	= verbal clause
أَنَّ + **noun or pronoun**	= nominal clause or verbal clause with the subject being in anteposition

Which one of these two structures must be used, depends on the meaning of the verb that precedes أَنْ / أَنَّ .

1. أَنَّ is employed after verbs

of **informing, expressing**:

to assure	أَكَّدَ II
to mention	ذَكَرَ
to announce	أَذَاعَ IV
to declare/state/announce	صَرَّحَ (بِ) II
to announce	أَعْلَنَ IV

of **knowing or believing**:

to know	عَرَفَ
to believe, to assume/to presume	اعْتَقَدَ VIII
to find out/to learn	عَلِمَ
to appear/to come to light, to become clear	اتَّضَحَ VIII

of **(sensory) perception**:

to grasp/to comprehend, to perceive/to realize	IV أَدْرَكَ
to see; to think	رَأَى
to hear	سَمِعَ
to notice/to remark etc.	III لاحَظَ

أَنَّ is frequently combined with prepositions, thus with لِ = لِأَنَّ "*because*", كَ = كَأَنَّ

"*as if*", مَعَ = مَعَ أَنَّ "*although*" etc. (☞ Adversative, Restrictive and Concessive

Sentences)

2. أَنْ is employed after the following **modal auxiliary verbs**:

it ought to be/should be (only the imperfect tense is common: (كان ينبغي *or* يَنْـــبَغِي)	VII اِنْبَغَى
to want	IV أَرَادَ
to be allowed/permitted (to do sth.)	(سُمِحَ لَهُ)
to be able (to do sth.)	X اِسْتَطَاعَ
to be possible, feasible (for sb.), to be able to	IV أَمْكَنَ
must, to have to (the imperfect tense is nearly exclusively in use: (كان يجب *or* يَجِبُ)	وَجَبَ (عَلَى)

and after verbs depicting **demanding, ordering, suggesting, wishing, hoping,
doubting, fearing, or an emotion** a.o. as well:

to hope (for)		أَمَلَ
to be possible or likely	*(mostly passive)*	VIII اِحْتَمَلَ / يُحْتَمَلُ
to fear		خَافَ
to wish		رَجَا
to make happy		سَرَّ
to request, to call (upon sb.)		طَلَبَ
to suggest		VIII اِقْتَرَحَ

After some verbs, أَنْ or أَنَّ can be employed alternatively, depending on whether the predicate expresses a statement or an action, the execution of which is in the future and which is wished or expected, but is not quite certain:

He wrote to me that the delegation arrived yesterday.	كَتَبَ لِي أَنَّ الْوَفْدَ وَصَلَ أَمْسِ.
He wrote to me that the delegation arrives tomorrow.	كَتَبَ لِي أَنَّ الْوَفْدَ سَيَصِلُ غَدًا.
He wrote to me that the delegation would (or was (due) to) arrive tomorrow.	كَتَبَ لِي أَنْ سَيَصِلَ الْوَفْدُ غَدًا.

If we except بَعْدَ أَنْ (and مُنْذُ أَنْ) + perfect tense, rarely will a verb in the perfect tense follow أَنْ. It occurs in sentences which announce a statement that is located at the beginning or at the end of a speech. Arabic بأَنْ + perfect tense = English "... by ... -ing"

He began his election campaign by describing ...	... بَدَأَ حَمْلَتَهُ الاِنْتِخَابِيَّة بِأَنْ وَصَفَ ...
He concluded his speech by proclaiming ...	... اِخْتَتَمَ كَلِمَتَهُ بِأَنْ أَعْلَنَ ...
He concluded his speech by requesting Dr. ... (to do sth.) ...	... أَنْهَى كَلِمَتَهُ بِأَنْ طَلَبَ مِن الدُّكْتُـور ...

Thus also after the verb سَبَقَ "to precede":

He had already said before ...	... لَقَدْ سَبَقَ لَهُ أَنْ قَالَ ...

أَنْ preceded by لا is contracted to أَلاَّ:

I am afraid that he will not reach his goal.	أَخْشَى أَلاَّ يَصِلَ إِلَى هَدَفِه.

Impersonal Expressions with أَنَّ :

It is very likely that	أَغْلَبُ / أَكْثَرُ الظَّنِّ أَنَّ
The truth is that	أَلْحَقُّ / الْحَقِيقَةُ أَنَّ
It is true that	صَحِيحٌ أَنَّ
There is no doubt that	لا شَكَّ أَنَّ
The reality is that	أَلْوَاقِعُ أَنَّ
It is obvious that	يَتَّضِحُ أَنَّ

It is worth mentioning that		يَسْتَحِقُّ الذِّكْرُ أَنَّ

Impersonal Expressions with أَنْ :

He has to	عَلَيْهِ أَنْ
It is necessary that	لا بُدَّ أَنْ
It is not to be singled out that	لا يُسْتَبْعَدُ أَنْ
He has a right to, is entitled to	لَهُ أَنْ
He has to	يَجِبُ أَنْ
It is probable that	يُحْتَمَلُ أَنْ
It is hoped	يُرْجَى أَنْ
It is reported	يُقَالُ أَنْ
It is enough to	يَكْفِي أَنْ
It is possible that	يُمْكِنُ أَنْ
It is desirable, necessary that	يَنْبَغِي أَنْ
It is expected that	يُنْتَظَرُ أَنْ

(☞ Participles as Nominal Predicate مِنَ ال...)

WORD ORDER

The normal word order in the verbal sentence is verb - subject. If the subject is emphasized in the main clause, it is placed in front of the verb, and the particle إِنَّ is set in front of the subject. Consequently, the word order is:

إِنَّ + **subject** + **verb** + **(object)**.

Moreover, this word order occurs without employing the particle إِنَّ if the main clause is introduced by a conjunction (فَ، وَ).

The word order subject - verb - without a particle in anteposition - is typical in headlines in newspapers.

The particle إِنَّ causes the subject to be in the accusative.

(They have told us:) The delegation visited the city of London yesterday.	(قَالُوا لَنَا) إِنَّ الوَفْدَ زَارَ مَدِينَةَ لندن أَمْس.

The particle إِنَّ is used after the verb قَالَ "*to tell, to say*" to introduce direct speech. Since "*to tell, to say*" is mostly followed by indirect speech in English, the illustrative sentence is translated best by: "*They have told us that the Arab delegation ...*" When reading unvocalized texts, it must be observed that one does not read the إِنَّ after قَالَ as أَنَّ ("*that*").

A personal pronoun instead of a noun can follow إِنَّ ; its affixed form is used, which is also the case after أَنَّ :

pl.	sg.
إِنَّهم، إِنَّهُنَّ، إِنَّكُمَا، إِنَّكم، إِنَّكُنَّ، إِنَّنا / إِنَّا	إِنَّه، إِنَّها، إِنَّهُمَا، إِنَّكَ، إِنَّكِ، إِنَّنِي/إِنِّي

The object in the shape of a noun can also be replaced by a clause. Such a soc. objective clause (☞ Objective Clauses) is often introduced by the conjunction أَنَّ "*that*", after which the noun is in the accusative:

The friend has written that Muhammad has arrived in Berlin.	كَتَبَ الصَّدِيقُ أَنَّ مُحَمَّداً وَصَلَ إِلَى برلين.
I have heard that the delegation arrived yesterday.	سَمِعْتُ أَنَّ الْوَفْدَ وَصَلَ أَمْس.

The word order in the objective clause invariably is **subject - verb - (object)** which is introduced by أَنَّ. Consequently, a verb **never** occurs immediately after أَنَّ.

	subordinate clause				main clause	
لندن.	إلى	وَصَلَ	مُحَمَّداً	أَنَّ	الصَّدِيقُ	كَتَبَ
		verb	subject			
objective clause					subject	verb
أَمْسِ.		وَصَلَ	الْوَفْدَ	أَنَّ	ــــتُ	سَمِعْــ
		verb	subject			
objective clause					(subject +)	verb

The function of an objective clause can also be fulfilled by a nominal sentence. The normal word order does not change. The subject follows أَنَّ in the accusative, as is the case in the verbal sentence. The predicate remains in the nominative:

I have heard that Muḥammad is ill.	سَمِعْتُ أَنَّ مُحَمَّداً مَرِيضٌ.

TOPIC AND COMMENT (أَلْجُمْلَةُ ذَاتُ الْوَجْهَيْن)

a. Anteposition of the Object

The normal word order in the Arabic language is verb - subject - object. The anteposition of the subject, i.e. the word order subject - verb - object, is possible.

Another construction frequently used both in Standard Arabic and, more importantly, in oral usage renders the anteposition of any object possible (أَلْجُمْلَةُ ذَاتُ الْوَجْهَيْن "*the double-sided sentence*"). This useful stylistic pattern allows one to emphasize a special topic.

In such constructions, the object in the nominative case is placed first in the sentence followed by the comment in the form of a statement or a question. The corresponding affixed pronoun is inserted in the vacant place of the object of the original sentence. This allows one to emphasize any topic and makes a complex sentence clearer. The succession of two nouns (subject and object) is avoided. There is a pause after the part of the sentence which is placed in front when spoken. For such sentences, English often achieves the emphasis with the passive.

The prime minister welcomes the Arab guests (or passive: the Arab guests are welcomed ...).	يُرَحِّبُ رَئِيسُ الْوُزَرَاءِ بِالضُّيُوفِ الْعَرَبِ. ⇦ الضُّيُوفُ الْعَرَبُ يُرَحِّبُ بِهِمْ رَئِيسُ الْوُزَرَاءِ.
The politicians support the relations with this country. *The relations with this country are supported by the politicians.*	يُؤَيِّدُ السِّيَاسِيُّونَ الْعَلَاقَاتِ مَعَ هَذَا الْبَلَدِ. ⇦ أَلْعَلَاقَاتُ مَعَ هَذَا الْبَلَدِ يُؤَيِّدُهَا السِّيَاسِيُّونَ.
I accomplished my tasks.	أَنْجَزْتُ وَاجِبَاتِي. ⇦ وَاجِبَاتِي أَنْجَزْتُهَا.

How much I love my mother!	كَمْ أُحِبُّ أُمِّي. ⇦ أُمِّي كَمْ أُحِبُّهَا.
Have you seen this film?	هَلْ شَاهَدتَّ هَذَا الْفِلْمَ؟ ⇦ هَذَا الْفِلْمُ هَلْ شَاهَدتَّهُ؟

The position of the object at the beginning of the sentence is also known in Indo-European languages. Constructions of this nature are known by *Nominativus absolutus* and *Nominativus* or *Casus pendens*. Topic and comment is also found in colloquial English: *"Tom, he's met the teacher."*

b. Anteposition of the 2nd Term of a Genitive Construction

The 2nd term of a genitive construction can be placed at the beginning of the sentence as well. The corresponding affixed pronoun replaces it again.

The visit of the delegation begins on Wednesday.	تَبْدَأُ زِيَارَةُ الْوَفْدِ يَوْمَ الْأَرْبِعَاءِ. ⇦ أَلْوَفْدُ تَبْدَأُ زِيَارَتُهُ يَوْمَ الْأَرْبِعَاءِ.
The new models have fixed prices. (lit.: the prices of the new models are fixed).	أَسْعَارُ الْمُودِيلاَتِ الْجَدِيدَةِ مُحَدَّدَةٌ. ⇦ أَلْمُودِيلاَتُ الْجَدِيدَةُ أَسْعَارُهَا مُحَدَّدَةٌ.
The picture has beautiful colours. (lit.: the colours of the picture are beautiful).	أَلْوَانُ الصُّورَةِ جَمِيلَةٌ. ⇦ أَلصُّورَةُ أَلْوَانُهَا جَمِيلَةٌ.

This possibility of detaching a noun from a complex sentence is also given with regard to other groups of words (above all prepositional phrases):

I have bought many books in (from) this bookstore.	اشْتَرَيْتُ مِنْ هَذِهِ الْمَكْتَبَةِ كُتُبًا كَثِيرَةً. ⇦ هَذِهِ الْمَكْتَبَةُ اشْتَرَيْتُ مِنْهَا كُتُبًا كَثِيرَةً.
I have met only three of these students.	قَابَلْتُ ثَلاَثَةً مِنْ هَؤُلاَءِ الطُّلاَّبِ فَقَطْ. ⇦ هَؤُلاَءِ الطُّلاَّبُ قَابَلْتُ ثَلاَثَةً مِنْهُمْ فَقَطْ.

In such sentences, إِنَّ can be used to put more emphasis on the topic. A following verb in the perfect tense is mostly preceded by قَدْ.

I entered this house two years ago.	إِنَّ هَذَا الْبَيْتَ قَدْ دَخَلْتُهُ قَبْلَ سَنَتَيْنِ.
I saw this plan in the university.	إِنَّ هَذِهِ الْخُطَّةَ قَدْ رَأَيْتُهَا فِي الْجَامِعَةِ.
This program will be realized in future.	إِنَّ هَذَا الْبَرْنَامَجَ سَيُحَقَّقُ فِي الْمُسْتَقْبَلِ.

c. If certain parts of an interrogative sentence are placed in front, it comes to the word order noun - interrogative particle or interrogative adverb - predicate:

Where did you buy this book from?	مِنْ أَيْنَ اشْتَرَيْتَ هَذَا الْكِتَابَ؟
	⇦ هَذَا الْكِتَابُ مِنْ أَيْنَ اشْتَرَيْتَهُ؟

If the subject of the interrogative sentence is emphasized by being placed in front, the pronoun which refers to it appears in the nominal sentence in the form of the independent pronoun:

Are the prices fixed?	هَلِ الْأَسْعَارُ مُحَدَّدَةٌ؟
	⇦ أَلْأَسْعَارُ هَلْ هِيَ مُحَدَّدَةٌ؟

In the verbal sentence it is completely missing:

When did the Sudanese delegation arrive at the airport?	مَتَى وَصَلَ الْوَفْدُ السُّودَانِيُّ إِلَى الْمَطَارِ؟
	⇦ أَلْوَفْدُ السُّودَانِيُّ مَتَى وَصَلَ إِلَى الْمَطَارِ؟

d) The particle ف after the introducing أَمَّا is also a means to emphasize a certain

topic (☞ The Particle ف)

As for the conference, it is extremely boring.	أَمَّا الْمُؤْتَمَرُ فَهُوَ مُمِلٌّ لِلْغَايَةِ.

ف and و can also precede the collocations used to emphasize a certain topic:

As for the solution, ...	وَ/ فَأَمَّا الْحَلُّ فَقَالَ ...
As far as the budget is concerned, ...	وَ/ فَفِيمَا يَتَعَلَّقُ بِالْمِيزَانِيَّةِ ف ...
As for the book, ...	وَ/ فَفِيمَا يَخُصُّ الْكِتَابَ ف ...

CONDITIONAL SENTENCES (أَلْجُمَلُ الشَّرْطِيَّةُ)

Arabic makes the distinction between real and unreal conditions. The construction of the conditional sentence consists of the conditional clause proper = conditional (أَلشَّرْطُ) and of the result clause (أَلْجَوَابُ) as the logical consequence of the condition.

The Real Conditional Sentence

In the real conditional sentence the condition is regarded as actually given or as possible with respect to its feasibility. The most common Arabic conjunction employed for introducing such a conditional sentence is إِذَا *"if"*.
The construction is as follows:

(فَعَلَ stands for the perfect tense, يَفْعَلُ for the imperfect tense)

English		Arabic		
conditional	result clause	result clause	conditional	
a) present	present	فَعَلَ	فَعَلَ	إِذَا
b) present	present	يَفْعَلُ	فَعَلَ	إِذَا
c) present	perfect	يَكُونُ قَدْ فَعَلَ	فَعَلَ	إِذَا
d) present	future	فَسَوْفَ يَفْعَلُ	فَعَلَ	إِذَا
e) present	future	فَسَيَفْعَلُ	فَعَلَ	إِذَا
f) present	imperative	فَافْعَلْ	فَعَلَ	إِذَا

Accordingly, the Arabic perfect tense always has a present function in these conditional sentences.

a)	*If you give me the Arabic book, I will give you my book.*	إِذَا أَعْطَيْتَنِي الْكِتَابَ الْعَرَبِيَّ أَعْطَيْتُكَ كِتَابِي.
b)	~	إِذَا أَعْطَيْتَنِي الْكِتَابَ الْعَرَبِيَّ أُعْطِيكَ كِتَابِي.
c)	*If this news is true, the delegation left yesterday.*	إِذَا صَحَّ هَذَا الْخَبَرُ يَكُونُ الْوَفْدُ قَدْ غَادَرَ أَمْسِ.
d)	*If this news is true, the delegation will leave tomorrow.*	إِذَا صَحَّ هَذَا الْخَبَرُ فَسَوْفَ يُغَادِرُ الْوَفْدُ غَدًا.
e)	~	إِذَا صَحَّ هَذَا الْخَبَرُ فَسَيُغَادِرُ الْوَفْدُ الْقَاهِرَةَ غَدًا.
f)	*If you meet them, inform them immediately.*	إِذَا قَابَلْتَهُمْ فَأَطْلِعْهُمْ فَوْرًا.

The perfect tense (فَعَلَ) following إذَا may also be replaced by كَانَ + imperfect

tense (كَانَ يَفْعَلُ). Its actual function as present tense is preserved. This

construction particularly occurs with modal auxiliary verbs.

If you want to travel, speak with the director.	إذَا كُنْتَ تُرِيدُ أَنْ تُسَافِرَ فَاحْكِ مَعَ الْمُدِيرِ.

كَانَ following إذَا , with an actual function as present tense, is also employed in

the nominal conditional.

If Muḥammad is present, I will ask him.	إذَا كَانَ مُحَمَّدٌ مَوْجُودًا أَسْأَلُهُ.

فَ , if employed for the purpose of introducing a result clause, precedes قَدْ, لَنْ

and لَيْسَ as well as nominal sentences. This is in addition to its preceding سَ and

سَوْفَ and the imperative:

If the car is there, we will travel immediately, of course. (lit.: it is natural that we ...).	إذَا كَانَتِ السَّيَّارَةُ مَوْجُودةً فَمِنَ الطَّبِيعِيِّ أَنْ نُسَافِرَ فَوْراً.
If I complete my work by Sunday, I will have fulfilled my duty.	إذَا أَنْهَيْتُ عَمَلِي حَتَّى يَوْمِ الأَحَدِ فَقَدْ أَنْجَزْتُ وَاجِبِي.
If you visit it once, you will never forget it.	إذَا زُرْتَهَا مَرَّةً فَلَنْ تَنْسَاهَا أَبَداً.

The result clause may also be a verbal clause preceded by فَإِنَّ + subject.

If you give me your book, I will give you my book.	إذَا أَعْطَيْتَنِي كِتَابَكَ فَإِنَّنِي أُعْطِيكَ كِتَابِي.

Negation: The perfect tense following إذَا is replaced by لَمْ + jussive. The result

clause is negated either by لَمْ + jussive or by لَا, لَنْ or لَيْسَ .

If you do not give me your book, I will not give you my book.	إذَا لَمْ تُعْطِنِي كِتَابَكَ فَلَمْ أُعْطِكَ/لَا أُعْطِيكَ كِتَابِي.
If you do not give me your book, I will (surely) not give you my book.	إذَا لَمْ تُعْطِنِي كِتَابَكَ فَلَنْ أُعْطِيَكَ/ فَسَوْفَ لَا أُعْطِيكَ كِتَابِي.

If كَانَ يَفْعَلُ occurs in the conditional, its negation is not expressed by كَانَ being

negated, but by the imperfect tense negated by لَا (لَا يَفْعَلُ).

If you do not want to travel, discuss (the matter) with the director.	إِذَا كُنْتَ لَا تُرِيدُ أَنْ تُسَافِرَ فَاحْكِ مَعَ الْمُدِيرِ .

A condition relating to the past naturally occurs rather seldom. The Arabic construction then requires the past perfect (كَانَ قَدْ فَعَلَ) after إِذَا . Its negation is not expressed by كَانَ being negated, but by the verb form فَعَلَ being negated by means of لَمْ (لَمْ يَفْعَلْ).

If you have bought this car, you have chosen a good model.	إِذَا كُنْتَ قَد اشْتَرَيْتَ هَذِهِ السَّيَّارَةَ فَقَد اخْتَرْتَ / تَكُونُ قَد اخْتَرْتَ مُودِيلاً جَيِّداً .
If you have not read this book yet, you do not know the problems.	إِذَا كُنْتَ لَمْ تَقْرَأْ هَذَا الْكِتَابَ بَعْدُ فَإِنَّكَ لَا تَعْرِفُ الْقَضَايَا .

The clause introduced by إِذَا and the result clause are interchangeable. The conditional then follows the result clause, which formally turns into a dependent main clause. The basic rule that the verb after إِذَا must be in the perfect tense remains unaffected. There are no particular rules for the construction of the main clause regarding structure or tense.

I (will) (surely) give you my book if you give me your book.	(إِنَّنِي،سَوْفَ) أُعْطِيكَ كِتَابِي إِذَا أَعْطَيْتَنِي كِتَابَكَ .
Inform them immediately if (= in case) you meet them!	أَطْلِعْهُمْ فَوْراً إِذَا قَابَلْتَهُمْ .
You will be able to read the news-papers if you learn every day.	سَتَسْتَطِيعُ أَنْ تَقْرَأَ الْجَرَائِدَ إِذَا كُنْتَ تَتَعَلَّمُ كُلَّ يَوْمٍ .

Another conjunction employed for the introduction of a real conditional sentence is إِنْ *"if"*. However, it is used far less than إِذَا in modern Arabic,. The perfect tense or the jussive is employed in the conditional, i.e. after إِنْ , and likewise in the result clause. لَمْ must be used to negate such sentences. The rules mentioned regarding إِذَا , also apply to the introduction of the result clause by means of فَ, and to interchangeability.

If you give me your book, I will give you my book.	إِنْ أَعْطَيْتَنِي / تُعْطِنِي كِتَابَكَ فَأُعْطِيكَ/ فَأُعْطِكَ كِتَابِي .
If you do not give me your book, I will not give you my book (either).	إِنْ لَمْ تُعْطِنِي كِتَابَكَ فَلَمْ أُعْطِكَ كِتَابِي .

If you meet them, inform them!	إنْ قَابَلْتَهُمْ فَاطْلِعْهُمْ.
I will give you the book if Muhammad does not ask for it.	سَأُعْطِيكَ الْكِتَابَ إنْ لَمْ يَطْلُبْهُ مُحَمَّدٌ.

"If not/otherwise/or else" is rendered by وَإِلَّا (وَإِنْ لا):

Let us go otherwise we shall be late.	لِنَذْهَبْ وَإِلَّا فَتَأَخَّرْنَا / فَسَوْفَ نَتَأَخَّر.

إذَا and إنْ being equivalent to the English conjunctions *"if, whether"* are also used

for introducing indirect questions. Furthermore, هَلْ إذَا and مَا إذَا and also فِيمَا or

عَمَّا إذَا are available after سَأَلَ and فَكَّرَ

We do not know whether he was there.	لا نَعْرِفُ إذَا / مَا إذَا / إنْ / هَلْ كَانَ هُنَاكَ.
He asked them if he was there.	سَأَلَهُمْ عَمَّا إذَا كَانَ هُنَاكَ.
He considered if she was there.	فَكَّرَ فِيمَا إذَا كَانَتْ مَوْجُودَةً.

عَلَى أَنْ and في حَالَة/ بِشَرْطِ أَنْ / عَلَى شَرْطِ أَنْ / شَرِيطَةَ أَنْ in the sense of *"provided*

(that), on the condition that, in the event of, in case of", followed by the imperfect
tense (subjunctive), are also employed to form real conditional sentences.

I will travel tomorrow, provided the symposium begins immediately.	سَأُسَافِرُ غَداً بِشَرْطِ أَنْ / عَلَى شَرْطِ أَنْ / شَرِيطَةَ أَنْ / عَلَى أَنْ تَبْدَأَ النَّدْوَةُ فَوْراً.
in case of his absence	في حَالَةِ غِيَابِه

Besides إذَا and إنْ , there are several other words, mostly interrogative pronouns

or words derived from interrogative adverbs, which can introduce a conditional
sentence, e.g.

in the sense of "where(so)ever"	حَيْثُمَا
in the sense of "how(so)ever"	كَيْفَمَا
in the sense of "if something"	مَا
in the sense of "if someone"	مَنْ
in the sense of "what(so)ever"	مَهْمَا

مَنْ and مَا have their English equivalents in the interrogative pronouns "*who*" and "*what*", which contain a conditional sense as well (*he who [= if someone] seeks, finds*).

The Unreal Conditional Sentence (اِمْتِنَاعُ الشَّرْطِ)

Sentences in which the condition has not been realized or cannot be realized are called unreal conditional sentences. In Arabic, the unreal conditional sentence is introduced by means of the conjunction لَوْ . Both, in the conditional and in the result clause, the perfect tense is mostly used to express unreal conditions in the present and future tense. The result clause may be introduced by the emphasizing particle لَ :

If you gave me this book, I would read it.	لَوْ أَعْطَيْتَنِي هَذَا الْكِتَابَ لَقَرَأْتُهُ.
If you walked in/through the city now, you would know its beauty.	لَوْ سِرْتَ الآنَ فِي الْمَدِينَةِ لَعَرَفْتَ جَمَالَها.

Unlike in the real conditional sentence, the perfect tense following the conjunction لَوْ may also express the past tense in the unreal conditional sentence.

If they had used force, the conference would have failed.	لَوِ اسْتَخْدَمُوا الْعُنْفَ لَفَشِلَ الْمُؤْتَمَرُ.

The context must decide which tense is represented by the perfect tense in each particular case. The same applies to constructions with كَانَ + imperfect tense. However, in the conditional or in the result clause, the past perfect (كَانَ قَدْ فَعَلَ) may be employed in order to clarify the temporal relation.

Nowadays, the past conditional كَانَ سَيَفْعَلُ "*would have done*" is used in such sentences:

He would have died if he had known the reason.	كَانَ سَيَمُوتُ لَوْ عَلِمَ السَّبَبَ.

The conditional and the result clause are interchangeable, just as is the case in the real conditional sentence. The result clause turns into an independent main clause again. In this case, the verb does not necessarily take on the perfect tense.

I would give him my book if he gave (or had given) me his book.	إِنَّنِي سَأُعْطِيهِ كِتَابِي لَوْ أَعْطَانِي كِتَابَهُ.

The unreal conditional sentence may be turned into a nominal construction by the conjunction أَنَّ being placed behind لَوْ . The former is followed by the noun, then by the verb.

If Muḥammad had visited me, I would have given him the book.	لَوْ أَنَّ مُحَمَّداً زَارَنِي لأَعْطَيْتُهُ الْكِتَابَ / لَكُنْتُ قَدْ أَعْطَيْتُهُ الْكِتَابَ.
If Muḥammad visited me tomorrow, I would give him the book.	لَوْ أَنَّ مُحَمَّداً سَيَزُورُنِي غَداً لأَعْطَيْتُهُ الْكِتَابَ.

The unreal conditional sentence is negated by means of لَمْ in the conditional, and by لَمْ or by مَا emphasized by the particle (لَمَّا = لَ) in the result clause.

If the plane had not been late, it would (not) have arrived in Cairo at 6 o'clock.	لَوْ لَمْ تَتَأَخَّرِ الطَّائِرَةُ لَوَصَلَتْ (لَمَا وَصَلَتْ) إلَى الْقَاهِرَة فِي السَّاعَة السَّادِسَة.
If Muḥammad had not come to me yesterday, I would not have been able to give him the book.	لَوْ لَمْ يَأْتِ مُحَمَّدٌ إلَيَّ أَمْسِ / لَوْ أَنَّ مُحَمَّداً لَمْ يَأْتِ إلَيَّ أَمْسِ لَمَا اسْتَطَعْتُ / لَمَا كُنْتُ أَسْتَطِيعُ أَنْ أُعْطِيَهُ الْكِتَابَ.

لَوْ followed by لا (= لَوْلا) without a verb means "*if it were not or had not been for ...*".

If it had not been for Muḥammad / him, I would not have completed the work; if it were not for Muḥammad / him, I would not complete the work.	لَوْلا مُحَمَّدٌ / لَوْلاهُ لَمَا أَنْهَيْتُ الْعَمَلَ.

Sentences with كَمَا لَوْ كَانَ / كَمَا لَوْ أَنَّ

Arabic makes use of كَمَا لَوْ كَانَ / كَمَا لَوْ أَنَّ "*as if*" in unreal equations.

He treated him as if he were a medical doctor.	عَالَجَهُ **كَمَا لَوْ كَانَ** طَبِيباً.
He looked at them as if he met them before this day.	نَظَرَ إِلَيْهِمْ **كَمَا لَوْ كَانَ** قَدِ الْتَقَى بِهِمْ قَبْلَ هذا الْيَوْمِ.
The ministers vote as if the president was ruling them.	وَيُصَوِّتُ الْوُزَرَاءُ **كَمَا لَوْ كَانَ** الرَّئِيسُ يُسَيْطِرُ عَلَيْهِمْ.
He speaks about him as if he were a speaking living being.	وَيَتَحَدَّثُ عَنْهُ **كَمَا لَوْ كَانَ** كَائِناً حَيّاً يَنْطُقُ.
It seemed as if the children were the main concern.	وَكَانَ يَبْدُو **كَمَا لَوْ أَنَّ** الأَطْفَالَ هُمُ الشُّغْلُ الشَّاغِلُ.

We find لَوْ also in combination with (يَا) حَبَّذَا meaning "*how nice it would be if*" followed by a verb in the perfect or imperfect tense:

How nice it would be if he met them/should meet them.	(يَا) حَبَّذَا لَوِ اجْتَمَعَ / يَجْتَمِعُ بِهِمْ.
How nice it would be if he was new.	(يَا) حَبَّذَا لَوِ يَكُونُ جَدِيداً.

Nowadays, we find لَوْ followed by يَكُونُ denoting what should take place in the future:

If only he would be his successor.	لَوْ يَكُونُ خَلِيفَتُهُ.
I wished there were a new resolution.	أَتَمَنَّى لَوْ يَكُونُ هُنَاكَ قَرَارٌ جَدِيدٌ.

EXCEPTIVE SENTENCES (أَلْمُسْتَثْنَى)

Exceptive sentences in Arabic are sentences in which almost always a negative statement relating to the subject, object or predicate is restricted.

The most common Arabic exceptive particle is إِلَّا (< إِنْ لَا). The English translation is *"except for/that, but"* or *"only"*. Other exceptive particles are غَيْرَ, سِوَى, عَدَا, مَا عَدَا, فِيمَا عَدَا, خَلَا and حَاشَا. However, خَلَا and حَاشَا are no longer used in contemporary Arabic.

In the negative exceptive, the noun excepted by إِلَّا is in the same case as the restricted noun:

No Arab friends attended the event except the Egyptian students; of the Arab friends only the Egyptian students came (lit.: did not come ... but ...).	لَمْ يَحْضُرِ الأَصْدِقَاءُ الْعَرَبُ إِلَى الْحَفْلَةِ إِلَّا الطُّلَابُ الْمِصْرِيُّونَ.

The nominative follows إِلَّا, because the restricted noun (أَلْأَصْدِقَاء), as a subject of لَمْ يَحْضُرْ, takes on the nominative, too.

I do not fear anything but cold weather; I only fear cold weather.	لَا أَخَافُ مِنْ أَيِّ شَيْءٍ إِلَّا (مِنَ) الطَّقْسِ الْبَارِدِ.

The word أَلطَّقْس takes on the genitive after the preposition مِن, which does not need to be repeated.

Quite often, the restricted nouns are not mentioned at all. The excepted noun is the logical complement to the whole sentence, which makes it understandable.

Only the Egyptian students attended the event (lit.: did not attend the event but ...).	لَمْ يَحْضُرِ الْحَفْلَةَ إِلَّا الطُّلَابُ الْمِصْرِيُّونَ.

The nominative follows إِلَّا; the government of يَحْضُرُ affects the logical complement الطُّلَّابُ.

I will only buy the two Arabic books.	لَا أَشْتَرِي إِلَّا الْكِتَابَيْنِ الْعَرَبِيَّيْنِ.

The accusative follows إِلَّا; the government of اِشْتَرَى affects the logical complement الْكِتَابَيْنِ.

I am only afraid of the cold weather.	لَا أَخَافُ إِلَّا مِنَ الطَّقْسِ الْبَارِدِ.

The government of خَافَ by means of مِن is preserved and affects the logical complement الطَّقْسِ.

إلَّا preceded by the negation مَا and the following pronoun هُوَ/هِيَ also occurs in a nominal construction:

These words are only (= nothing but) an expression of his fear.	هَذِهِ الْكَلِمَاتُ مَا هِيَ إِلَّا تَعْبِيرٌ عَنْ خَوْفِه.

A pronoun, a prepositional phrase or a whole sentence or clause may also follow إلَّا , instead of a noun.

Pronoun

Only he knows that.	لَا يَعْرِفُ ذَلِكَ إِلَّا هُوَ.

Prepositional phrase

We are only superior to them because of our knowledge.	لَا نَتَفَوَّقُ عَلَيْهِمْ إِلَّا بِسَبَبِ مَعْرِفَتِنَا.
No contacts with them except within the narrowest limits.	لَا اتِّصَالَاتِ مَعَهُمْ إِلَّا فِي أَضْيَقِ الْحُدُودِ.

إلَّا + temporal prepositional phrase is equivalent to the English "*only, not until*":

He returned only after 2 days.	لَمْ يَرْجِعْ إِلَّا بَعْدَ يَوْمَيْنِ.

Sentences/Clauses
a) Objective clause

I only want to say ...	لَا أُرِيدُ إِلَّا أَنْ أَقُولَ ...

b) Conditional sentence

You will only complete the work if you work every day.	لَنْ تُنْهِيَ الْعَمَلَ إِلَّا إِذَا عَمِلْتَ كُلَّ يَوْمٍ.

c) Temporal clause

He did not inform them about his illness until he had (already) overcome it.	لَمْ يُطْلِعْهُمْ عَلَى مَرَضِهِ إِلَّا بَعْدَ أَنْ تَغَلَّبَ عَلَيْهِ.
We were not informed of this visit until the delegation arrived.	لَمْ نَعْلَمْ بِهَذِهِ الزِّيَارَةِ إِلَّا عِنْدَمَا وَصَلَ الْوَفْدُ.

A restrictive construction with إلَّا is also possible with other types of subordinate clauses.

The positive exceptive is less common. The excepted noun takes the accusative here - the construction is translated into English by "except, but".

All students but Muhammad came. lit.: *All students came except Muhammad.*	جَاءَ كُلُّ الطُّلَّابِ إِلَّا مُحَمَّدًا.

2. Other exceptive particles

Other exceptive particles, not as common as إِلَّا , are سِوَى and غَيْر in the negative exceptive. They are generally followed by the genitive:

Only the Syrian friends stayed.	لَمْ يَبْقَ سِوَى الأَصْدِقَاء السُّورِيِّينَ.
Only Muḥammad helped me.	لَمْ يُسَاعِدْنِي غَيْرَ مُحَمَّدٍ.
I understood all the texts except an old one.	فَهِمْتُ كُلَّ النُّصُوصِ غَيْرَ نَصٍّ قَدِيمٍ.
I remember all the sentences except one.	أَحْفَظُ كُلَّ الْجُمَلِ سِوَى جُمْلَةٍ وَاحِدَةٍ.
Nobody came except the teacher.	لَمْ يَحْضُرْ أَحَدٌ غَيْرَ الْمُعَلِّمِ.
I didn't meet with anyone except the journalist.	لَمْ أَلْتَقِ بِأَحَدٍ غَيْرَ/سِوَى الصُّحُفِيِّ.
I only told the truth.	لَمْ أَقُلْ غَيْرَ / سِوَى الْحَقِّ.

فِيمَا عَدَا or مَا عَدَا، عَدَا are also exceptive particles for the positive exception. They are followed by either the genitive or the accusative.

All but the Lebanese delegation left the city.	غَادَرَ كُلُّهُمُ الْمَدِينَةَ مَا عَدَا الْوَفْدَ اللُّبْنَانِيِّ.
I bought all the books except two.	اشْتَرَيْتُ الْكُتُبَ كُلَّهَا عَدَا كِتَابَيْنِ.
I read all the books except two.	قَرَأْتُ كُلَّ الْكُتُبِ مَا عَدَا كِتَابَيْنِ.

مُجَرَّد and فَقَط

فَقَط and مُجَرَّد *"only, merely, solely"* are used instead of (لا) ... إِلَّا . فقط , unlike إِلَّا , does not except anything from a general statement; but, as an emphasizing particle, particularly stresses the statement of a comparatively small quantity, number, period or distance.

only 10 days	عَشَرَةُ أَيَّامٍ فَقَطْ
only 21 persons	وَاحِدٌ وَعِشْرُونَ شَخْصًا فَقَطْ

مُجَرَّد takes the construct state and **precedes** nouns, which are almost always indefinite. If the construction is part of a prepositional phrase, the preposition **precedes** it:

With only a letter, we received the papers. / One letter was enough to get the papers.	حَصَلْنَا عَلَى الأَوْرَاقِ بِمُجَرَّدِ رِسَالَةٍ.

In many dialects, *"bass"* is used instead of فَقَط .

CLAUSES OF TIME (TEMPORAL CLAUSES)

Clauses of time are introduced by means of conjunctions which indicate that the action of the subordinate clause takes place

1. at the same time as the action of the main clause takes place (*when, as soon as = time, while, as long as = duration, whenever = reiteration*)
2. before the action of the main clause (*after, since, when*)
3. or after the action of the main clause (*until, before*).

1. Temporal Clauses of Simultaneousness

Simultaneousness of the actions expressed by the main and the subordinate clause is expressed by the following conjunctions:

عِنْدَمَا + **verb in the perfect tense** (or كَانَ + imperfect tense or participle) = **when**

When I was playing, Muhammad came.	عِنْدَمَا كُنْتُ أَلْعَبُ جَاءَ مُحَمَّدٌ.

The clause introduced by عِنْدَمَا may precede the main clause or follow it:

Muhammad came when I was playing.	جَاءَ مُحَمَّدٌ عِنْدَمَا كُنْتُ أَلْعَبُ.

The possibility of the temporal clause being placed in front of or behind the main clause also applies to all following clauses introduced by a temporal conjunction.

عِنْدَمَا + **verb in the imperfect tense** = **as soon as**

I will inform them about this matter as soon as I meet them.	سَأُطْلِعُهُمْ على هذه القَضية عِنْدَمَا أَجْتَمِعُ بِهِمْ.

عِنْدَمَا + imperfect tense, often in a conditional sense = *"when, if"*.

حِينَ or حِينَمَا + **verb in the perfect or imperfect tense** have the same meaning as

عِنْدَمَا does. In journalese عِنْدَمَا is found far more frequently. حِينَمَا and حِينَ are more representative of individual style.

بَيْنَمَا + **verb in the perfect tense** (or كَانَ + imperfect tense or participle) or **imperfect tense** = *"while"*

I did the work while Muhammad was absent.	أَنْجَزْتُ الْعَمَلَ بَيْنَمَا كَانَ مُحَمَّدٌ غَائِباً.
I do the work while Muhammad is absent.	أُنْجِزُ الْعَمَلَ بَيْنَمَا يَكُونُ مُحَمَّدٌ غَائِباً.

بَيْنَمَا also introduces clauses of contrast, like the English *"whereas"* does:

Export has increased whereas import has decreased.	إِرْتَفَعَ التَّصْدِيرُ بَيْنَمَا انْخَفَضَ الاسْتِيرَادُ.

Temporal clauses of simultaneousness are furthermore introduced by means of the following conjunctions:

As soon as, when	*He escaped as soon as the army came.*	هَرَبَ **حَالَمَا** جَاءَ الْجَيْشُ.	حَالَمَا
while, as long as, when (very rare)	*They still speak about peace while they are witnessing the destruction of the country.*	مَا زَالُوا يَتَكَلَّمُونَ عَنِ السَّلَامِ **رَيْثَمَا** يَشْهَدُونَ عَلَى دَمَارِ الْبَلَدِ.	رَيْثَمَا
as long as	*We stay here as long as he is in the town.*	نَبْقَى هُنَا **طَالَمَا** هُوَ فِي الْمَدِينَةِ.	طَالَمَا
when, as	*He spent the nights in the clubs in Paris when the people were suffering from starvation.*	سَهِرَ فِي نَوَادِي بَارِيس **فِيمَا** يُعَانِي الشَّعْبُ مِنَ الْجُوعِ.	فِيمَا
whenever	*Whenever he came/ comes the audience laughed/ laughs.*	**كُلَّمَا** جَاءَ/يَجِيءُ ضَحِكَ/ يَضْحَكُ الْحُضُورُ.	كُلَّمَا
when, as	*When they arrived they entered the school.*	**لَمَّا** وَصَلُوا دَخَلُوا الْمَدْرَسَةَ.	لَمَّا
hardly…, no sooner … than	*The army had hardly arrived when he escaped.*	**مَا أَنْ** وَصَلَ الْجَيْشُ **حَتَى** هَرَبَ.	مَا أَنْ …حَتَى
as long as, while	*We stay here as long as he is in the town.*	نَبْقَى هُنَا **مَا دَامَ** فِي الْمَدِينَةِ.	مَا دَامَ
so long as… not, unless	*The war is unavoidable unless the positions do not change.*	أَلْحَرْبُ حَتْمِيَّةٌ **مَا لَمْ** تَتَغَيَّرِ الْمَوَاقِفُ.	مَا لَمْ

مَا دَامَ is conjugated in the perfect tense like قَامَ, accordingly:

So long as/while I (you (both) /he/she (both)/we/you/they) am/ are here, he will not sleep.	مَا دُمْتُ (دُمْتَ/دُمْتُمَا/دُمْتِ/دَامَ/دَامَا/دَامَتْ/ دَامَتَا/دُمْنَا/دُمْتُمْ/دُمْتُنَّ/دَامُوا/دُمْنَ) هُنَا لَنْ يَنَامَ.

Another syntactic possibility of expressing the simultaneousness of the main clause and the subordinate clause consists in the so-called circumstantial clause (☞ *Hāl*).

The following nouns in the accusative case are used in temporal clauses of simultaneousness with respect to a certain time:

in the hour when	*He arrived in the hour when the president died.*	وَصَلَ **سَاعَةَ** مَوْتِ الرَّئِيسِ.	سَاعَةَ:
at the time when	*He arrived at the time when the president died.*	وَصَلَ **وَقْتَ** مَوْتِ الرَّئِيسِ.	وَقْتَ:
on the day when	*He arrived on the day when the president died.*	وَصَلَ **يَوْمَ** مَوْتِ الرَّئِيسِ.	يَوْمَ:

2. Temporal Clauses of Anteriority

بَعد أَنْ + verb in the perfect tense = **"after"**

I went home after I had done the work.	ذَهَبْتُ إِلَى الْبَيْتِ **بَعْدَ أَنْ** أَنْجَزْتُ الْعَمَلَ.

Rarely لَمَّا fulfils the same function:

After the train arrived he welcomed the guests.	**لَمَّا** وَصَلَ الْقِطَارُ رَحَّبَ بِالضُّيُوفِ.

عِنْدَمَا and حِينَمَا can be used in the sense of *"when, after"* for the purpose of expressing anteriority, too. In many cases it is neither possible to differentiate them clearly from بَعْدَ أَنْ *"after"* nor from لَمَّا *"when, after"*, which is seldom used in Standard Arabic nowadays. However, in spoken language the latter occurs very frequently.

مُنْذُ (أَنْ) + verb in the perfect tense = **"since"**

I have been (and am still) working as an interpreter since I graduated from university.	لا أَزَالُ أَشْتَغِلُ مُتَرْجِماً **مُنْذُ أَنْ** تَخَرَّجْتُ مِنَ الْجَامِعَةِ.

3. Temporal Clauses of Posteriority

قَبْلَ أَنْ + verb in the imperfect tense (subjunctive) = **"before"**

I (will) ask my father before I write the letter.	أَسْأَلُ أَبِي **قَبْلَ أَنْ** أَكْتُبَ الرِّسَالَةَ.

حَتَّى + verb in the perfect tense (usually) = **"until"**

He worked until he had accomplished the tasks.	عَمِلَ **حَتَّى** أَنْجَزَ الْوَاجِبَاتِ.

رَيْثَمَا + verb in the imperfect tense (usually) = **"until"** (rather rare)

The election was postponed until the conference came to an end.	تَمَّ تَأْجِيلُ الانْتِخَابِ **رَيْثَمَا** يَنْتَهِي الْمُؤْتَمَرُ.

Frequently a prepositional construction (☞ Infinitve) is chosen - especially for the purpose of expressing anteriority and posteriority -, accordingly

بَعْدَ إِنْجَازِه الْعَمَلَ / لِلْعَمَلِ instead of	بَعْدَ أَنْ أَنْجَزَ الْعَمَلَ
حَتَّى إِنْجَازِه الْوَاجِبَاتِ / لِلْوَاجِبَاتِ instead of	حَتَّى أَنْجَزَ الْوَاجِبَاتِ
قَبْلَ كِتَابَتِه الرِّسَالَةَ / لِلرِّسَالَةِ instead of	قَبْلَ أَنْ يَكْتُبَ الرِّسَالَةَ
مُنْذُ تَخَرُّجِي مِنَ الْجَامِعَةِ instead of	مُنْذُ (أَنْ) تَخَرَّجْتُ مِنَ الْجَامِعَةِ

CONCESSIVE SENTENCES

There are several conjunctions to express concession in Arabic. The most important are the following:

even if, even though	(حَتَّى) وَلَوْ
wherever	أَيْنَمَا
despite, in spite of the fact that	بِالرَّغْمِ مِنْ أَنَّ
despite, in spite of	رَغْمَ
despite, in spite of	رَغْمَ أَنَّ
despite, in spite of	عَلَى الرَّغْمِ مِنْ أَنَّ
however	كَيْفَمَا
whenever	مَتَى مَا
although	مَعَ أَنَّ
whoever	مَنْ
whatever	مَهْمَا
even if, even though	وَإِنْ

The rules for the construction of unreal conditional sentences introduced by إِنْ or لَوْ respectively, apply for وَإِنْ / (حَتَّى) وَلَوْ as well. The main clause usually precedes the subordinate clause.

I will not accomplish the work, even if I work every day.	سَوْفَ لا أُنْجِزُ الْعَمَلَ وَإِنْ عَمِلْتُ كُلَّ يومٍ.
I will not accomplish the work, even if I work every day.	سَوْفَ لا أُنْجِزُ الْعَمَلَ (حَتَّى) وَلَوْ عَمِلْتُ كُلَّ يومٍ.
I will complete the work, even if nobody helps me.	سَأُنْهِي الْعَمَلَ وَإِنْ لَمْ يُسَاعِدْنِي أَحَدٌ.
I will complete the work, even if nobody helps me.	سَأُنْهِي الْعَمَلَ (حَتَّى) وَلَوْ لَمْ يُسَاعِدْنِي أَحَدٌ.

وَلَوْ = "*not (even) a single*" may also emphasize a negated statement:

He has not given me (any money), and had it only been one dinar = he has not given me a single dinar.	لَمْ يُعْطِنِي (نُقُوداً) وَلَوْ دِينَاراً وَاحِداً.

I will not ask him for a single book.	لَنْ أَطْلُبَ مِنْهُ وَلَوْ كِتَاباً وَاحِدًا.

مَهْمَا is always followed by the perfect tense, or sometimes by the jussive of كَانَ.

A following main clause is mostly introduced by فَ (فَإِنَّ):

We will travel whatever the difficulties will be.	سَوْفَ نُسَافِرُ مَهْمَا كَانَتِ الصُّعُوبَاتُ.
Whatever the difficulties will be, we will travel.	مَهْمَا كَانَتِ الصُّعُوبَاتُ فَسَوْفَ نُسَافِرُ.
Whatever you try, you will not succeed.	مَهْمَا حَاوَلْتَ فَإِنَّكَ لن تَنْجَحَ.
Whatever the case will be, he is the president.	مَهْمَا يَكُنْ مِنَ الأَمْرِ فَهُوَ الرَّئِيسُ.
Whatever the reason is, we will continue the efforts.	مَهْمَا يَكُنْ السَّبَبُ فَإِنَّا نُوَاصِلُ الْجُهُودَ.

The other conjunctions introducing concession can be placed first or second. The sequence of tenses depends on the intended meaning:

He continued the war despite all the menaces.	وَاصَلَ الْحَرْبَ رَغْمَ كُلِّ التَّهْدِيدَاتِ.
He delivered his lecture although he knew the consequences.	أَلْقَى الْمُحَاضَرَةَ رَغْمَ أَنَّهُ كَانَ عَرَفَ الْعَوَاقِبَ.
He entered the battle despite the superiority of the enemy.	دَخَلَ الْمَعْرَكَةَ عَلَى الرَّغْمِ مِنْ تَفَوُّقِ الْعَدُوّ.
The president is abroad although the country is on the verge of complete bankruptcy.	أَلرَّئِيسُ فِي الْخَارِجِ بِالرَّغْمِ مِنْ أَنَّ الْبَلَدَ عَلَى وَشْكِ الإِفْلاسِ التَّامِّ.
Although she refuses her responsibility she will continue to practise the same politics.	مَعَ أَنَّهَا تَرْفُضُ مَسْؤُولِيَّتَهَا فَإِنَّهَا تَسْتَمِرُّ فِي مُمَارَسَةِ نَفْسِ السِّيَاسَةِ.
We will fight them wherever we find them.	سَنُكَافِحُهُمْ أَيْنَمَا وَجَدْنَاهُمْ.
However he works, he will not succeed.	كَيْفَمَا يَعْمَلُ لَنْ يَنْجَحَ.
We will welcome them whenever we see them.	سَنُرَحِّبُ بِهِمْ مَتَى مَا نَرَاهُمْ.
We will know whoever was responsible for the problems.	سَنَعْرِفُ مَنْ كَانَ مَسْؤُولاً عَنِ الْمَشَاكِلِ.

ADVERSATIVE SENTENCES

Arabic uses the following particles for adversative sentences:

but, however	He came but he forgot the book.	جَاءَ (وَ)لٰكِنَّهُ نَسِيَ الْكِتَابَ.	(وَ)لٰكِنَّ
but, however (mostly after negations)	He doesn't attend the lectures but all the parties.	لا يَحْضُرُ الدُّرُوسَ (وَ)لٰكِنْ كُلَّ الْحَفَلات.	(وَ)لٰكِنْ
but (not)	They did not take his house but his car.	ما أَخَذُوا مِنْهُ الْبَيْتَ بَلِ السَّيَّارَةَ.	بَلْ
but not	The director is generous but not ignorant.	الْمُدِيرُ كَرِيمٌ (وَ)لا جَاهِلٌ.	(وَ)لا

The Particle ف can also render an adversative meaning:

He stood there but nobody moved.	وَقَفَ هُنَاكَ فَلَمْ يَتَحَرَّكْ أَحَدٌ.
He was in the capital but he did not meet the president.	كَانَ فِي الْعَاصِمَة فَلَمْ يَجْتَمِعْ بِالرَّئِيسِ.

Nowadays, the past conditional سَيَفْعَلُ كَانَ = "*would have done*" is also used in adversative sentences:

He would have become crazy but he knew the solution.	كَانَ سَيُصْبِحُ مَجْنُوناً لٰكِنَّهُ عَرَفَ الْحَلَّ.

RESTRICTIVE SENTENCES

The following conjunctions serve the purpose of linking a clause with a restrictive clause. The English equivalents are: "*however, but, nevertheless, ... (al)though, yet*".

He explained the situation but he refused to mention any details.	شَرَحَ الْوَضْعَ غَيْرَ أَنَّه رَفَضَ أَنْ يَذْكُرَ أَيَّةَ تَفَاصِيل.	غَيْرَ أَنَّ
The Minister has met with the persons responsible; however, the resolution of the government still stands.	إِنَّ الْوَزِيرَ قَدْ قَابَلَ الْمَسْؤُولِينَ إِلاَّ أَنَّ قَرَارَ الْحُكُومَة لا يَزَالُ قَائِماً.	إِلاَّ أَنَّ
We wanted this solution although we didn't know the consequences.	أَرَدْنَا هٰذَا الْحَلَّ عَلَى أَنَّنَا لَمْ نَعْرِفِ الْعَوَاقِبَ.	عَلَى أَنَّ
This is reasonable although we prefer other solutions.	هٰذَا مَعْقُولٌ بَيْدَ أَنَّنَا نُفَضِّلُ حُلُولاً أُخْرَى.	بَيْدَ أَنَّ
Politics is only for fools.	إِنَّمَا السِّيَاسَةُ لِلْأَغْبِيَاء.	إِنَّمَا

CLAUSES OF REASON

Clauses of reason are commonly introduced by the following conjunctions for *"since, because, for, inasmuch as/in that ..."*. A following verb may be in any tense.

He did not write because he was ill.	لَمْ يَكْتُبْ **لِأَنَّهُ** كَانَ مَرِيضاً.	لِأَنَّ ، لِأَنَّهُ
He does not write because he sleeps in classes.	لَا يَكْتُبُ **إِذْ أَنَّهُ** يَنَامُ في الدَّرْسِ.	إِذْ ، إِذْ أَنَّ، إِذْ أَنَّهُ
He does not write because he sleeps in classes.	لَا يَكْتُبُ **حَيْثُ أَنَّهُ** يَنَامُ في الدَّرْسِ.	حَيْثُ، حَيْثُ أَنَّ، حَيْثُ أَنَّهُ
Since he had studied in Egypt, he spoke the Egyptian dialect.	**بِمَا أَنَّهُ** كَانَ يَدْرُسُ في مصرَ فَقَدْ تَكَلَّمَ اللَّهْجَةَ المِصْرِيَّةَ.	بِمَا أَنَّ، بِمَا أَنَّهُ
This plan is good for it opens up new prospects.	هذه الخُطَّةُ جَيِّدَةٌ **ذلكَ أَنَّهَا** تَفْتَحُ آفاقاً جَديدةً.	ذلكَ أَنَّ، ذلكَ أَنَّهُ
Since those books were new, they were not used.	**وَلَمَّا** كَانَتْ تِلْكَ الْكُتُبُ جَديدَةً **فَإِنَّهَا** لا تُسْتَعْمَلُ. *	لَمَّا

* If لَمَّا is used in clauses of reason (☞ Clauses of Time) it is mostly followed by كَانَ and فَ + verb or فَإِنَّ + noun or suffix in the second part of the sentence.

Clauses of reason can also be introduced by the particle فَ (فَاءُ السَّبَبِيَّةُ) with the meaning of *"because, for, and then, and so, hence/ therefore"*. It is used nearly as frequently as لِأَنَّ and is employed in the secondary clause following the main clause. It is also often introduced by فَ as a new independent sentence.

He did not take part in the classes, and so he failed in the examination.	لَمْ يَحْضُرِ الدُّرُوسَ فَفَشِلَ في الامْتِحَانِ.
The government cannot solve the problems because it does not know their causes.	لا تَسْتَطِيعُ الحُكُومَةُ حَلَّ المَشَاكِلِ، فَهِيَ لا تَعْرِفُ أَسْبَابَهَا.
He was two hours late, and so he did not get the licence.	تَأَخَّرَ بِسَاعَتَيْنِ فَلَمْ يَحْصُلْ عَلَى الرُّخْصَةِ.

If preceding a verb in the perfect tense فَ is often followed by قَدْ having a causative meaning:

I left the school because I was afraid of the director.	خَرَجْتُ مِنَ الْمَدْرَسَةِ فَقَدْ كُنْتُ أَخَافُ مِنَ الْمُدِيرِ.

The same is true with فَإِنَّ :

I left the school because I was afraid of the director.	خَرَجْتُ مِنَ الْمَدْرَسَةِ فَإِنَّنِي كُنْتُ أَخَافُ مِنَ الْمُدِيرِ.

THE ATTRIBUTIVE RELATIVE CLAUSE (أَلصِّلَةُ وَالصِّفَةُ)

Not only a word or a group of words, but also a whole clause can be added to a noun as an attributive adjunct. The relative clause is the form of the attributive clause that occurs most frequently.

There are two types of attributive relative clauses:

a) relative clauses which are employed as attributive adjuncts related to definite nouns (صِلَةٌ).

b) relative clauses which are employed as attributive adjuncts related to indefinite nouns (صِفَةٌ).

a) صِلَةٌ

If the relative clause is the modifier of a definite noun, it is preceded by a relative pronoun.

There is the same agreement in state between a noun and an attributive clause as there is between a noun and an adjectival attributive adjunct. If the antecedent is definite, the adjective is defined by the article أل, the relative attributive clause by the soc. relative pronoun. The term relative pronoun is therefore not quite correct, because it expresses, above all, the definiteness of the attributive clause in addition to characterizing gender and number. However, the relative pronoun does not indicate the syntactic function (of the modified antecedent) in the relative clause.

The relative pronouns (أَلْأَسْمَاءُ الْمَوْصُولَةُ) are:

after a masc. noun in the singular	اَلَّذِي
after a fem. noun in the singular and after plurals which denote non-persons	اَلَّتِي
after a masc. noun in the plural which denotes persons	اَلَّذِينَ
after a fem. noun in the plural which denotes persons	اَللَّاتِي، اَللَّوَاتِي
after a masc. dual	اَللَّذَان
after a fem. dual	اَللَّتَان

Whereas the four first-mentioned forms are neutral as to case, the two dual forms are inflected. When following a noun in the genitive or accusative, they are اَللَّتَيْنِ / اَللَّذَيْنِ. The article ال is the first component of the relative pronoun, therefore the initial *Hamza* of اَلَّذِي، اَلَّتِي etc. is *Hamzat waṣl*.

اَلَّذِي، اَلَّتِي etc. are equivalent to the English relative pronouns *"who, which, that"* in the nominative. The noun which is modified by the relative clause is the subject of this clause at the same time.

the student who came from Iraq	اَلطَّالِبُ الَّذِي جَاءَ مِنَ الْعِرَاقِ
the student (f.) who came from Iraq	اَلطَّالِبَةُ الَّتِي جَاءَتْ مِنَ الْعِرَاقِ
the students who came from Iraq	اَلطُّلَّابُ الَّذِينَ جَاؤُوا مِنَ الْعِرَاقِ
the students (f.) who came from Iraq	اَلطَّالِبَاتُ اللَّاتِي جِئْنَ مِنَ الْعِرَاقِ
the two students who came from Iraq	اَلطَّالِبَانِ اللَّذَانِ جَاءَا مِنَ الْعِرَاقِ
the two students (f.) who came from Iraq	اَلطَّالِبَتَانِ اللَّتَانِ جَاءَتَا مِنَ الْعِرَاقِ

A literal translation of the Arabic examples makes the difference in word order in the Arabic and in the English relative clause clear to us. In Arabic: Normal word order of the verbal sentence, accordingly "the student who he has come", in English: Inverted word order, consequently "the student who has come".

اَلَّذِي ، اَلَّتِي etc. are also employed in sentences when the subject is not identical with the antecedent. In English, the relative pronoun is in the genitive or objective (as an indirect or direct object or the complement of a preposition) in these cases. In the Arabic language, the affixed pronoun in the relative clause makes the connection with the antecedent.

the friend whom I have met	اَلصَّدِيقُ الَّذِي قَابَلْتُهُ
the (girl)friend whom I have met	اَلصَّدِيقَةُ الَّتِي قَابَلْتُهَا
the friends whom I have met	اَلْأَصْدِقَاءُ الَّذِينَ قَابَلْتُهُمْ
the two friends whom I have met	اَلصَّدِيقَانِ اللَّذَانِ قَابَلْتُهُمَا
the friend (to) whom I have written a letter	اَلصَّدِيقُ الَّذِي كَتَبْتُ لَهُ رِسَالَةً
the (girl)friend (to) whom I have written a letter	اَلصَّدِيقَةُ الَّتِي كَتَبْتُ لَهَا رِسَالَةً

the friends (to) whom I have written a letter	ألأَصْدِقَاءُ الَّذِينَ كَتَبْتُ لَهُمْ رِسَالَةً
the (girl)friends (to) whom I have written a letter	ألصَّدِيقَاتُ اللَّاتِي كَتَبْتُ لَهُنَّ رِسَالَةً
the friend whose doctor I have met	ألصَّدِيقُ الَّذِي قَابَلْتُ طَبِيبَهُ
the (girl)friend whose doctor I have met	ألصَّدِيقَةُ الَّتِي قَابَلْتُ طَبِيبَهَا
the friends whose doctor I have met	ألأَصْدِقَاءُ الَّذِينَ قَابَلْتُ طَبِيبَهُمْ
the two (girl)friends whose doctor I have met	ألصَّدِيقَتَانِ اللَّتَانِ قَابَلْتُ طَبِيبَهُمَا
the friend with whom I have been to the theatre	ألصَّدِيقُ الَّذِي كُنْتُ مَعَهُ فِي الْمَسْرَحِ
the friends with whom I have been	ألأَصْدِقَاءُ الَّذِينَ كُنْتُ عِنْدَهُمْ
with the two friends from whom I have received the books	عِنْدَ الصَّدِيقَيْنِ اللَّذَيْنِ أَخَذْتُ الْكُتُبَ مِنْهُمَا
the (girl)friend at whose house I was	ألصَّدِيقَةُ الَّتِي كُنْتُ فِي بَيْتِهَا

Forms which are defined in a different way than by the article could also be employed in place of الصَّدِيقَةُ ، الأَصْدِقَاءُ ، الصَّدِيقُ etc. which were chosen as an example, e.g. صَدِيقُ مُحَمَّدٍ، صَدِيقِي a.o.

b) صِفَةٌ

If the relative clause is the modifier of an indefinite noun, **no** relative pronoun is used. There is agreement in state here, as well. The antecedent is indefinite, consequently the attributive clause does not get a sign of definition either.

Word order and the affixed pronoun are just as they are in the syndetic relative clause:

I have read an article in the newspaper in which it says: ...	قَرَأْتُ فِي الْجَرِيدَةِ مَقَالَةً جَاءَ فِيهَا ...
I have met a friend who came from London.	قَابَلْتُ صَدِيقاً وَصَلَ مِن لندن.
There are delegations in the hotel who came from the Arab countries.	فِي الْفُنْدُقِ وُفُودٌ وَصَلَتْ مِنَ الْبُلْدَانِ الْعَرَبِيَّةِ.
a present which I have sent to my friend	هَدِيَّةٌ أَرْسَلْتُهَا إِلَى صَدِيقِي

THE NOMINAL RELATIVE CLAUSE

In addition to the attributive relative clause, there is another type of relative clause known as the nominal relative clause which is also utilized in the English language. It is introduced here by the determinative-relative pronoun *"who, which"*.

"Honour to whom honour is due" (to the one honour is due to),

or, when related to indefinite quantities, by the generalizing-relative pronoun *"who"* or *"what"*.

Who (everyone who) visits us will be welcome.

What (that which) he did was not right.

A conditional sense is frequently discernible in this context.

He who seeks shall find. (If someone seeks, he shall find.)

Idleness rusts the mind. (If someone is idle, his mind will rust).

These relative clauses are introduced in the Arabic language by the determinative-relative pronoun

اَلَّذِي pl. اَلَّذِينَ (related to persons, seldom to non-persons) *he ... who / the one ... who; they ... who / the ones ... who; that ... which / the one ... which;*

by the generalizing-relative pronoun

مَنْ (related to persons) *(he) who / who(ever); someone who;*

and the generalizing-relative pronoun

مَا (related to non-persons) *what; that ... which / the one ... which; something.*

Such sentences can fulfil the syntactic function of:

a) a subject

What happened to me yesterday will not happen to me again.	مَا حَدَثَ لِي أَمْسِ لَنْ يَحْدُثَ لِي مَرَّةً ثَانِيَةً.
The one who delivered the speech is my friend.	اَلَّذِي أَلْقَى الكَلِمَةَ صَدِيقِي.

b) an object

We know who is holding the negotiations.	نَعْرِفُ مَنْ يُجْرِي الْمُحَادَثَاتِ.

c) a predicate or

This is (that which)/what happened to me.	هَذَا مَا حَدَثَ لِي.

d) the 2nd term of a genitive construction,

He told us all he knew.	حَكَى لَنَا كُلَّ مَا عَرَفَ.

e) be construed in subordination to a preposition.

He has told us about the things he has seen there.	حَكَى لَنَا عَمَّا شَاهَدَ هُنَاكَ.
The price of it is 10 pounds including electricity.	سِعْرُهَا عَشْرُ لِيرَاتٍ بِمَا فِي ذَلِكَ الْكَهْرَبَاءِ.

A construction in which مَنْ and مَا are modified by a post-positive مِنْ + noun is typical for Arabic.

We know (that which)/what is in them (in their souls) of doubts = We know which doubts they entertain.	نَعْرِفُ مَا فِي أَنْفُسِهِم مِن شُكُوكٍ.
You came with the ones who (were) with you of the men = you came with the men who were with you.	جِئْتَ بِمَنْ عِنْدَكَ مِنَ الرِّجَالِ.
that which they have of apparatuses = the apparatuses they have.	مَا عِنْدَهُم مِنْ أَجْهِزَةٍ

Nominal relative clauses of this kind are preferred to the corresponding attributive relative clauses in many cases.

attributive:	نَعْرِفُ الشُّكُوكَ الَّتِي تُوجَدُ فِي أَنْفُسِهِمْ.
nominal:	نَعْرِفُ مَا فِي أَنْفُسِهِم مِن شُكُوكٍ.
attributive:	جِئْتَ بِالرِّجَالِ الَّذِينَ (كَانُوا) عِنْدَكَ.
nominal:	جِئْتَ بِمَنْ عِنْدَكَ مِنَ الرِّجَالِ.
attributive:	أَلْأَجْهِزَةُ الَّتِي (تُوجَدُ) عِنْدَهُمْ
nominal:	مَا عِنْدَهُم مِنْ أَجْهِزَةٍ

Furthermore, مِنْ + affixed pronoun + مَنْ / مَا belongs to the nominal relative clause constructions:

there are some among them who …	مِنْهُمْ مَنْ …
there is something among them which …	مِنْهَا مَا …

مَا and مَنْ are contracted with some prepositions:

$$ \text{فِيمَا} \quad < \quad (\text{فِي} + \text{مَا}) \text{،} \qquad \text{مِمَّا} \quad < \quad (\text{مِنْ} + \text{مَا}) $$

$$ \text{مِمَّنْ} \quad < \quad (\text{مِنْ} + \text{مَنْ}) \text{،} \qquad \text{عَمَّا} \quad < \quad (\text{عَنْ} + \text{مَا}) $$

مَنْ can denote singular or plural and مَا can denote something masculine or feminine:

I asked who (m. sg.) visited me.	سَأَلْتُ مَنْ زَارَنِي.
I asked who (f. sg.) visited me.	سَأَلْتُ مَنْ زَارَتْنِي.
I asked who (m./f. dual) visited me.	سَأَلْتُ مَنْ زَارَانِي / زَارَتَانِي.
I asked who (m. pl.) visited me.	سَأَلْتُ مَنْ زَارُونِي.

I asked who (f. pl.) visited me.	سَأَلْتُ مَنْ زُرْنَنِي.
I liked what (m. sg.) I saw.	أَعْجَبَنِي مَا رَأَيْتُهُ.
I liked what (inanimate f. sg. or plural) I saw.	أَعْجَبَتْنِي مَا رَأَيْتُها.

Some phraseology in the form of nominal relative clauses:

forever and ever, for all time and time to come	إِلَى مَا شَاءَ الله
after approximately one year (lit.: after the passing of what approximates one year)	بَعْدَ مُرُورِ مَا يُقَارِبُ عَاماً وَاحِداً
including (lit.: with that which is in it)	بِمَا فِي ذَلِكَ
including	بِمَا فِيه
as for/to..., with regard to, as regards ..., as far as ... is concerned	فِيمَا يَخُصُّ
Mesopotamia	مَا بَيْنَ النَّهْرَيْن
whatever God intends, God knows what	مَا شَاءَ الله
it is worth mentioning (lit.: of that which is worth mentioning that ...)	مِمَّا هُوَ جَدِيرٌ بِالذِّكْرِ أَنْ
it must be mentioned (lit.: of that the remarking of which is necessary)	مِمَّا يَجِبُ مُلَاحَظَتُهُ أَنْ

Perhaps, Maybe, Possibly
There are three basic possibilities to render "*perhaps, maybe, possibly*" in Arabic:

Introducing nominal and verbal sentences (perfect and imperfect tense)	رُبَّمَا
Preceding the imperfect tense	قَدْ
Preceding a noun or affixed pronoun followed by the imperfect tense	لَعَلَّ

Examples:

Perhaps the president is now in Cairo.	رُبَّمَا الرَّئِيسُ الآنَ فِي الْقَاهِرَة.
He possibly moved yesterday.	رُبَّمَا تَحَرَّكَ أَمْسِ.
He will possibly move tomorrow.	رُبَّمَا يَتَحَرَّكُ غَدًا.
Maybe he sleeps, maybe not.	قَدْ يَنَامُ قَدْ لا يَنَامُ.
He may be there.	قَدْ يَكُونُ هُنَاكَ.

The director may be in the school.	لَعَلَّ الْمُدِيرُ فِي الْمَدْرَسَةِ.
Maybe, he is in the school.	لَعَلَّهُ فِي الْمَدْرَسَةِ.
Maybe, he travels tomorrow.	لَعَلَّهُ يُسَافِرُ غَدًا.

Too big, too long etc.

Arabic has no direct equivalent for such expressions like *"too big, too long"* etc. Other contextual constructions are used to render the same meaning:

This bag is too big / bigger than it should be. I need a smaller bag.	هَذِه الشَّنْطَةُ كَبِيرَةٌ / أَكْبَرُ مِمَّا يَنْبَغِي. أَحْتَاجُ إِلَى شَنْطَة أَصْغَرَ.
This lesson is too long / longer than it should be. I prefer shorter lessons.	هَذَا الدَّرْسُ طَوِيلٌ/ أَطْوَلُ مِمَّا يَنْبَغِي. أُفَضِّلُ الدُّرُوسَ الْقَصِيرَةَ.
This suit is somewhat too big for me.	هَذِه الْبَدْلَةُ كَبِيرَةٌ عَلَيَّ نَوْعًا مَا.

CARDINAL NUMBERS (ٱلْأَعْدَادُ الْأَصْلِيَّةُ)

The Arabic numerals are written in the following way:

0	1	2	3	4	5	6	7	8	9	10
٠	١	٢	٣	٤	٥	٦	٧	٨	٩	١٠

Sometimes the numerals are written as follows: ١٢٣٤٥٦٧٨٩

Compound numbers which are expressed by numerals are written from left to right as in English: 1994 ⇨ ١٩٩٤

Cardinal Numbers 0 – 10 :

٦	ستّة	sitta	٠	صفر	ṣifr
٧	سبعة	sab'a	١	واحد	wāḥid
٨	ثمانية	tamāniya	٢	اثنان	itnāni
٩	تسعة	tis'a	٣	ثلاثة	talāta
١٠	عشرة	'ašara	٤	أربعة	arba'a
			٥	خمسة	ḫamsa

The Arabic words for the cardinal numbers **1** and **2** are adjectives and agree as such with the principal noun in case, state, gender and number:

	2		1	
	f.	m.	f.	m.
n.	إثْنَتَان	إثْنَان	وَاحِدَةٌ	وَاحِدٌ
g.	إثْنَتَيْنِ	إثْنَيْنِ	وَاحِدَة	وَاحِد
a.	إثْنَتَيْنِ	إثْنَيْنِ	وَاحِدَةً	وَاحِداً

The initial *Hamza* of اثْنَان is a *Hamzat waṣl*: مَعَ اثْنَيْنِ مِنْهُم

وَاحِدَةٌ / وَاحِدٌ are not employed as an indefinite article, but are strictly used as numerals: كِتَابٌ وَاحِدٌ one book.

إثْنَان / إثْنَتَان rarely occur as an attributive adjunct (they are at most, added to the noun as an emphasis), as duality is already expressed by the dual form of the latter.

According to grammatical rules numbers **3 - 10** are regarded as diptotes in abstract counting. Consequently the correct pronunciation would be *wāhidun, itnāni, talātatu, arba'atu, hamsatu* etc. In general, however, the endings are dropped in oral usage.

1 and **2** are adjectives. By contrast **3 - 10** are nouns. Each number from **1-10** has a masculine and a feminine form. The numbers are used in abstract counting as shown, i.e. **1** and **2** in their masculine, **3 -10** in their feminine forms.

The rule of so-called polarity applies to **3 - 10** in connection with a noun as the counted item, i.e., a masculine word is preceded by the feminine form of the number, a feminine word by the masculine form of the number.

The number and the noun are the 1ˢᵗ and the 2ⁿᵈ term of a genitive construction. The noun is indefinite and takes the genitive plural.

in connection with a feminine noun		in connection with a masculine noun
ثلاثُ فتيات	٣	ثلاثةُ رجالٍ / مُعلِّمينَ
أرْبعُ فتيات	٤	أرْبعةُ رجالٍ / مُعلِّمينَ
خمْسُ فتيات	٥	خمْسةُ رجالٍ / مُعلِّمينَ
ستُّ فتيات	٦	ستَّةُ رجالٍ / مُعلِّمينَ
سبْعُ فتيات	٧	سبْعةُ رجالٍ / مُعلِّمينَ
ثماني فتيات	٨	ثمانية رجالٍ / مُعلِّمينَ
تسْعُ فتيات	٩	تسْعةُ رجالٍ / مُعلِّمينَ
عَشْرُ فتيات	١٠	عَشَرةُ رجالٍ / مُعلِّمينَ

This rule about polarity also applies when the noun does not immediately follow the number or is not mentioned at all.

three of them	ثَلاثةٌ مِنْهُمْ	*three men*	ثَلاثةٌ رجَالٍ
I have seen three.	رأَيْتُ ثَلاثةً	*three of the men*	ثَلاثةٌ مِنَ الرِّجَالِ

11-19 are indeclinable (مَمْنُوع من الصرْف) with the exception of **12**. There is agreement in gender, not polarity in gender, between the numeral *m.* عَشَرَ *f.* عَشْرَةَ which denotes ten and the following noun.

The noun takes the **accusative singular**.

in connection with a feminine noun		in connection with a masculine noun
إِحْدَى عَشْرَةَ فتاةً	١١	أحد عَشَرَ رجُلاً
إِثْنَتا عَشْرَةَ فتاةً	١٢	إِثْنا عَشَرَ رجُلاً
ثلاثَ عَشْرَةَ فتاةً	١٣	ثلاثةَ عَشَرَ رجُلاً
أرْبعَ عَشْرَةَ فتاةً	١٤	أرْبعةَ عَشَرَ رجُلاً
خَمْسَ عَشْرَةَ فتاةً	١٥	خَمسةَ عَشَرَ رجُلاً
ستَّ عَشْرَةَ فتاةً	١٦	ستَّةَ عَشَرَ رجُلاً
سبْعَ عَشْرَةَ فتاةً	١٧	سبْعةَ عَشَرَ رجُلاً
ثمانيَ عَشْرَةَ فتاةً	١٨	ثمانيةَ عَشَرَ رجُلاً
تسْعَ عَشْرَةَ فتاةً	١٩	تسْعةَ عَشَرَ رجُلاً

The rule of polarity in gender which applies to **3 - 10** also applies to **13 - 19** in so far as the masculine number denoting the unit is connected with the feminine number denoting ten and, vice versa the feminine number denoting the unit with the masculine number denoting ten. Accordingly polarity in gender exists within the two terms of these compound numbers. On the other hand, there is agreement in **11** and **12**: A masculine number denoting the unit is connected with a masculine number denoting ten, and a feminine number denoting the unit with a feminine number denoting ten.

The dual inflection occurs in the genitive and accusative of **12**:

I went there with twelve girls.	ذهبْتُ إلى هُناك مع اثْنَتَيْ عَشْرَةَ فتاةً.
I saw twelve men there.	رأيْتُ هُناك اثْنَيْ عَشَرَ رجُلاً.

10 is masc. عَشْر , fem. عَشْرَة , whereas it is عَشَر and عَشْرَة when it functions as a component of the compound numbers **11-19**.

The numbers **20 - 99** are followed by the noun in the accusative singular as well. The numbers **20, 30, 40** up to **90** which denote tens have the form of the sound masculine plural (n. ون— , g., a. ين—). The units compounded with them follow the rules stated above, i.e. there is agreement in gender between **1** and **2** which denote units and the counted item, polarity in gender between the numbers **3 - 9** which denote units and the counted item.

The word order is different from modern English; units come before tens.

in connection with a feminine noun		in connection with a masculine noun
عِشْرُونَ فتاةً	٢٠	عِشْرُونَ رجُلاً
إحْدَى وعِشْرُونَ فتاةً	٢١	واحِدٌ / أحدٌ وعِشْرُونَ رجُلاً
إثْنتان وعِشْرُونَ فتاةً	٢٢	إثْنان وعِشْرُونَ رجُلاً
ثلاثٌ وعِشْرُونَ فتاةً	٢٣	ثلاثةٌ وعِشْرُونَ رجُلاً
ثلاثُونَ فتاةً	٣٠	ثلاثُونَ رجُلاً
إحْدَى وثلاثُونَ فتاةً	٣١	واحِدٌ / أحدٌ وثلاثُونَ رجُلاً
إثْنتان وثلاثُونَ فتاةً	٣٢	إثْنان وثلاثُونَ رجُلاً
ثلاثٌ وثلاثُونَ فتاةً	٣٣	ثلاثةٌ وثلاثُونَ رجُلاً
أرْبعُونَ فتاةً	٤٠	أرْبعُونَ رجُلاً
خَمْسُونَ فتاةً	٥٠	خَمْسُونَ رجُلاً
سِتُّونَ فتاةً	٦٠	سِتُّونَ رجُلاً
سَبْعُونَ فتاةً	٧٠	سَبْعُونَ رجُلاً
ثَمَانُونَ فتاةً	٨٠	ثَمَانُونَ رجُلاً
تِسْعُونَ فتاةً	٩٠	تِسْعُونَ رجُلاً

The whole hundreds (i.e. **100, 200, 300** ...), the numbers thousand, million, billion when functioning as the 1st term of a genitive construction are construed with the following noun in the genitive singular. The numbers **300, 400,... 900**, each of which is constructed out of the respective units and the word for hundred, مائة or مئة (*pronounced mi'a[tun]*), as a genitive construction, are written together.

Since the rule about polarity applies here as well, these take the masculine form when preceding مائة, and the feminine form when preceding ألْف، مَلْيُون، مِلْيار. The plural of the three last-named words is آلاف، مَلايينُ، مِلْيارات. The plural of مائة is مئات, which, however, is only used in the meaning of "hundreds".

مائة is in the singular when the numerals **300 - 900** are formed, although numbers **3 - 9** are otherwise construed with the plural:

١٠٠٠	أَلْفُ رجُلٍ	١٠٠	مائةُ رجُلٍ
٢٠٠٠	أَلْفا رجُلٍ	٢٠٠	مائَتا رجُلٍ
٣٠٠٠	ثلاثةُ آلاف رجُلٍ	٣٠٠	ثَلاثُمائة رجُلٍ
١٠٠٠٠٠٠	مَلْيُونُ رجُلٍ	٩٠٠	تِسْعُمائَة رجُلٍ

The order in compound numbers is thousand + hundred + unit + ten, which are connected by a copulative و respectively. If the units **3 - 9** or **10** are there, polarity in gender is to be observed.

١٠٣	مائةٌ وثَـــلاثةُ رجَـــالٍ
١١٢	مِائةٌ واثْنَتا عشْرَةَ فتاةً
٢٠٠	مائَتا دولار
٢١٠	مائَتان وعَشَرَةُ أشْخاصٍ
٣٠٠	ثَلاثُمائة يورو
٤٨٦	أَرْبعُمائة وستُّ وثمانُونَ لَيرةً
١٧٥٩	أَلْفٌ وسبْعُمائة وتِسْعةٌ وخَمْسُونَ عاماً
٢٠٠٠	أَلْفا سنة
٨٠٠٠	ثَمانِــيةُ آلاف ديـــنـــارٍ
١١٠٠٠	أَحَدَ عَشَرَ أَلْفَ جُنَيهٍ
٢٠٠٠٠٠	مائَتا أَلْف
٣٢٥٠٠٠	ثَلاثُمائة وخَمْسةٌ وعشْرُونَ أَلْفاً

The complete reading of "*I met 143 men.*" would be as follows:

قَابَلْتُ مائةَ رَجُلٍ وَثَلاثَةَ رِجَالٍ وَأَرْبَعِينَ رَجُلاً.

instead of

قَابَلْتُ مائةَ وَثَلاثَةَ وَأَرْبَعِينَ رَجُلاً.

With regard to numbers **101, 102, 1001, 1002**, the abstract count differs somewhat from the construction number + noun as counted item:

أَلْفٌ وواحِدٌ	but:	أَلْفُ لَيْلة ولَيْلَةٌ	مائةٌ وواحِدٌ	but:	مائةُ دينار ودينارٌ
أَلْفٌ واثْنتانِ	but:	أَلْفُ لَيْلة ولَيْلتانِ	مائةٌ واثْنان	but:	مائةُ دينارٍ ودِيناران

The numbers are
in the **genitive:**

after prepositions	مَعَ ثَلاثَةِ رِجَالٍ
after nouns	صَاحِبُ ثَلاثَةِ بُيُوتٍ
after the numbers 3 – 10	ثَلاثَةُ آلافٍ
and the hundreds	مِائَةُ أَلْفٍ

and in the **accusative:**

after verbs (as the object)	رَأَيْتُ ثَلاثَةَ رِجَالٍ
after إِنَّ and أَنَّ	أَعْرِفُ أَنَّ ثَلاثَةَ رِجَالٍ ...
after the numbers 11 – 99	وَاحِدٌ وَعِشْرُونَ أَلْفاً

The declension of 8 is: nominative and genitive ثَمَانٍ, accusative ثَمَانِياً and when definite أَلثَّمَانِيَ or أَلثَّمَانِي.

THE YEARS

The years are in the genitive after the words سَنَةٌ and عَامٌ "*year*". Polarity in gender, which applies to numbers **3 - 10**, and agreement in gender, which applies to numbers **1** and **2** are to be observed again with regard to them.

in the year 1990	فِي سَنَةِ أَلْفٍ وتِسْعِمائَةٍ وتِسْعِينَ
in the year 1991	فِي سَنَةِ أَلْفٍ وتِسْعِمائَةٍ وإِحْدَى وتِسْعِينَ
in the year 1991	فِي عَامِ أَلْفٍ وتِسْعِمائَةٍ ووَاحِدٍ وتِسْعِينَ
in the year 1992	فِي سَنَةِ أَلْفٍ وتِسْعِمائَةٍ واثْنَتَيْنِ وتِسْعِينَ
in the year 1992	فِي عَامِ أَلْفٍ وتِسْعِمائَةٍ واثْنَيْنِ وتِسْعِينَ
in the year 1993	فِي سَنَةِ أَلْفٍ وتِسْعِمائَةٍ وثَلاثٍ وتِسْعِينَ
in the year 1993	فِي عَامِ أَلْفٍ وتِسْعِمائَةٍ وثَلاثَةٍ وتِسْعِينَ
in the year 2002	فِي سَنَةِ أَلْفَيْنِ واثْنَتَيْنِ
in the year 2002	فِي عَامِ أَلْفَيْنِ واثْنَيْنِ
in the year 2007	فِي سَنَةِ أَلْفَيْنِ وسَبْعٍ

in the year 2007	في عَامِ أَلفَيْنِ وسبعةٍ
in the year 2015	في سَنَةِ أَلفَيْنِ وخَمسَ عشْرةَ
in the year 2015	في عَامِ أَلفَيْنِ وخَمسةَ عَشَر

The numbers are also read from the right to the left:

في عَامِ ثَلَاثَةَ وَتِسعِينَ وَتِسعمائةٍ وألفٍ ⇦ 1993

The states of the Maghrib mostly use the same numerals used in Europe and America; and their use is not restricted to dates.

If the word combination consisting of a number and a noun is to be definite (3 men > the 3 men), the number follows the noun. The noun takes the plural then in any case. The rule about polarity is not affected by this.

أَلرِّجَالُ الثَّلَاثَةُ، أَلفَتَيَاتُ الثَّلَاثُ، أَلأَشْخَاصُ الثَّلَاثَةَ عَشَرَ
أَلمُدُنُ المائةُ ، أَلكُتُبُ الألفُ

The construction which consists of a number defined by the article + ´a noun without an article is also frequently found:

أَلثَّلَاثَةَ عَشَرَ شَخْصاً، أَلثَّلَاثَةُ رِجَالٍ

When referring to indefinite numbers (*some, ...odd*) from **3 – 9** بِضْعة/بِضْع and after **10** نَيِّفٌ is used:

He came back after some years.	عَادَ بَعْدَ بِضْعِ سَنَوَاتٍ.
He lived in a hotel after some months.	عَاشَ بَعْدَ بِضْعةِ أَشْهُرٍ في فُنْدُقٍ.
some twenty, twenty odd	عِشْرُونَ وَنَيِّفٌ / نَيِّفٌ وَعِشْرُونَ
some thousand, thousand odd	أَلفٌ وَنَيِّفٌ / نَيِّفٌ وَأَلفٌ

FRACTIONAL NUMBERS

The fractional numbers $^1/_3$, $^1/_4$, $^1/_5$ ... $^1/_{10}$ are formed out of the corresponding cardinal number according to the pattern فُعْلٌ pl. أَفْعَالٌ:

$^2/_3$	ثُلثَان	$^1/_3$	ثُلْثٌ / أَثلَاثٌ
$^3/_4$	ثَلَاثَةُ أَرْبَاعٍ	$^1/_4$	رُبْعٌ / أَربَاعٌ
$^2/_5$	خُمُسَان	$^1/_5$	خُمْسٌ / أَخْمَاسٌ
$^4/_5$	أَرْبَعةُ أَخْمَاسٍ	$^1/_6$	سُدُسٌ / أَسْدَاسٌ
$^5/_6$	خَمْسَةُ أَسْدَاسٍ	$^1/_7$	سُبْعٌ / أَسْبَاعٌ

Only the fractional number $^{1}/_{2}$: نِصْف is not derived from the cardinal number.

Fractions, in which the denominators are greater than 10 are paraphrased by means of the preposition عَلى or by جُزْء مِن "*a part of*":

$^{1}/_{11}$	وَاحِدٌ عَلى أَحَدَ عَشَرَ / جُزْءٌ مِنْ أَحَدَ عَشَرَ
$^{5}/_{12}$	خَمْسَةُ عَلى اثْنَيْ عَشَرَ
$^{7}/_{100}$	سَبْعَةُ عَلى مِائة / سَبْعَةُ أَجْزاءٍ مِن مِائة

NUMERAL ADVERBS OF REITERATION

The numeral adverbs indicating reiteration are expressed by مَرَّة + cardinal number:

once, one time	مَرَّةٌ واحِدةٌ	thrice, three times	ثَلاثَ مَرَّاتٍ
twice	مَرَّتَيْنِ	four times	أَرْبَعَ مَرَّاتٍ

THE NUMERAL PATTERN فُعَالِيٌّ

Such adjectives often denote the number of parts belonging to a thing:

quadriliteral verb	أَلفِعل الرُّباعِيُّ	*biliteral interpreting*	ترجمة ثُنائيّة
Five-Year-Plan	الخُطّة الخُماسِيّة	*triliteral committee*	أَللجنة الثُّلاثيّة

THE NUMERAL PATTERN مُفَعَّلٌ

This pattern has the form of the passive participle of Form II. If derived from numerals, it denotes the shape of squares or things:

the pentagonal house	أَلْبَيْتُ الْمُخَمَّسُ	*The Golden Triangle*	أَلْمُثَلَّثُ الذَّهَبِيُّ
the hexagonal pillar	أَلْعَمُودُ الْمُسَدَّسُ	*square mile*	مِيلٌ مُرَبَّعٌ

DECIMAL NUMBERS

The decimal numbers are written with a comma and usually spoken as follows:

3.9	٣٫٩	ثلاثةٌ فاصِلةٌ تسعةٌ (من عشرةٍ)
4.25	٤٫٢٥	أربعةٌ فاصِلةٌ خمسةٌ وعشرون (من مئةٍ)
7.123	٧٫١٢٣	سبعةٌ فاصِلةٌ مئةٌ وثلاثةٌ وعشرون (من ألفٍ)

The decimals can also be read with the prepositions ب or مع :

3.9	٣٫٩	ثلاثةٌ مع / بفاصِلة تسعةٍ (من عشرةٍ)

Table 54 : CARDINAL NUMBERS (SUMMARY)

	In connection with a feminine noun	in connection with a masculine noun	
1	واحِدة، إحْدَى	واحِد، أَحَد	١
2	اثْنَتان	اثْنان	٢
3	ثلاث	ثلاثة	٣
4	أَرْبع	أَرْبعة	٤
5	خَمْس	خَمْسة	٥
6	سِتّ	سِتّة	٦
7	سَبْع	سَبْعة	٧
8	ثمان (ثَماني)	ثَمانِية	٨
9	تِسْع	تِسْعة	٩
10	عَشَرْ	عَشَرة	١٠
11	إحْدَى عَشْرَةَ	أَحَدَ عَشَرَ	١١
12	اثْنَتا عَشْرَةَ	اثْنا عَشَرَ	١٢
13	ثلاثَ عَشْرَةَ	ثلاثةَ عَشَرَ	١٣
14	أَرْبعَ عَشْرَةَ	أَرْبعةَ عَشَرَ	١٤
15	خَمْسَ عَشْرَةَ	خَمْسةَ عَشَرَ	١٥
16	سِتَّ عَشْرَةَ	سِتَّةَ عَشَرَ	١٦
17	سَبْعَ عَشْرَةَ	سَبْعةَ عَشَرَ	١٧
18	ثَماني عَشْرَةَ	ثَمانِية عَشَرَ	١٨
19	تِسْعَ عَشْرَةَ	تِسْعةَ عَشَرَ	١٩
20		عِشْرُونَ	٢٠
21	إحْدَى وعِشْرُون	واحِدٌ / أَحدٌ وعِشْرُون	٢١
22	اثْنَتانِ وعِشْرُون	اثْنانِ وعِشْرُون	٢٢

23	ثلاثٌ وعِشْرُون		ثلاثةٌ وعِشْرُون	٢٣
30		ثلاثون		٣٠
40		أَرْبعون		٤٠
50		خَمسون		٥٠
60		سِتّون		٦٠
70		سبْعون		٧٠
80		ثمانون		٨٠
90		تِسْعون		٩٠
100		مئةٌ، مائَة		١٠٠
101	مئة وواحدة		مئة وواحد	١٠١
102	مئة واثْنتانِ		مئة واثنان	١٠٢
103	مئة وثلاث		مئة وثلاثة	١٠٣
200		مئتا(ن)		٢٠٠
300		ثلاثُمائة		٣٠٠
1000		أَلْف ج آلاف		١٠٠٠
1001	أَلْف وواحدة		أَلْف وواحد	١٠٠١
1002	أَلْف واثْنتانِ		أَلْف واثْنان	١٠٠٢
1003	أَلْف وثلاث		أَلْف وثلاثة	١٠٠٣
1100			أَلْف ومئة	١١٠٠
1200			أَلْف ومئتا(ن)	١٢٠٠
1300			أَلْف وثلاثُمائة	١٣٠٠
2000		أَلْفا(ن)		٢٠٠٠
3000		ثلاثةُ آلاف		٣٠٠٠

10 000	عَشْرَةُ آلاف	١٠٠٠٠
11 000	أَحَدَ عَشَرَ أَلْف (اً)	١١٠٠٠
100 000	مئة أَلْف	١٠٠٠٠٠
200 000	مئتا أَلْف	٢٠٠٠٠٠
1 000 000	مَلْيون ج ملايينُ	١٠٠٠٠٠٠
1 000 000 000	مِلْيار ج مِلْيارات	١٠٠٠٠٠٠٠٠٠

ORDINAL NUMBERS (الأَعْداد التَّرْتيبِيَّة)

Ordinal Numbers from 1-10:

	f.	m.		f.	m.
1ˢᵗ	أُولَى	أَوَّلُ	6ᵗʰ	سَادِسَة	سَادِس
2ⁿᵈ	ثَانِيَة	ثَانٍ	7ᵗʰ	سَابِعَة	سَابِع
3ʳᵈ	ثَالِثَة	ثَالِث	8ᵗʰ	ثَامِنَة	ثَامِن
4ᵗʰ	رَابِعَة	رَابِع	9ᵗʰ	تَاسِعة	تَاسِع
5ᵗʰ	خَامِسَة	خَامِس	10ᵗʰ	عَاشِرة	عَاشِر

The ordinal numbers of **1** and **2** are adjectives of the pattern فاعِل *fā'il* and are subject to the rules of agreement. They are (if the numerals are definite):

	2.		1.	
	f.	m.	f.	m.
n.	أَلثَّانِيَةُ	أَلثَّانِي	أَلأُولَى	أَلأَوَّلُ
g.	أَلثَّانِيَةِ	أَلثَّانِي	أَلأُولَى	أَلأَوَّلِ
a.	أَلثَّانِيَةَ	أَلثَّانِيَ	أَلأُولَى	أَلأَوَّلَ

The numeral adverbs "*first(ly)*" and "*secondly*" are expressed by the indefinite accusative of the ordinal number: أَوَّلاً ، ثَانياً

ثانٍ, definite أَلثَّانِي, is declined like ثَمَانٍ, definite أَلثَّمَانِي.

Ordinal numbers from 11-19:

	f.	m.
11th	حَادِيَةَ عَشْرَةَ	حَادِي عَشَرَ
12th	ثَانِيَةَ عَشْرَةَ	ثَانِي عَشَرَ
13th	ثَالِثَةَ عَشْرَةَ	ثَالِثَ عَشَرَ
14th	رَابِعَةَ عَشْرَةَ	رَابِعَ عَشَرَ
15th	خَامِسَةَ عَشْرَةَ	خَامِسَ عَشَرَ
16th	سَادِسَةَ عَشْرَةَ	سَادِسَ عَشَرَ
17th	سَابِعَةَ عَشْرَةَ	سَابِعَ عَشَرَ
18th	ثَامِنَةَ عَشْرَةَ	ثَامِنَ عَشَرَ
19th	تَاسِعَةَ عَشْرَةَ	تَاسِعَ عَشَرَ

The numbers 11th - 19th are not inflectional.

THE NUMERAL ADVERBS

sixth	سَادِساً	*first*	أَوَّلاً
seventh	سَابِعاً	*second*	ثَانِياً
eighth	ثَامِناً	*third*	ثَالِثاً
ninth	تَاسِعاً	*fourth*	رَابِعاً
tenth	عَاشِراً	*fifth*	خَامِساً

After **10** the ordinal number in connection with expressions like "*item*" or "*article*" is used:

$$ أَلْنُّقْطَةُ الرَّابِعَةَ عَشْرَةَ / أَلْمَادَّةُ الْعِشْرُونَ $$

The Arabic ordinal numbers are treated like adjectives with regard to syntax. Accordingly they follow the noun, and there is agreement in case, state, gender and number between them and the noun. Unlike the case of the cardinal numbers, there is is no polarity in gender in the ordinal numbers.

in connection with a feminine noun		in connection with a masculine noun	
the 1ˢᵗ year	أَلسَّنَةُ الْأُولَى	the 1ˢᵗ day	أَلْيَوْمُ الْأَوَّلُ
		1ˢᵗ Tishrīn (October)	تِشْرِينُ الْأَوَّلُ
		2ⁿᵈ Kānūn (January)	كَأنُونُ الثَّانِي
the 2ⁿᵈ year	أَلسَّنَةُ الثَّانِيَةُ	the 2ⁿᵈ day	أَلْيَوْمُ الثَّانِي
the 3ʳᵈ year	أَلسَّنَةُ الثَّالِثَةُ	the 3ʳᵈ day	أَلْيَوْمُ الثَّالِثُ
the 10ᵗʰ year	أَلسَّنَةُ الْعَاشِرَةُ	the 10ᵗʰ day	أَلْيَوْمُ الْعَاشِرُ
the 11ᵗʰ year	أَلسَّنَةُ الْحَادِيَةَ عَشْرَةَ	the 11ᵗʰ day	أَلْيَوْمُ الْحَادِيَ عَشَرَ
the 12ᵗʰ year	أَلسَّنَةُ الثَّانِيَةَ عَشْرَةَ	the 12ᵗʰ day	أَلْيَوْمُ الثَّانِيَ عَشَرَ
the 19ᵗʰ year	أَلسَّنَةُ التَّاسِعَةَ عَشْرَةَ	the 19ᵗʰ day	أَلْيَوْمُ التَّاسِعَ عَشَرَ

The ordinal numbers for **1ˢᵗ**, i.e. أَوَّل , is frequently connected with the following noun in the form of a genitive construction and is neutral as to gender in this case: i.e. *"for the 1ˢᵗ time"* = لِأَوَّلِ مَرَّةٍ

The ordinal numbers from **2-10** also occasionally precede the noun just as أَوَّل does.

The ordinal numbers of the tens (20ᵗʰ, 30ᵗʰ, . . . 90ᵗʰ), hundreds, thousands etc. are expressed by means of the cardinal numbers.

in connection with a feminine noun		in connection with a masculine noun	
the 20ᵗʰ year	أَلسَّنَةُ الْعِشْرُونَ	the 20ᵗʰ day	أَلْيَوْمُ الْعِشْرُونَ
the 100ᵗʰ year	أَلسَّنَةُ الْمِائَةُ	the 100ᵗʰ day	أَلْيَوْمُ الْمِائَةُ
the 1000ᵗʰ year	أَلسَّنَةُ الْأَلْفُ	the 1000ᵗʰ day	أَلْيَوْمُ الْأَلْفُ

but:　the 20 days

　　　the 1000 years

أَلْأَيَّامُ الْعِشْرُونَ

أَلسَّنَوَاتُ الْأَلْفُ

The ordinal numbers over **20** in which units occur as well, consist of ordinals (units) and cardinal numbers (tens).

Take note of the numeral **1** in ordinal numbers like **21ˢᵗ**, **31ˢᵗ** etc. in this context.

in connection with a masculine noun	
the 21st day	أَلْيَوْمُ الْحَادِي وَالْعِشْرُونَ
the 22nd day	أَلْيَوْمُ الثَّانِي وَالْعِشْرُونَ
the 31st day	أَلْيَوْمُ الْحَادِي وَالثَّلَاثُونَ
the 38th day	أَلْيَوْمُ الثَّامِنُ وَالثَّلَاثُونَ
in connection with a feminine noun	
the 21st year	أَلسَّنَةُ الْحَادِيَةُ وَالْعِشْرُونَ
the 22nd year	أَلسَّنَةُ الثَّانِيَةُ وَالْعِشْرُونَ
the 31st year	أَلسَّنَةُ الْحَادِيَةُ وَالثَّلَاثُونَ
the 38th year	أَلسَّنَةُ الثَّامِنَةُ وَالثَّلَاثُونَ

Ordinal numbers over 100 naturally occur rarely. They are either paraphrased or expressed in terms of the preposition بَعْدَ *"after"*:

the 101st day	أَلْيَوْمُ الْأَوَّلُ بَعْدَ الْمِائَة

DATES

Dates are expressed by means of the ordinal numbers:

on May 1st (*lit.:* on the 1st day of the month of May)   فِي الْيَوْمِ الْأَوَّلِ مِنْ شَهْرِ مَايُو

In general, a shortened form is chosen that does not contain the words يوم and شهر:

فِي الْأَوَّلِ مِنْ آيَّار

An even shorter form usually appears in newspapers, official letters etc.:

فِي ٢٠ تَمُّوز ، فِي ١ أَيَّار

The month can be represented by the corresponding numeral as well, so that the Arabic date does not differ from the form used in America and Europe:

1/5/2004 = فِي ٢٠٠٤/٥/١

In the region of the Maghrib the form 01/05/2004 is also typical.

To find out the date, the following question is asked:

What is today's (tomorrow's) date?	مَا هُوَ تَارِيخُ الْيَوْمِ (الْغَدِ) ؟

The answer is e.g.:

Today (tomorrow) is May 1st.	أَلْيَوْمَ (غَدًا) الْأَوَّلُ مِنْ أَيَّار.

THE TIME

The ordinal numbers are also used with regard to the time. They serve the purpose of stating the full hours:

at 2 o'clock	في السَّاعَة الثَّانِيَة
at 5 o'clock	في السَّاعَة الخَامِسَة
at 10 o'clock	في السَّاعَة العَاشِرة
at 11 o'clock	في السَّاعَة الحَادِيَة عَشْرَةَ

Only 1 o'clock is expressed by the cardinal number: في السَّاعَة الوَاحِدة

There are some more differentiations in Arabic besides 1.00 p.m., 2.00 p.m. ... 12.00 p.m. with regard to indicating the time.

The words   مَسَاءً ، ظُهْراً ، بعد الظُّهْر ، قَبْلَ الظُّهْر ، صَبَاحاً   are added in the following way:

at 1.00 a.m.	في السَّاعَة الوَاحِدَة صَبَاحاً
at 9.00 a.m.	في السَّاعَة التَّاسِعَة صَبَاحاً
at 10.00 a.m.	في السَّاعَة العَاشِرَة قَبْلَ الظُّهْر
at 11.00 a.m.	في السَّاعَة الحَادِية عَشْرَةَ قَبْلَ الظُّهْر
at 12.00 a.m.	في السَّاعَة الثَّانِية عَشْرَةَ ظُهْراً
at 1.00 p.m.	في السَّاعَة الوَاحِدة بَعْدَ الظُّهْر
at 5.00 p.m.	في السَّاعَة الخَامِسَة بَعْدَ الظُّهْر
at 6.00 p.m.	في السَّاعَة السَّادِسَة مَسَاءً
at 12.00 p.m.	في السَّاعَة الثَّانِية عَشْرَةَ مَسَاءً

ألسَّاعَة is often omitted, and في التَّاسِعَة صَبَاحاً / مَسَاءً is spoken. The use of the corresponding cardinal number is widespread in colloquial language as well.

The corresponding words for ¼ (رُبْع), ⅓ (ثُلْث) and ½ (نِصْف) are used in indications of time containing 15, 20 and 30 minutes. They are added by means of the conjunctions و or إلَّا. The noun is in the accusative after إلَّا .

at 2.30	فِي السَّاعَةِ الثَّانِيَةِ وَالنِّصْفِ
at 3.15	فِي السَّاعَةِ الثَّالِثَةِ وَالرُّبْعِ
at 4.20	فِي السَّاعَةِ الرَّابِعَةِ وَالثُّلْثِ
at 4.45 (a quarter to 5)	فِي السَّاعَةِ الخَامِسَةِ إلَّا الرُّبْعَ
at 5.40 (a third to 6)	فِي السَّاعَةِ السَّادِسَةِ إلَّا الثُّلْثَ

Time by minutes is indicated in the same way by means of وَ or إلَّا with the corresponding cardinal numeral and the word for minute (دَقِيقَة) being added.

at 1.05	فِي السَّاعَةِ الوَاحِدَةِ وَخَمْسِ دَقَائِقَ
at 7.12	فِي السَّاعَةِ السَّابِعَةِ وَاثْنَتَي عَشْرَةَ دَقِيقَةً
at 8.25	فِي السَّاعَةِ الثَّامِنَةِ وَخَمْسٍ وَعِشْرِينَ دَقِيقَةً
at 8.35 (25 min. to 9)	فِي السَّاعَةِ التَّاسِعَةِ إلَّا خَمْساً وَعِشْرِينَ دَقِيقَةً
at 9.42 (18 min. to 10)	فِي السَّاعَةِ العَاشِرَةِ إلَّا ثَمَانِي عَشْرَةَ دَقِيقَةً
at 10.55 (5 min. to 11)	فِي السَّاعَةِ الحَادِيَةَ عَشْرَةَ إلَّا خَمْسَ دَقَائِقَ

The indication of time "*... minutes to half past ...*" or "*... past half past ...*" is possible in Arabic, namely up to 9 minutes to or past the half hour:

five minutes to half past five	فِي السَّاعَةِ الخَامِسَةِ وَالنِّصْفِ إلَّا خَمْسِ دَقَائِقَ
nine minutes past half past six	فِي السَّاعَةِ الخَامِسَةِ وَالنِّصْفِ إلَّا خَمْسِ دَقَائِقَ

The time is asked for by

What time is it (now)?	كَمِ السَّاعَةُ؟ or by أَلسَّاعَةُ كَمْ (الآنَ)؟

The answer is:

It is 1.15 now.	أَلسَّاعَةُ (الآنَ) الوَاحِدَةُ وَالرُّبْعُ.
It is 12.30 now.	أَلسَّاعَةُ (الآنَ) الثَّانِيَةَ عَشْرَةَ وَالنِّصْفُ.
It is 3.50 now. (10 min. to 4)	أَلسَّاعَةُ (الآنَ) الرَّابِعَةُ إلَّا عَشْرَ دَقَائِقَ.

ALPHABETICAL NUMBERING

Arabic has a special order for letters when expressing numbers a), b), c) etc. The order is different from the alphabet and mostly given in the form of the following meaningless string of words.

أَبْجَدْ هَوَّزْ حُطِّي كَلَمَنْ سَعْفَصْ قَرَشَتْ ثَخَذْ ضَظَعْ

***Table 55*: ORDINAL NUMBERS (SUMMARY)**

1st	أَوَّل م أُولَى
2nd	ثانٍ (الثاني) م ثانِيَة
3rd	ثالث م ثالثة
4th	رابع م رابعة
5th	خامس م خامسة
6th	سادس م سادسة
7th	سابِع م سابعة
8th	ثامِن م ثامنة
9th	تاسع م تاسعة
10th	عاشِر م عاشِرة
11th	حادي عَشَرَ م حادية عَشْرَةَ
12th	ثانِيَ عَشَرَ م ثانِية عَشْرَةَ
13th	ثالثَ عَشَرَ م ثالثة عَشْرَةَ
14th	رابعَ عَشَرَ م رابعة عَشْرَةَ
15th	خامسَ عَشَرَ م خامسة عَشْرَةَ
16th	سادسَ عَشَرَ م سادسة عَشْرَةَ
17th	سابعَ عَشَرَ م سابعة عَشْرَةَ
18th	ثامنَ عَشَرَ م ثامنة عَشْرَةَ
19th	تاسعَ عَشَرَ م تاسعة عَشْرَةَ
20th	عِشْرونَ
21st	حادٍ وعِشْرونَ (الحادي والعِشْرونَ) م حادية وعِشْرونَ
22nd	ثانٍ وعِشْرونَ (الثاني والعِشْرونَ) م ثانِية وعِشْرونَ

23rd		ثالِث وعِشْرونَ م ثالِثة وعِشْرونَ
40th		أَرْبَعونَ
100th		مِئة، مائة
101st		مِئة وواحِد(ة)، أَوَّل (أُولَى) بَعْدَ المِئة
102nd		مِئة واثْنان (اثْنتان)، ثان (ثانِية) بَعْدَ المِئة
103rd		مِئة وثلاث(ة)، ثالِث(ة) بَعْدَ المِئة
1000th		أَلْف
1100th		أَلْف ومِئة، مِئة بعد الأَلْف

THE NAMES OF THE DAYS AND THE MONTHS

The days of the week are:

	On . . .			*On . . .*	
Thursday	يَوْمَ الْخَميسِ	أَلْخَميسُ	*Sunday*	يَوْمَ الأَحَد	أَلأَحَدُ
Friday	يَوْمَ الْجُمْعة	أَلْجُمْعةُ	*Monday*	يَوْمَ الاثْنَيْنِ	أَلاثْنَيْنِ
Saturday	يَوْمَ السَّبْتِ	أَلسَّبْتُ	*Tuesday*	يَوْمَ الثَّلاثاء	أَلثَّلاثاءُ
			Wednesday	يَوْمَ الأَرْبَعاء	أَلأَرْبَعاءُ

The months have different names in the Arab world. Some countries use a system similar to Europe. The usage is different even within the same country.

	Syr./Iraqi	*Eg.*		*Syr./Iraqi*	*Eg.*
July	تَمُّوزُ	يُولِيُو	*January*	كانُونُ الثَّاني	يَنايِرُ
August	آبُ	أَغُسْطُسُ	*February*	شُباطُ	فِبْرايِرُ
September	أَيْلُولُ	سِبْتَمْبَرُ	*March*	آذارُ	مارِسُ
October	تِشْرِينُ الأَوَّلُ	أُكْتُوبَرُ	*April*	نيسانُ	أَبْريلُ
November	تِشْرِينُ الثَّاني	نُوفَمْبَرُ	*May*	أَيَّارُ	مايُو
December	كانُونُ الأَوَّلُ	ديسَمْبَرُ	*June*	حَزَيْرانُ، حُزَيْرانُ	يُونِيُو

Most of the names of months are diptotes. They are regarded as proper names and are definite without having an article.

THE MONTHS OF THE ISLAMIC CALENDAR

The names of the twelve months of the Islamic calendar are as follows:

number of days	name of the month	number of the month	number of days	name of the month	number of the month
(30)	رَجَبٌ	7th	(30)	مُحَرَّمٌ	1st
(29)	شَعْبَانُ	8th	(29)	صَفَرٌ	2nd
(30)	رَمَضَانُ	9th	(30)	رَبِيع الأوَّل	3rd
(29)	شَوَّالٌ	10th	(29)	رَبِيع الثَّانِي	4th
(30)	ذُو الْقَعْدَة	11th	(30)	جُمَادَى الأُولَى	5th
(29)	ذُو الْحجَّة	12th	(29)	جُمَادَى الآخِرَةُ	6th

These names are used in newspapers and publications belonging to Islamic and state institutions.

The basic unit of the Islamic year is a *"moon year"*. It consists of twelve months with alternating 30 and 29 days. The duration of a moon year is about 354 days. The Islamic calendar starts with the 16th of July of the *"sun year"* 622, the year of the *Hijra* of the Prophet Mohammed from Mecca to Medina. The last month of the year, which consists of 30 days in leap years, is the month of the pilgrimage to Mecca.

The following abbreviations are used to designate the Muslim and the Christian year:

AH (Anno Hegriæ)	ألسَّنَةُ الْهِجْرِيَّةُ / هِجْرِيًّا	هـ
AD	ألسَّنَةُ الْمِيلادِيَّةُ / مِيلادِيًّا	م

The two main holidays of the Islamic year are:

10th *of Ḏū l-Hijja*	The Feast of Immolation, or Greater Bairam	عِيدُ الأَضْحَى / ألْعِيدُ الْكَبِيرُ
1st *of Shawwāl*	The Feast of Breaking the Ramaḍān Fast, or the Minor Feast	عِيدُ الفِطْر / ألْعِيدُ الصَّغِيرُ

The following approximate calculations can be used to transform *Hijra* (moon) years (H) into Gregorian (sun) years (G) and vice versa.

$$G = H - \frac{H}{33} + 622 \qquad\qquad H = G - 622 + \frac{G - 622}{32}$$

GRAMMATICAL INDEX (ENGLISH)

(The numbers of the pages which focus on the topics concerned are indicated in bold type.)

GRAMMATICAL INDEX (ARABIC)

(The numbers of the pages which focus on the topics concerned are indicated in bold type.)